BEFORE YOU SUE

BEFORE YOU SUE

How to Get Justice Without Going to Court

FLETCHER KNEBEL and
GERALD S. CLAY

QUILL
WILLIAM MORROW
NEW YORK

Library of Congress Cataloging-in-Publication Data

Knebel, Fletcher.
  Before you sue: how to get justice without going to court /
Fletcher Knebel and Gerald S. Clay.
      p. cm.
    ISBN 0-688-08669-1
    1. Compromise (Law)—United States—Popular works.   2. Dispute resolution (Law)—United States—Popular works.   I. Clay, Gerlad S.
II. Title.
KF9084.Z9K53   1989
347.73'9—dc19
[347.3079]

88-39317
CIP

Printed in the United States of America

First Quill Edition

1 2 3 4 5 6 7 8 9 10

BOOK DESIGN BY MINA GREENSTEIN

To Ruth, Lou, and Constance

Foreword

A major accomplishment of this book is the enthusiasm it arouses for mediation as a worthy method of resolving a great many legal disputes, frequently permitting aggrieved parties to save substantial sums in legal fees and much time in anguished concentration on a lawsuit.

At a time when our court systems are overburdened by the heavy demands cast upon them, when final adjudications all too often take years, and when the expense of litigation is beyond the reach of so many, mediation offers bright hope. When the main thoroughfares for legal proceedings become glutted, it is time to look to secondary avenues. Fortunately, mediation is now an available approach—in over 350 programs in 42 states, as well as for a growing number of practitioners in American law firms.

This work should allay the unfounded fears of those who can benefit from mediation and yet are unfamiliar with it. Its simple procedures are described, its nonbinding nature is explained, and its increasing acceptance across the nation is proof of its splendid performance where it has been used.

Far more people should utilize mediation and reap its advantages. In these pages we find the social value of quieting neighborhood disputes, lessening family controversies, and reducing the burden that conventional litigation places on the taxpayer. We also grasp the potential for quick, inexpensive settlement of thousands of the day-to-day commercial disputes that clog the country's courts of law and disrupt the vital economic life of the country.

The beauty, indeed the excellence, of *Before You Sue: How to Get Justice Without Going to Court* is the very pleasant manner in which its serious message is developed. Examples of a hard-fought lawsuit and a strongly contested mediation are portrayed vividly and realistically. The pitfalls and strengths of each approach come to light. The descriptions of lawyers, of law office preparations, client anxieties, courtroom drama, and mediation exchanges are excellent and afford the reader a wonderful insight into the give and take and the consequences of legal conflicts. There is here, enough compelling force to draw the reader to the final page.

Justice is one of the cardinal virtues. It should be the prime goal of organized society. Those who strive for it—as a principle of fairness in human dealings or in the administration of the law—are fulfilling a noble mission. Toward those ends and in these pages, the authors, Fletcher Knebel and Gerald S. Clay, have made a laudable contribution.

—Lawrence H. Cooke

Former Chief Judge, New York State, and Chairman, National Conference of Chief Justices

May 19, 1987

Contents

Don't Sue, Settle

1

If you've been wronged, cheated, mistreated, or bullied in violation of law, you hire an attorney, file a lawsuit, and seek retribution and damages in the civil courtrooms of the land.

That scenario is dear to the American heart. Most of us believe that we will find justice in the county or federal courthouse. We have faith in the fairness of judges and juries of our peers. Critics may call us the most litigious people on earth, but we hold that the system pays off for us in time of need. When harmed in dispute, we rally to the law's old battle cry: Sue the bastards!

It is the thesis of this book that if you respond in this fashion whenever you suffer a perceived injustice, you usually will do yourself more harm than good. We believe, and hope to persuade you also in the following pages, that in the overwhelming number of cases you will be better off to seek relief outside the formal legal system. We intend to show you that in most situations, you'll serve yourself far better by taking the path of mediation.

In mediation, you and your foe select a third party who sits down with both disputants and helps you work out a mutually satisfactory agreement that resolves the differences. Mediation, in its essence, is as simple as the previous sentence, but in its operation, it can be as subtle, intricate, and infinitely varied as humanity itself.

If you're a person in the white heat of early indignation over a wrong suffered at the hands of another, you'll probably read the preceding paragraph with vast skepticism. You even may resent the very suggestion that you should sit in the same room and talk to the person who has harmed you so severely. "What, talk it out with that bandit? You think I'm a wimp or what? No way. I'm taking him to court where he'll get what he deserves!"

The authors know how you feel because we've been there. We too have wanted to haul the miscreant into court and make him pay through the nose for all the damage he's done us. But we have learned that the legal system, protector though it is of many individual liberties and rights, just does not provide swift and automatic redressing of the thousands of wrongs suffered daily in this country.

One of us is a lawyer who has practiced in the adversarial legal system for twenty years and who recently has turned increasingly to mediation as a surer, saner, safer, and far less traumatic way to obtain satisfaction for injuries suffered. The other is a writer who in his former newspaper career covered courts, trials, judges, and lawyers, including the politics of the law, in several states and the nation's capital.

In theory the U.S. system of civil justice should provide a forum for the timely redressing of all but a few wrongs. It has widely dispersed and well-financed facilities open to everyone and with few exceptions it dispenses justice evenhandedly without the favoritism or gross disregard of individual rights so characteristic of tyrannies and dictatorial regimes.

In practice our vaunted civil justice system often fails us. Our civil courts provide a forum for adjudication of only a small percentage of the millions of wrangles that annually disrupt the economic and social life of the nation. Complaints against our legal system are as old as the republic, and in England, from which we inherit the bulk of our law, satirists were decrying the complexities of British justice more than 300 years ago. In recent times, especially since World War II, the process of civil litigation has become so cumbersome, slow, and unresponsive to this nation's needs that even stars of the system, such as the former Chief Justice of the United States, Warren Burger, have called for reforms and greatly increased use of alternative methods of settling disputes.

Why You Should Avoid the Courthouse

Back to you. Let's assume you've just been cheated or dealt a low economic blow in apparent violation of the law. Why should you follow our advice by avoiding the courts and seeking your satisfaction outside the conventional legal system?

Because a legal traffic jam has slowed progress through the courts to a crawl. Envision your favorite expressway at evening rush hour during a heavy rain and you'll come up with an apt comparison. In few jurisdictions can your lawsuit come to trial in less than eighteen months. In most the gap is more than two years and in some counties in the nation you must wait four years and more before your case can be heard by judge and jury.

Because fighting a lawsuit to conclusion costs a lot of money. Few lawyers charge less than $100 an hour, the $150-an-hour fee is now common in urban areas, and many specialists and members of elite firms charge $300 an hour and up. If you are suing for amounts in the $100,000 range, your lawyer may easily spend 100 to 300 hours in such pretrial preparations as interrogatories, depositions, motions, and conferences. That means $15,000 and up before you even get to court.

Because you have scant idea in your initial white heat of anger how much stress, trauma, and sagging spirits your lawsuit may cause you as it goes through its various phases. You may have some ragged nights and certainly the suit, if properly pursued, will take a big chunk of your time.

Because you have no assurance, after all your expenditures of time, money, and emotional reserves, that you'll win your case. As remote as the possibility seems now, you stand a chance of losing. The courts do not exist to validate your own perception of right and wrong.

Because the odds are heavy that no matter how grievously you may have been wronged, you'll wind up settling your case anyway. The civil case that actually goes through trial in this country is a rarity. Ninety-five percent of all lawsuits filed are dropped, settled, or otherwise disposed of before a trial decision. The pressure to settle is strong, from judges, from lawyers, and at last from weary suers themselves. If you pay no attention to any other part of this book, you'll get your money's worth if you'll ponder this question: *Since the odds of my case being settled are better than nine to one anyway, why don't I save myself time, money, and stress by mediating the matter at the outset?*

Because the chances of you being 100 percent right and your opponent being 100 percent wrong are extremely slim. Though in your early anger over your aggravation, this may seem farfetched, the fact remains that you undoubtedly have less than a totality of the law on your side. This means that a small to large factor of uncertainty will propel you toward settlement eventually.

Because conditions may change radically during your march to the courtroom. In these years you may lose heart, get sick, switch interests, or run out of money to pay your lawyer. Your foe may die or go bankrupt.

Because there is always the chance during the pretrial process of discovery that your opponents will find out something about you that reflects adversely on you and which you'd rather never came to light. Very few of us have conducted ourselves in a completely blameless manner. Put it this way: The chances of you coming out of your case as pure and unsullied as you went in are almost nil.

Because there's a good chance that the law's adversarial system, which pits you against your foe as one warrior against another, will aggravate rather than lessen the tensions between you and your opponent. This may have but little significance if you're fighting a stranger whom you'll never see again, but most suits involve parties who have some kind of a continuing relationship—husbands and wives, business partners, business executives and their suppliers or customers, companies and their employees, neighbors, city hall and its citizens.

People who have been through prolonged bitter lawsuits know the tremendous toll that the experience can exact on the psyche of a principal, be he or she a winner or loser. All kinds of unforeseen traumas await the traveler along the twisting jungle trails of the law—humiliation on the witness stand; refusal of supposedly close friends to give supporting testimony; staggering costs of depositions, motions, interrogatories; long talks with attorneys; the incessant moral tug-of-war between telling the truth and advancing one's cause; sleepless nights; the hours, days, and sometimes weeks lost at work, wasting time on miniscule side issues brought up by opponents; grappling with that bizarre foreign language, legalese; the maddening pedestrian pace of the average lawsuit; the complex rules that bar seemingly pertinent evidence and testimony.

It is no wonder that many people who "win" a lawsuit wind up dissatisfied with the outcome, disillusioned with our system of civil justice, and disgusted with both the courtroom and its functionaries.

So Right It Hurts

So why don't more people seek settlement at the outset? Big Ego covers a good deal of the answer. The human ego operates through that small voice that tells you over and over again how right you are. It also never fails to remind you how wrong your foe is.

Other factors play a part. Friends and family, eager to see you vindicated, may push you toward a courtroom showdown. You, after all, will do the fighting and agonizing. They won't. Visions of a huge jury award may dance in your head. Your lawyer, part of a legal establishment geared to trial by combat, may steer you to litigation. But Ego's small voice, never once admitting the possibility of self error, plays the chief role.

Sample. You see a thirty-year-old house that you intend to refurbish and rent as an investment. You look it over with a real estate agent who has advertised the place. He warns you the place needs work. On the other hand, at $150,000, it looks like a steal. Even better, in the bargaining, you get it for $140,000. At settlement, you pay $30,000 down and the rest on a mortgage.

A week after closing, as you take a contractor through the house to plan alterations, he points out some major deficiencies not visible on the surface. The main plumbing line is about to rust through, windowsills have interior rot, the furnace can't stand one more winter, and some amateur-installed wiring, in violation of local codes, has turned the place into a firetrap. Having counted on some $5,000 for modifications, you now find you'll first have to spend $40,000 to make the place safe and sound.

Enraged, you storm to a lawyer. You want to sue the bastards, both seller and real estate agent. Settle, mediate, or compromise? Not on your life. No way is it your fault. Quite simply, you've been defrauded by the seller and his fast-talking accomplice, the realtor.

When a friend asks you whether you're not partially to blame for not having given the house a thorough inspection in the company of an advising contractor before buying, you say absolutely not. It was the legal obligation of the seller and agent to come clean on the actual condition of the house, you contend. Sure, the agent warned you, but did he or the seller mention the invisible problems? No. You know they're wrong because Ego's small voice keeps telling you: "You're right. You're right. Go get 'em, tiger."

At the outset almost everyone overestimates his or her chances of winning a lawsuit. Consumed by anger, convinced he's been flagrantly wronged, knowing little of the law's hazards and often told by his lawyer that he has a good case, the aggrieved can't wait to tell his story to judge and jury and collect the handsome fine they'll levy on the other litigant for victimizing such a worthy citizen.

Vilhelm Aubert, a scholar who studied the attitude of suers, wrote of the "moral tinge" of lawsuits.

> To predict loss in a courtroom would normally imply doubt concerning one's own moral right. . . . some litigants may choose to court total loss rather than expose themselves to suspicions of guilty conscience. This attitude may imperceptibly blend with a more genuine moral stubbornness, and unwillingness to bargain about one's moral rights. It may be considered morally wrong, even, to yield without a command from the court.

Aubert adds another reason for suing—the sheer excitement of risking time and money on an uncertain outcome. The courtroom, as well as the racetrack and the casino, has its lure for gamblers.

A few potential litigants may be attracted to the lawsuit by still another feature. For some of those leading drab uneventful lives far from the glittering parade of celebrities and powerful movers and shakers of our society, the courtroom offers the chance for a leading dramatic role, however brief the run.

We recognize the many psychological barriers to settlement in the mind of the person who feels grievously and legally wronged, but we believe it would be a mistake to rush into a lawsuit. There are, of course, issues and grievances that are better carried to judgment in a court of law than settled along the way. But they are few in number, very few in number. The great mass of complaints, especially those of a commercial nature, should be settled before they get to court.

The last fifteen years have seen the rise of many alternative methods of resolving disputes in America, so that today formal litigation is but one of a number of roads to satisfaction for the wrong that has been done you. We, the authors, are convinced that one of these roads, mediation, will bring you the resolution you seek faster, cheaper, and with far less agonizing stress than will the conventional lawsuit.

The Myth of Winning

2

"Winning isn't everything, it's the only thing."
—VINCE LOMBARDI

Before going into the core of this book, where we take you behind the scenes in law offices to examine the merits of mediating your dispute rather than filing a lawsuit and plunging into litigation, we want to place the American legal process in the psychology of the times.

No American quotation of our era so misrepresents the essence of modern life as that ascribed to the late Vincent Lombardi, coach of the Green Bay Packers, who purportedly tossed off the famous line about winning. The sole purpose of the game, the remark implied, was not the playing of it, but the winning of it.

However pertinent the comment might be for professional sports— and even there it fails to reflect reality by a wide margin—as a metaphor for life, Lombardi's enshrinement of victory is junk psychology.

For every minute of our lives bent toward winning, we spend hours and days adjusting, accommodating, compromising, turning from combat, maneuvering, striving, helping, being helped, joining, collaborating, side-stepping, negotiating, loving, hanging out, and just plain being. Most of society's rituals, customs, and advisories on behavior, the social grease that lubricates the mechanics of living together, serve to avoid rather than incite the struggles that result in winners and losers.

A society truly dedicated to the pursuit of individual and collective victory for all its members would present an arena of unrelenting hostile confrontation marked by brutality, bloodshed, and warfare. The theology of winning ultimately shapes a nation so savage and ruthless that even the John Wayne—Rambo disciples of machismo would flee its borders in search of more tender precincts in which to rear their young. The last large nation committed to total victory, remember, was Nazi Germany.

Games and sports, as prevalent and popular as they are in the age of television, belong to a world apart. Games take place in a highly artificial, structured environment. They have rigid rules designed to yield winners and losers in every contest. But life beyond games features elastic rules, limitless ambiguity, and wide areas where winning becomes irrelevant and the pursuit of victory seems ludicrous at best and perilous at worst.

Consider three basic human institutions honored around the world: friendship, mateship, and family. Friendship, one of life's most common and fulfilling relationships, flourishes in the absence of winners and losers. The best way to nurture a friendship is to give and take, expose one's vulnerability, confide, share, and support without judging. The sure way to destroy a friendship is to attempt to "win" through domination or manipulation.

Marriage or unlicensed mateship enriches the partners to the degree that neither person seeks to "win" by exerting control over the other. By contrast, the divorce courts bulge with combatants who followed the time-tested tactics for winning; bulling ahead without regard to another person's interests or sensibilities; refusing to negotiate; taking an inflexible stance to prove oneself right; declining to adjust, give ground, or compromise; insisting on having one's way; and never surrendering except as a stratagem to gain a larger advantage.

Within the family, the world's most valued and powerful human institution, people get along by constant compromise and conciliation and by balancing one another's wants and interests. In fact, family life mirrors a never-ending, subtle, largely subconscious, process of human adjustment. The bargaining and negotiation go on day after day, hour by hour, minute by minute, as family members seek the utmost in individual freedom and personal gain while retaining the maximum of support. A sure way to alienate other members, losing their help and protection and risking being drummed out of the clan, is to pursue a strategy designed for winning.

In personal life, so in the outside world. In the vast realm of commerce, from dusty Third World markets to the financial canyons of lower Manhattan, the transfer of money, goods, and services proceeds by negotiation. Compromise, not victory, saturates the marketplace. While the seller wants the highest price, he or she can't set the price beyond the means of all buyers or so high as to antagonize the customers. The seller who charges all that the traffic will bear at the moment will see customers stampede to his or her competitor at the first opportunity. For the fate of cartels that push prices skyward, see OPEC and the 1986 collapse of the oil prices it had rigged. The most successful business houses are those that supply their products at reasonable prices to many customers over long periods of time. The least successful squeeze the customer, extort the maximum in dollars, and pay scant attention to the interests of those they deal with. Commerce does not tolerate winners and losers for long. When the seller outpoints, outthinks, outmaneuvers, and outplays the buyer in the manner of the winning football coach, the commercial game ends with the "winner" often filing for bankruptcy. He or she has enraged and alienated all the buyers.

The producer or seller does compete, of course, against rivals for the consumer's dollar. Although this phase of commerce is customarily described in terms of winning or losing, a whole range of factors, including laws, custom, geography, and labor unions, combine to thwart victory or defeat. The desire to avoid a maiming struggle against competitors so often prevailed over the yen for combat in early industrial America that Congress felt compelled to pass the antitrust laws to restore equilibrium to the marketplace. This same fondness for accommodation in place of warfare—some enforcement people call it conspiracy—provides a continuing test of antitrust laws and theories.

Negotiation, compromise, adjustment predominate almost everywhere, at work, in courtship, in worship, in leisure pursuits aside from games, in domestic politics, and in the international forums. Only when diplomacy fails do we go to war.

In America, however, the prevailing workaday practice of accommodation marches under battle flags. Even while we negotiate, bend, palaver, and maneuver, we use the lexicon of warfare. We "win" the point, "lose" the deal, "capture" the market percentage, "rout" the opposition, stage an advertising "blitz," "shoot down" the front office proposal, and suffer a barrage of "flak" for our best ideas. For many years a conductor on a train out of Princeton, New Jersey, enjoined his morning commuters to New York "to knock 'em dead in there today," a command presumably covering such incendiary white-collar missions as dictating, word processing, conferring, telephoning, advising, complaining, acceding, and from time to time thinking.

In matters of steamy romance, we say that Joe "lost" because the woman he was courting rejected his proposal and married Hank instead. Actually the world still holds some two and a half billion women for Joe, one of whom will agree to wed him, help him produce offspring, home, and family and perhaps even share a few hours or years of marital bliss with him. So Joe lost only in the sense that Lee Iacocca failed to sell a copy of his popular autobiography to the first customer to enter a bookstore.

The vocabulary of combat is carried over into such endeavors as self-development and group enterprises so that we say he or she "won the battle" if the person quits drinking and joins Alcoholics Anonymous or kicks a drug habit. Or a congregation "wins for the Lord" if it raises sufficient money to build a new church. Actually such usage is metaphorical for in its strict original sense winning involves the existence of a loser. Our dictionary's first definition of "win" is "to achieve victory over others in a competition." Achieving a goal or succeeding in rearranging one's life in a more orderly fashion is not the kind of winning we're talking about here.

Our military establishment does, of course, "win" or "lose" wars. The Pentagon gained a spectacular triumph of arms over Japan in 1945. However, witnessing today's tidal wave of made-in-Japan products flooding the land, and the widening Japanese ownership of U.S. industry and real estate, Americans may wonder about the nature of victory.

Short of war, modern life holds only restricted fields in which winning over losers is the goal. Games, both physical and mental, yes. Bidding on contracts, yes. Gambling, yes. Beauty, endurance, and muscle-bulging contests, yes. Running for political office, yes.

Going to court to seek redress of perceived wrongs, yes. . . . And then again, no.

The Myth of the Courtroom Victory

On the face of it, our system of civil justice would seem to offer America's largest and most pervasive institution committed to clear rules of winning and losing. Every working day in this most litigious of all societies, Americans bombard the nation's state and federal courthouses with some 58,000 new lawsuits. Each day, Monday through Friday, produces 58,000 new plaintiffs, armies of new defendants, 58,000 new cases for the care and feeding of 700,000 lawyers scattered through thousands of law firms and legal divisions of corporations, institutions, and governments.

These suits may take anywhere from one to ten years to grind through congested courthouses and appeals courts to a conclusion, but when they do, they will yield some 58,000 winners and 58,000 losers every day, won't they?

No, they won't. Ninety-five percent of the fifteen million new civil lawsuits brought each year in the United States will never trigger a verdict by judge or jury. Only about 5 percent of the contested cases will reach a conclusion that produces a clear winner and loser.

Ninety-five out of every hundred civil lawsuits filed in the courthouses of the nation will be dropped, thrown out of court, or settled. The vast majority of them will be settled by negotiation between the contending parties just as they have been for many decades past. Some litigants will settle soon after the filing of the suit, some during the lengthy waiting period before trial, some on the courthouse steps as the parties and their witnesses gather to do legal battle, and some, under the judge's pressure, even while the case is being tried.

These numbers and percentages paint an astounding picture. Here is a huge institution erected to the judicial process. It is designed and built to pit adversary against adversary and to produce winners and losers—those found to have behaved properly under the law and those found to have acted improperly—after an exceedingly complex, cumbersome, costly, and often leisurely procedure. And yet this layered establishment of justice performs its vaunted function only occasionally.

It is as though the New York Yankees and the Boston Red Sox, meeting to work at baseball under their lucrative contracts, produced a winner only one game out of twenty. The rest of the contests ended in tie scores. Under these negotiated terms, sometimes the Red Sox were awarded the most home runs and the fatter batting averages and sometimes the Yankees.

If it is a myth that most endeavors in life are to be "won" or "lost" against others in our society, and we believe that it is, it is no less a myth that the American system of civil justice provides a forum for legal combat in which litigants battle to victory or defeat. True, there are a small number of victors and vanquished coming out of the nation's courtrooms, but they are vastly outnumbered by the mass of litigants who sue in anger, then settle in relative tranquility some months or years later. They decide to settle because they come to realize, as their lawyers already knew, that few cases match absolute right versus absolute wrong. There's a good bit of legal right in almost every contestant's brief and there's a good bit of legal wrong in the position too. Life is a bundle of ambiguities and nowhere do the cloudy doubts and dualities proliferate as they do in the law of the land.

Although much of this book deals with the legal profession, this is not to be read as another of the attacks on lawyers that have been going on for centuries and in which Charles Dickens joined in 1853 with his brilliant satire of an interminable lawsuit in *Bleak House*. We respect lawyers. One of us practices law for a living and the other is the father of a successful attorney in San Francisco. It is the system of civil justice under which lawyers work that we find so unwieldy, torpid, costly, emotionally draining, and generally unresponsive to the needs of those it was designed to help.

We seek, in the remainder of this book, to introduce you to an alternative system, one that is private and much faster and cheaper. For the great majority of users it has produced gratifying results. We hope to persuade you to sidestep the traditional system of fighting it out in court and to take your complaint to an attorney who will guide

you to mediation where final agreements are sealed between participants who neither win nor lose.

We argue the case for mediation rather than litigation chiefly through
presenting two cases of persons who believe they have suffered severely, unfairly, and in violation of the law at the hands of others.
One person chooses the path of litigation leading, she hopes, to vindication and redress of wrongs by judge and jury. The other opts for
a quick mediation of her grievance, taking her case before a mediator
who helps the disputants and their lawyers find common ground.
These two cases are fictional because we wished to make them representative of the main themes played out day after day in the privacy
of the nation's law offices as clients struggle toward a resolution of
their problems. The names and issues are fictional, but what tran-
spires in these stories is duplicated many times over each week
throughout the country.

We hope that we can persuade you to early negotiation and settlement of your grievance, but if we fail, we wish you good luck on
your lawsuit. You'll need it, for the litigating path to the courthouse
is long, painful, and very, very expensive.

The Lawsuit Way

3

Part One: *First Meeting of Lawyer and Client*

William F. Hutchinson sits at a desk awaiting Oretta Long, a widowed businesswoman with a grievance against some in-laws. On the wall behind him hangs a framed diploma from Stanford Law School, a photograph of Jennifer, his wife, together with the towheaded twin boys, Kevin and Danny, and a print of a sun-baked Mexican town by Tamayo. The upholstered leather armchairs match the adobe shade of the fabric wall covering. An unostentatious office, but done in good taste, it denotes solidity and reliability without underlining the message.

An attorney in general practice, Bill Hutchinson specializes in business law in the firm of Devereaux, Goldstein, Hutchinson & Tong, a partnership of seven men (actually each the owner of his own professional corporation) backed by a cadre of law associates, paralegals, secretaries, clerks, and messengers with offices on Wilshire Boulevard near Beverly Hills. The law firm is quite close to the national average in size.

Bill earns around $125,000 a year, about $20,000 above the average for members of the American Bar Association, according to an *ABA Journal* survey, and far above the $60,000 average for the legal profession as a whole. However, he earns well below the annual income of the senior partners of many big corporate law firms. In certain exceptional corporate litigation, lead attorneys earn more than $500 an hour.

Bill is in his forties, an even-tempered, friendly man with an incisive mind. Lawyers rank among the best and the brightest in America and Bill stood in the upper half of his class at law school. If anything, Bill's mind has sharpened since graduation and of course he benefits by some twenty years of practical experience. He's in good physical shape, honing his trim body at racquetball, tennis, and a weekly softball game.

The minute he sees Mrs. Long, Bill senses that she's in a fighting mood. A smartly dressed woman with an air of sophistication, she wears her anger as she might a fur. She's attractive, poised, and confident in manner. Bill guesses her age at about forty-five.

Noting her glance at his family photograph, Bill talks for a moment about his wife and sons, then leads her into a conversation about herself. She has come here because she liked the work of Ira Goldstein, one of Bill's partners, a specialist in estates and wills, who guided her through probate when her husband died some years ago. Still, Bill knows little about her and he wants her to talk about herself and family so that he can size her up, get a fix on her personality.

Articulate with an orderly mind despite her underlying anger, Oretta Long has been widowed six years, has a teenage daughter, Amy, with whom she lives in Santa Monica in the four-bedroom stone ranch-style home left her by Frank. She is seeing several men, but has no current marriage intentions. She grew up in Oregon, daughter of two schoolteachers, was graduated from San Diego State University, and worked briefly in the insurance business before she married. Oretta Long settles back in the chair near Bill's desk and opens a dispatch case.

"You brought the papers, I see," he says.

She nods and places two documents on his desk. "The will and the contract."

"I got only a snapshot view from our phone conversation," Bill uncaps a fountain pen and squares a long yellow pad before him.

"Why don't you give me the particulars. Take your time and give me all the facts you think are relevant."

"I've just had the rug yanked out from under me, Mr. Hutchinson." Her eyes flash. "I had a perfectly valid contract and they broke it."

"Bill, please. Let's start back when your husband died."

"Okay. Frank died six years ago March. We were married for fifteen years, a good partnership at work as well as at home. At work, I did all the selling in the early years."

The story develops. Frank Long died at age fifty, leaving her the house, a car, some cash, and one third of a prosperous women's sports apparel business. The other two thirds went on equal shares to two younger half brothers of Frank Long, Arthur and Wendell. Under a stock redemption agreement, the brothers used proceeds of company-held insurance on Frank's life to buy out Oretta's one-third interest in the business. She received $900,000 in the deal that had been contemplated as a possibility by Frank Long.

"Was the buyout amicable?" asks Bill.

"Oh yes. I'd always been on good terms with the half brothers, not real close, you know, but friendly enough."

In a relaxed atmosphere, she relates, Arthur, Wendell, and Oretta Long drew up a homemade signed agreement under which she would continue marketing the sportswear line in the western states. She would be paid a salary of $30,000 plus 15 percent of her gross sales and would operate on an expense account covering costs "of travel, lodging, and entertainment normal in the trade." The contract was to extend for ten years.

All went smoothly the first four years, although Wendell, who handled company finances, did complain about her flying first class and stopping at the best hotels. She told him that she had "to go first class" to get the business, Arthur sided with her and that ended the matter, she thought.

"But things changed a lot in this last year," Oretta continues. "I started selling on the East Coast, Connecticut, New York, and a lot of shops in Florida, and the half brothers refused to pay me the agreed fifteen percent. Instead they paid me just ten percent. They claimed it cost them more to service the East Coast. . . . Bull!" She flared. "Slightly higher shipping costs, yes, but I shot the volume up with lots of new outlets in Florida.

"Then another stingy thing. If a wholesaler or store returned stuff unsold, Wendell wouldn't give me any commission on it. Fair enough. But then I found out he also knocked off my percentage when a store returned defective goods, you know, badly sewn seams, tears, soil marks. That's not fair and he knows it."

Bill refers to the signed agreement, notes that it says merely that Oretta is to be paid 15 percent "on the gross sales price" of the business she brings in. At first glance, this appears to indicate that Wendell Long did not violate the agreement. Damaged clothes did not become part of "gross sales."

"How long has he been doing that?" asks Bill.

"Just since last summer."

"Earlier it had been his practice to pay you your percentage, damaged, soiled, or not?"

"That's right. Then another thing happened. Wendell called me in and said they'd decided that from now on I had to fly economy class. He also put a limit on other expense account items so that I can't stop at a first-rate hotel and can't take customers to dinner at the best restaurants. I told him that going the El Cheapo route would lose us customers. The argument went on from there. We were going at it hot and heavy when Arthur showed up. He said they'd talk it over and let me know their decision."

She sniffs. "Some decision! Last month I got a formal letter from the half brothers, saying they were terminating our arrangement because of 'my uncooperative attitude' and that my final check would be put in the mail." Oretta fishes about in her dispatch case. "Yes, here's the letter." She hands it to the lawyer.

Bill glances through the letter, then asks: "Does that bring us up to date?" He taps his pencil on the yellow pad. "Anything else?"

"That's it. . . . Oh, no. Wait a sec. I have a lot of old customers that I don't bother to call on anymore. They're so sold on the line that they just send in their orders out of our semiannual sales pamphlet. Last year Wendell knocked them off my percentage list. He said if I didn't call on the customer, the sale was a 'company sale' and no salesman could get a cut." She shrugs in disgust. "Can you believe it?"

Hutchinson shakes his head in sympathy. "So, effectively, you've been fired in the fifth year of a ten-year contract?"

"Right. Kicked out without so much as a thank-you." Oretta Long fluffs her shoulder-length brown hair, takes a silver cigarette case from her handbag. "Mind if I smoke?"

"Go right ahead." Bill, a nonsmoker who watches his health, does mind. On the other hand, he can see that his client is seething at the mere recollection of her treatment at the hands of the brothers.

While Oretta lights a cigarette and savors the first few puffs, Bill Hutchinson continues his running speculation about his new client. Is she the type who'll slog the case through to the finish, or tire of the game after a few weeks? What is she really after here, money, apologies to a bruised ego, vengeance? Will she enjoy or detest the legal process? Some clients embrace a lawsuit as a kind of robust avocation, forever prompting or second-guessing the attorney.

He gathers that she has sufficient resources to carry a lawsuit through to the end. His intuition tells him that she is basically honest. She is not overly emotional and although work is important to her, it is but one aspect of her life. He doubts a lawsuit would become an all-consuming passion with her. She feels wronged, seeks justice, and wants action taken. She knows very little about the legal system and will be inclined to trust him.

All in all, she'll make a good client, he believes. Bill reads the letter of dismissal, this time with some care. "Aside from what they call your 'uncooperative attitude,' they don't appear to give any solid reason for letting you go."

"None at all." Angrily she blows a column of smoke toward the ceiling. "A couple of wimps. Afraid to tell me to my face."

"Did they have any cause at all to break the agreement? Anything they might claim against you?" Hutchinson searches his client for body language clues. Does her rancor have other more personal roots?

"Absolutely not. You know what this is all about, Mist—er—Bill?"

"Please tell me." He says it patiently, without irony.

"Wendell put his girlfriend—he's married, you know—on the sales payroll last year." She inhaled again, tapped the cigarette on an ashtray. "I'll bet ten to one she takes over my job. Look, I have nothing against the woman. She takes the hand she's dealt, but damn if I intend to get booted out, in violation of my contract, just to make room for the guy's mistress."

"Understood." Bill makes another note on his legal pad. "So you've been at home for the last month or so?"

"Yes. At first I had a feeling of relief almost. Now I could have the leisure—forced on me, to be sure—to do some of the things I'd been putting off. I worked out in the garden, spent more time with Amy, and had lunch with some of my old women friends. But, frankly, Bill, I'm not cut out for that kind of life. I need to be working. I enjoyed my job and I was good at it."

She explains how the sales job became part of her life. She helped Frank Long start the sportswear manufacturing company and at the beginning did all the marketing. Since Frank's death and the buyout by the half brothers, she has been making about $100,000 annually under the agreement. She enjoyed the work and the money and she thinks Arthur and Wendell Long should be made to pay through the nose for breaking their agreement and firing her without cause.

"Which brings us to the main point," says Bill. "Assuming that research shows that we have as good a legal case as it appears on the surface, what do you envision as a proper outcome? What, in short, do you want, Mrs. Long?"

"Oretta, please. Well, I do want my job back, as unhappy as I am with Arthur and Wendell. And I want money, Bill. A lot of it. Not so much for me, although I could use it, but the kind of money that will make them bleed a few quarts. I want them to go through what I have."

"I understand." How many new clients had sat in that chair and voiced the same desire in different words? Several hundred, at least. They came in under a full head of steam, vengeance in their hearts. They wanted to get even, to make those who had visited them with injuries (whether real or fancied) suffer, and they wanted to translate their own pain into collectible dollars.

Throughout this first hour, several trains of thought have been rolling through Bill Hutchinson's brain. While one part of his mind attends to the facts served up by Mrs. Long, another picks up psychological clues from the widow's body language. These tell him that her voiced desire to strike back at the half-brothers-in-law is not mere talk. The words spring from heated emotions. A third part of his mind toys with legal themes and still a fourth hovers over the most important aspect of the problem: **What's This Thing Worth?**

By worth Hutchinson doesn't mean his own fee, although he certainly includes that in his recurring assessment. Rather he centers on the core issue. When the case finally grinds to its conclusion, what will it bring to the aggrieved widow?

Actually, Bill's hidden guesstimator phrases the question differently: What kind of a deal can we make at settlement? For Bill Hutchinson, he of the keen mind and fit body, assumes from the outset that this case will be settled with the attorney for the Culprit Half Brothers sometime before an actual trial.

Bill knows as well as the next lawyer that the overwhelming number of civil suits, whatever their merits, wind up either dropped or settled. He knows that studies support what his own experience tells him—that of all the civil cases filed in the United States, less than 5 percent come to trial.

Negotiation plays such a major role on the stage of American litigation that Bill Hutchinson always assumes he'll settle his case. In the last ten years of his busy, prosperous career, he has had to try only eighteen of his lawsuits and twelve of those were settled before they reached a decision. Bill won four of the six that went all the way, although several of his winning clients complained bitterly about the process. Because of court congestion, none of the litigated cases got to trial in less than three years and two waited another year and a half for appeals. Only one of the winning clients collected more money than negotiation probably would have brought him. Several clients were appalled at the size of the legal bill. Trials cost money.

It is a striking irony of Bill Hutchinson's professional life that in a legal system geared for adversarial combat, producing a clear winner and loser, he spends the bulk of his time far from courts, negotiating quietly around a table or over the telephone. Trained at law school for courtroom strife in a tradition rooted in the dark ages of trial by fire, he tries not, rarely faces a jury. Untrained at law school for negotiation and compromise (he never took a course connected with these arts, since law schools only recently began offering studies in mediation and allied methods), he spends the bulk of his critical hours doing precisely that. Indeed Bill Hutchinson is not an attorney at all in the film/fiction/public image of that calling, but a negotiator who's skilled in the intricacies of the law. Yet he's typical of the great majority of his profession.

Strangely, even though his guesstimator searches ceaselessly for the probable settlement area while Mrs. Long sketches her predicament, Bill Hutchinson isn't aware of the process. The calculations and the search go on at a subliminal level far below the stratum that holds Bill's own image of himself. For Bill sees himself as a tough, though fair, legal warrior who'll always battle to win the maximum for his client. Bill thinks of himself not as a man who adjusts, concedes, and arranges, but as a courthouse winner and occasional champion.

Near the end of this first hour with the embattled Widow Long, a set of phrases surfaces from the deep recesses of Bill's mind—commission, broken contract, about $300,000. The words and figure flash as if projected on a huge theatrical sign on Manhattan's Broadway. Yeah, that's about it, Bill Hutchinson says to himself. Barring some unexpected angle, this case probably will be settled with Arthur and Wendell Long agreeing to pay Oretta somewhat more than half of the $500,000 she'd earn over the remaining five years of the agreement. As for Oretta's other complaints—tightening of the expense account, lower commission percentage on East Coast sales—Bill assumes they'll fall away like autumn leaves.

The reasoning behind this newly surfaced hunch zips through Bill's mind so swiftly he hardly recognizes it:

1. Though she's raging against the wicked half brothers now, Mrs. Long will cool off in the long months ahead before the case reaches the trial calendar. She will likely find that other interests and commitments supersede the lawsuit in the four or more years before the case drags to trial.

2. He sets the dollar figure much lower than her probable earnings because Bill assumes that the half brothers, as mean as Oretta may paint them, will come up with evidence showing that Oretta too did not live up to all elements of the agreement. No client in Bill's memory ever came into his office with hands as clean as Ivory Soap's vaunted purity. He's not sure what Oretta's lapses might have been, but he has some surmises. She may have puffed her expense accounts, maybe alienated some customers, perhaps done less well as a saleswoman than she believes. The possibilities are endless.

3. The brothers, on the other hand, having clearly violated an agreement and no doubt having no wish to see all their business practices aired in court to the benefit of competitors, will have no stomach for protracted litigation. No one wants all his or her business records combed by snooping paralegals. Specifically, Arthur and Wendell Long won't relish open talk in court

about shoddy goods shipped to retailers. Nor will they want their personal lives exposed. Wendell will recognize his vulnerability on the matter of the mistress-saleswoman.

Lawyer Hutchinson reveals nothing of his hidden prognosis of the case to his client. Any mention of settlement now would strike the outraged widow as defeatist. She would regard an attorney who spoke of negotiation at the outset as the kind of man who'd run from a fight, not at all the gladiator she seeks. Also Hutchinson dislikes admitting to himself that this case, seemingly a clear instance of right versus wrong, will eventually wind up settled in mottled ambivalence. Hutchinson, remember, sees himself as a fighting lawyer dedicated to the redressing of wrongs.

Bill lays his pencil aside and leans forward on his desk. "Oretta, subject of course to confirmation of all the facts here, it appears that we have a very good case against the brothers. There's no question that you've been dealt with unfairly, probably in violation of the law. The question is, how far do you want to go with this?"

"Well, I want that contract carried out. And I want to show the half brothers that they can't go back on their written word and get away with it." Oretta invariably says "half brothers" with a curl of scorn as if they belonged to some squalid lawless clan.

"Let me be candid about the possible costs," says Bill. "My fee is one hundred fifty dollars an hour and we bill the time of a law associate, who'll do much of the legal research and investigation, at seventy-five dollars an hour. To prepare adequately for a court appearance might involve as much as three hundred to four hundred hours at an average, let's say, of about one hundred ten dollars an hour. So we're looking at somewhere around forty thousand dollars, plus expenses." He smiles. "Of course, it would be considerably less if we can persuade the brothers by letter to honor their agreement."

"Fat chance!" Oretta snuffs out the last of her cigarette. "I understand you people don't work for nothing. Who does? The main thing is to make the half brothers honor our agreement and show me some respect for all the years I've given the company." She sets her jaw "Let's do whatever we have to. Let's go ahead."

"All right then. I'll need a retainer of seventy-five hundred dollars to begin the work." He glances at her and when she nods, he picks up his interoffice phone. "Janet, bring me a retainer contract."

Oretta reads through the statement, notes the phrase, "no results are guaranteed," signs the paper, and hands it to her lawyer.

"So then, let's get right to work." Bill lays the contract to one side. "Let me call in Susan Pennington. She's a bright young woman, a year out of Duke University Law School. If you two get along, I think she'd be ideal as the law assistant on this case."

Bill thinks Susan has just the sort of low-key sympathetic manner that would appeal to a woman suddenly plunged into the alien and often chilly waters of the law. Bill's prime concern here is his time. He judges that Oretta, a strong woman, will want to keep track of developments and he foresees numerous phone calls from her. He'd much prefer that the bulk of these calls be taken by Susan. At the moment, he has bigger fish to fry, two contract disputes in the multimillion range.

Bill introduces the two women. Susan Pennington has a warm, friendly manner that elicits an approving response from the new client.

Bill briefly outlines the circumstances for Susan, then takes the Arthur–Wendell–Oretta agreement and reads it aloud to both women. Wendell, says Oretta, typed the document while Arthur and Oretta stood at his shoulder offering terms and phrases as they went along. The paper was drawn without benefit of legal advice. A document composed on the assumption of lasting trust between the parties, it has ambiguous phrases. The agreement, for instance, does not define "gross sales" upon which Oretta's commission is based. The words "normal in the trade," used to describe Oretta's travel and entertainment, provide no guidelines, according to Oretta, who says that some salesmen of rival sportswear lines entertain and live extravagantly on the road, whereas others "nickel-and-dime" their way. Even the agreement to employ Oretta for ten years appears less than airtight. The contract says that "it is intended that this agreement shall extend for ten years."

"We may be in a bit of trouble here," says Bill. "They probably will contend that an intention does not constitute a solid commitment."

"I think we're in luck, Mr. Hutchinson," says Susan. "Actually, a jury last month brought in a verdict that hinged on intent. I happened to be researching the outcome in connection with a matter for

Mr. Devereaux. I think it'll support us." Her sunny look embraces Mrs. Long as a member of the team.

"See!" Bill Hutchinson beams at both women. "I knew Susan would be just the person for this case." After a few moments of chatter, he reads aloud the letter by which the two brothers discharged Oretta. They spoke of a "restructuring of the company's business," a "review of our marketing goals," and of "the need to economize." In this new scene, they might have retained Oretta, but her "uncooperative attitude" did not mesh with the new streamlined procedures. Therefore they were forced to terminate her services under "our arrangement." None of this oatmeal language surprises Bill.

"Note they don't use the word 'agreement' or 'contract.' Now it's an arrangement." Bill shakes his head over the camouflage. "You can bet a lawyer helped draft *that* letter."

"What about your attitude?" he asks Oretta. "Was it uncooperative? Did you refuse to work at any time or did you tell off one of the brothers?"

"Not at all." Oretta lights another cigarette. "I argued for my full commission and for a decent expense account, but I never quit work or turned away business. Actually, this last quarter I brought in more customers. Bill, every quarter since I've been selling the line, I've added to our customer list. The books of Bluebird Sportswear will prove the company has increased business steadily in my sales area."

Bill notes problems. The murky language of much of the agreement might permit the Long brothers to convince a jury they never planned a steel-banded contract. And her steamy arguments with Wendell, her superior, might well be construed as the kind of uncooperative behavior justifying her dismissal.

Hutchinson does not tell Oretta of his reservations. He feels that it would tend to erode her confidence in his ability to fight for her vindication. Anyway, at base, her legal position is strong.

"All right, Oretta. We'll get under way at once on this." He turns to his legal assistant. "Susan, let's draft our first letter to the Long brothers. I want it put in emphatic terms so that they know we mean business. We want Mrs. Oretta Long's full salary due under the contract and since sales are increasing and her commissions would go up in proportion, we require that Bluebird Sportswear pay her one hundred and fifteen thousand dollars a year for the next five years. We also want five hundred thousand for the damage caused to her career by the dismissal of Mrs. Long, totally unjustified, in violation of a written and signed contract. In addition, we demand access to the books of the company to ascertain whether, in fact, Mrs. Long has been paid her rightful fifteen percent commission in these last four years plus. Make that language forceful, but then end it on a conciliatory note that envisions a cooperative attitude on both sides, so that we won't have to resort to litigation."

"Are those numbers satisfactory, Oretta?" Bill asks. When she nods, he explains that the threat of a lawsuit, even when phrased in a backhanded fashion, often proves effective in bargaining for results.

"And Susan, let's begin researching the law, particularly with respect to 'lost business opportunities.' " Hutchinson speaks in a tone of crisp command. He knows the value of drama and if he can't perform on the broad public stage of a courtroom, he can put on a miniact for his client. "We want to look at informal written agreements, expense accounts, interpretations of 'gross sales' and conspiracy."

The mention of conspiracy startles Oretta and Bill hastens to reassure her that he's speaking in the broad legal meaning of the term and not of some Mafia plot. "If the Long brothers talked about firing you, they conspired," he says quietly.

"Also Susan, we want the theories on grounds for ousting competent successful employees and for punitive damages." Bill taps his legal pad as he reflects for a moment. "I can see a seven- or eight-count complaint and we want to be ready to file if they don't respond."

He turns full attention to Oretta Long again. "We'll give them ten days to respond," Oretta nods and smiles in agreement. "So, that's about it. We'll gear up for action at once, Oretta, and I'll keep you informed of developments. Don't expect anything before next week, though." He arises, comes around the desk, and places a hand on the widow's arm. "No communication with the half brothers, please, except through me. . . . You came to the right shop. We'll look after you and take good care of your interests."

Susan makes a fuss over the client, but this proves less than a chore. It's obvious that she likes Oretta and that the widow, with warmth beneath her sophisticated veneer, reciprocates the feeling.

Bill can envision the two women having a friendly drink together after the next meeting.

Oretta Long, buoyed and validated in her choler, leaves in an optimistic mood as the soft chimes of the wall clock strike four times. She has been here two hours, the last one with both lawyers. If she is aware that she already has spent $375, she doesn't show it.

The Mediation Way

4

New York
May 6

Part One: *First Meeting of Lawyer and Client*

Mark Bianchi is a Manhattan attorney. Like Bill Hutchinson across the country in Los Angeles, Bianchi practices law, largely contracts and other business matters. Like Hutchinson, he is in his mid-forties, has a comparable income, and works in a similar medium-size law firm, Archer, Gonzalez & Bianchi. He too is a family man with a wife and three children. He earned his law degree from Villanova Law School and like Hutchinson, he has a framed diploma hanging on his office wall. Also like Hutchinson, Bianchi keeps in shape, playing handball during many noon hours and golf on weekends.

There the resemblance ends, for Attorney Bianchi in recent years has been using a professional tool that Hutchinson has never tried and tends to belittle when he discusses it with other lawyers. Bianchi submits many of his cases to mediation, an informal process where a mediator facilitates discussion between the opposing parties to a dispute and helps them arrive at an agreement that avoids the long, thorny, and costly path of litigation.

In the last three years Bianchi has taken thirty-five of his clients to mediation with satisfactory settlements in all but eight cases. In two of those eight, the client decided to drop the matter. The other six cases went to court where one gained a substantial jury award, one suffered defeat, and four are still pending. In addition, Mark Bianchi himself has served as mediator in twenty-three commercial disputes, all but two of which resulted in agreement by the contesting parties.

Bianchi is no reformer or crusader for change. He believes America's civil legal system, fashioned for combat between warring foes, serves reasonably well for:

Those who believe their constitutional rights are being denied

Those whose grievances involve questions of public policy covering other citizens

Those who do have the law 100 percent on their side and are trying to collect a bad debt, deal with a nonpaying tenant, or force restitution from a crook who spurns their demands

Those disputants who are poles apart in their values, economic status, culture, and sometimes language

Those dissidents whose beliefs pit them against the conforming majority

Those not insignificant numbers of Americans who love the clamor and drama of the courtroom and who would rather have a jury validate their stance of rectitude—and demolish that of the opposing litigant—than win a million-dollar lottery

A good trial lawyer, Mark Bianchi will take a case to court and press it vigorously if his client insists, but in his view three-quarters of the aggrieved who walk into his office seeking the righting of wrongs would be better off submitting their complaints to the healing powers of mediation.

An occasional dabbler in scholarly legal theory, Bianchi has read in the law journals of the attacks on the mediation process by law professors of the Critical Legal Studies tribe. The CLSers, some of them foes of the capitalistic system, contend that mediation often reinforces existing social inequities and invites the oppressed to beg for scraps from the oppressors. It is ridiculous, they say, to expect the powerless to find justice in a mediation session with the powerful. Woe to the lamb that lies down with the lion.

While Bianchi tends to agree with some CLS points, he finds that none of them seem to apply to the great majority of his clients. For the most part he represents businessmen and women who share roughly the same values, ethics, and power and the same respect for that lubricant and goal of their commerce—money.

As a sample, Client Jake, owner of a plumbing supply house, claims that Distributor Fred violates federal antitrust laws by failing to give him the hefty discounts he gives Jake's competitors. Jake wants $150,000 damages. Client Grace, a builder–architect, contends that a subcontractor on a hospital project installed faulty wiring that caused several X-ray machines to malfunction. Since the hospital billed her for the repairs, she seeks $200,000 for reimbursement, damages, and legal fees. Clients Jim, Sarah, Hank, and George seek similar satisfaction in other fields. The list goes on and on.

To do business is to fall out, sooner or later, with suppliers, partners, rivals, or customers. No two parties to a deal put exactly the same interpretation on their signed contract. Businessmen and women labor under the same handicaps as the rest of us. Our motives are ambivalent, our language ambiguous, our characters flawed, and our written words imprecise despite the ministrations of troops of psychiatrists, preachers, and lawyers.

Attorney Bianchi finds that he serves his clients better by guiding them toward mediation or arbitration when possible. They wind up with approximately the same amount of money and ego satisfaction as they would gather in the inevitable pretrial negotiations that judges order, and they get there much faster and cheaper with far less wear and tear on the psychic engine.

Also Bianchi gets more personal satisfaction seeing his clients forge their own settlement than watching them agonize while losing or winning bitterly fought court battles. "Nobody wins, but nobody loses in mediation," he told his wife recently, "and it gives me a good feeling to be part of that."

The opening scene with Oretta Long in Bill Hutchinson's office differs only slightly from that which unfolds in the office of Mark Bianchi when a new client, Rosemary Wofford, brings her grievance to the initial meeting in New York on the same day that Oretta begins her action in Los Angeles.

Mrs. Rosemary Wofford resembles Oretta Long in many ways. She's an attractive, modishly dressed businesswoman in her early fifties. Although not a widow like Oretta, she is separated from her husband and lives with her two teenage sons in Princeton, New Jersey. Like Oretta, Rosemary Wofford comes with a flush of anger to her first meeting with an attorney. A woman friend recommended that she consult Bianchi in his law firm's office on East Fifty-third Street in Manhattan.

At Bianchi's urging, Rosemary Wofford prefaces her problem by telling something of herself. She grew up in Albany, attended Syracuse University for three years, worked for her younger brother for ten years, then married and became a housewife while she raised her two sons. She and her husband separated three years ago—a divorce is now imminent—and she went back to work for her brother a few months later.

In the years while she raised a family, her hard-driving brother Stephen Holloway built his home furnishings business into a prosperous chain of ten East Coast stores catering to the affluent. He handled only finely crafted furniture, elegant fabrics and draperies, and expensive carpeting, all offered along with an interior decorating service that had gained an elitist reputation in Southampton, Palm Beach, and fashionable residential towns near New York, Boston, and Washington, D.C.

Rosemary, always on good terms with her brother, but not, "you know, real close or cozy," returned to Holloway Interiors as manager of the Princeton, New Jersey, store. She and Stephen signed an agreement that stipulated she would be paid $65,000 a year plus a bonus of 15 percent of all net profits in excess of the store's net in the year before she was hired. For the year in question the store earned $72,000 net and Rosemary and Stephen both felt confident she could raise the figure to several hundred thousand dollars in profits in the years to come.

The terms of the agreement were to run for five years, says Rosemary, at which time it would be open for renegotiation or cancellation. Since they were brother and sister and trusted each other, they did not bother with a formally drafted legal document. Instead Stephen wrote the terms on a sheet of headquarters stationery, Rosemary made a few changes to which he had no objection, and then his secretary typed up an original with several copies. They both signed.

"We didn't think we'd ever have any trouble," she says, adding in a self-mocking tone, "Little did I know."

"Little do we all know." Bianchi clasps his hands behind his head. "Tell me about it."

Rosemary says it soon became apparent to her that she couldn't boost sales unless she widened the potential market and appealed to upper middle-class customers as well as the wealthy. "We had the old money as customers, but there just weren't enough really rich families moving into homes in our area and it's the newly moved people who provide the bulk of our business." The store's decorating specialist, a man who had worked for Holloway for twenty years, vehemently opposed her plan to offer several lines of furnishings priced substantially lower. After a number of emotional exchanges with the man, Rosemary discharged him.

"He told me the only reason he didn't quit before I could fire him was the six months' severance pay he got for being discharged."

Her strategy worked, she says. The first year she increased net profits by about $100,000, earning herself a $15,000 bonus. Another sizable increment appeared certain in this, the second year, but two months ago her brother fired her, charging that she had violated their understanding by "cheapening the Holloway Interiors name," dismissed an old and trusted employee, and sent "emotional shock waves" rolling through employees of the Holloway chain as well as through many of their valued customers. Stephen Holloway fired her with two months' salary advance and promptly rehired the employee she had let go.

Her ouster came after several arguments with Stephen. Since her dismissal, she has tried to see him a number of times, but he refuses on the telephone, contending that their "merchandising ideas are so far apart" that talk would be futile.

"That's about it," she concludes. "I'm fired with no ifs, ands or buts despite a contract that has more than three years to run."

"Did you have any discussions when you first went to work about the carriage trade nature of the business?" Mark Bianchi begins making notes on a large yellow pad. "For instance, did Stephen ever say specifically that you were to aim your sales pitch exclusively at high income customers?"

"Not that I remember." Rosemary reflects, frowning. "Of course,

I guess he took it for granted that I'd continue going for the wealthy crowd. That's where he'd made his money."

"You brought a copy of the contract with you?"

She nods and hands over a single sheet of paper. Bianchi reads the agreement aloud, pausing now and then to comment on various provisions. He emphasizes a phrase that describes Holloway Interiors as a "furniture and home decorating business of superior standards that is dedicated to offering the discriminating customer the finest in furnishings and interior decorating concepts."

He shakes his head when he finishes. "This is a loosely drawn agreement. For instance, do 'net profits' mean net before or after taxes?"

"We did have an argument about that after the first year." Recalling the incident brings color to Rosemary's cheeks. "I claimed my fifteen percent bonus should be based on a hundred and forty thousand dollars, the increase in our net profits before taxes, but Stephen said that net 'always' meant after taxes. So he based my bonus on one hundred thousand dollars, the net after taxes. I said, kind of kiddingly, that he was shuffling me out of some money. Stephen got mad, claiming I was accusing him of trying to cheat me, when he was only going by the standard definitions that all businesses adhered to."

"And did you get angry then?"

"Not really. You see, I was so sure that I'd produce another big increase this year that my income would go way up anyway. I was surprised Steve got so upset, but frankly I thought I'd be making so much money that it wouldn't matter."

"Did you check out your interpretation of 'net' with an accountant or tax attorney?"

"Yeah. A friend who's an accountant said that normally 'net profit' means after taxes, but that there are a lot of exceptions."

Bianchi nods. "That's right. And that's why I would have advised you to spell out in the contract exactly what you both agreed on, whether before or after taxes."

Rosemary looks embarrassed. "I should have checked the agreement with a lawyer before signing, I know. It just never occurred to me . . . my own brother."

Bianchi questions her for another half hour about the contract, her relationship with Stephen during her employment, her differences with the fired and subsequently rehired employee, and her intentions about work in the future. They reach a first-name basis during the process and feel quite comfortable with each other.

Like Bill Hutchinson, Mark Bianchi has his invisible guesstimator, a clump of brain cells that has been grinding away at the key question: **What's This Thing Worth?** At the end of his first hour and a half with Rosemary Wofford, Mark comes up with the figure $200,000—the maximum amount he thinks she reasonably could expect to collect from her brother at the end of litigation.

His reasoning parallels that of Hutchinson in estimating the probable outcome of Oretta Long's lawsuit. And Bianchi makes many of the same assumptions—that Rosemary would tire of a protracted legal battle, that she'd flinch at some of the facts Stephen Holloway's lawyers would dig up about her, and that Holloway would also recoil at having some of his practices revealed in court. Mark, like Hutchinson, knows the countless ways in which litigants lose heart for the fight and retreat at last into the den of settlement, often on the very eve of trial.

But unlike Bill Hutchinson, Mark Bianchi does not keep his first estimate a secret. He tells the client what has been running through his mind. He does it this way.

"Rosemary," he asks, "if Steve Holloway walked in here right now and offered to settle this thing this afternoon, what would you settle for?"

"Settle?" Rosemary is surprised, wary. "What do you mean? I wouldn't settle for anything less than my salary plus bonuses for the next three and a half years, as specified in the contract, plus a lot of bucks for the anguish he's caused me. I want Steve to know how it feels to hurt like I do."

"I know how you feel." Mark presses gently. "But just what does that mean in dollars? How much to do you want?"

"Well . . ." She hesitates. "I read about all those big awards from juries. I think I ought to get seven hundred and fifty thousand anyway." Fearing the amount may alarm the lawyer, she hastens to explain. "Steve broke that contract, practically ruined my career, and he should damn well be made to pay for it."

"What if he offered to give you your job back with a clearly worded contract?"

"No way." Rosemary makes the face of someone who has just un-expectedly bit into a lemon. "Steve and I are through. I saw what kind of man my brother is and I didn't like what I saw."

"But if he walked in here and offered you seven hundred and fifty thousand, you'd take it?"

"I would if he apologized." She flared. "He's got to acknowledge what he did."

"Understood. But translating your rightful due into dollars, you would consider seven fifty a fair offer?"

"If he did it right away, yes." She's still caught up in indignation. "But after a court trial, with your fees and expenses and all, I'd de-serve a lot more."

Bianchi catches a note of irritation in her voice. She doesn't want anymore of this quizzing by her attorney. After all, her manner seems to say, he's getting paid to come up with the answers. On the other hand, Mark has come to believe that it's his duty to force his new clients to think through their problems and their legal options.

"Rosemary," he says, "I think you've got a good case and there's no doubt in my mind that Stephen owes you under the law." He swivels in his chair and thrusts out his legs, informal prelude to a brotherly talk. "But there's lots of bad news too. I know you've heard about court delay and congestion. Well, here in New York, we've got a two-year delay. That is, on the day we file our lawsuit we're looking at just about two years until we can get into court before a judge and jury."

"God, I didn't know it was that long."

"Yep. Now in preparing for trial, we lawyers take advantage of a legal process called 'discovery.' That is, without even a court order, we can go into the other side's books and find out everything perti-nent to our complaint. Only difficulty is, the other side can do the same to us. So Stephen's lawyers will comb through your records and papers and interview your former employees and customers. Investi-gators will be going through your files for days."

"I didn't know that." She looks dismayed. "I thought that was just those big antitrust cases."

"No, yours too. And there's a high probability that they'll dig up something that won't look good in court."

"What, for instance? I'm not ashamed of my record in business."

"Could be most anything. Remember, this will be your adversary looking for what will make you look bad. Ever use expense money for something personal? Take someone to dinner who wasn't actually a customer? How about transportation? Didn't you tell me that your brother provided you a car for business as part of your agreement?"

"That's right. An Olds. Well, sure some of the mileage I put on the Olds was my own stuff, a few errands, nothing major."

"And expense account? Every nickel spent strictly on business?"

"Of course. Well, on my two buying trips to Chicago, naturally I phoned home to Tom and Joe, my sons, bought them a couple of shirts, piddling stuff like that. I did take my cousin Ed to dinner once. But I worked my tail off on those buying trips." She grows indignant again.

"I know, I know," Mark soothes. "But we have to expect that kind of attack once we get into court. How about social contact with any of your employees?"

She hesitates. "No. Well, nothing of any consequence."

"You see, your brother's lawyer will try to dig up something that makes you look less than businesslike. He'll try to picture you as a woman not to be trusted. . . . And that's just a token of what we face if we go the litigation route."

He describes the lengthy legal process, the complaint and the answer, the counterclaims, the flurry of motions, the depositions, the moves for more discovery, the waiting for trial, the picking of the jury, all climaxed by the judge's inevitable last-minute pressure on opposing lawyers to settle the case and help clear out the clogged channels of justice.

"All of this will be costing you money as we go along," says Mark. "My fee is a hundred fifty dollars an hour and my firm bills the services of a young law assistant, who'll do much of the legal drafting and research, at seventy-five dollars an hour. My guess is that it would take us in the neighborhood of two hundred hours to prepare properly for trial, so you face somewhere around twenty thousand dollars before we get before a judge. Once into court, our costs will run at about two thousand dollars a day. Figuring a five-day trial, we're looking at a total bill to you of about thirty thousand dollars."

"That's the great American legal system, right?" Rosemary makes a wry face. "I hate to see a price put on simple justice, but I'm determined to get my rights. Anyway, I guess there's no alternative."

"Oh, but there is, if we're lucky." Mark stops his apparently idle swiveling and leans across the desk. "There's mediation. I've taken a lot of my cases before a mediator. The last two, no more nor less involved than yours, were settled in a day. Do you know anything about it?"

She shakes her head. "But if it means sitting down with Steve, the ingrate, and talking politely to him, I'm against it. Do you know I used to lie for him to our parents when he was drinking in high school?"

"You would sit in the same room with Stephen, but I make our case for us and—"

Rosemary cuts in. "I don't want to bargain with the guy."

"Not even if it saves you twenty-five thousand dollars?"

"What do you mean?" Rosemary shows interest.

"I mean it's possible to go through mediation and get about the same sum you would after several years of litigation. You get results within six weeks and your expenses, compared to the trial route, are dirt cheap. In your case, probably under eight thousand dollars."

Bianchi explains the mediation process. Once the opposing parties agree to talk, they meet in a neutral office with a paid mediator who works with them in an effort to bring off a fair settlement. "No formality, no rules of evidence, no judge, no jury, just a fair-minded mediator using everyday common sense." He describes the mechanics of the simple procedure.

"So you start off at nine A.M., asking the seven hundred and fifty thousand dollars you want. Stephen starts off claiming he owes you nothing. By late that afternoon or perhaps the next day sometime, you both sign an agreement under which he pledges to pay you something fair, perhaps in a neighborhood somewhat below two hundred thousand." Mark writes the number on his legal pad. "That's just a guess, but it's an educated one. I've gone through lots of mediations now and I think I can forecast results with fair accuracy." He pauses. "There's even a chance that the mediator may suggest some kind of creative solution."

"Two hundred! That's a long way down from three quarters of a million." Rosemary looks glum. "Why do you want me to settle for so much less?"

"Because I think that's just about what you'd get if you filed suit, spent thirty thousand dollars, and then went through a trial two years from now. Nobody ever gets the big numbers they ask. And remember, the judge will put on pressure for a compromise at the last minute before trial anyway."

Rosemary does not respond at once. This is a new idea for her and she wants to think about it. Also she's a bit suspicious.

"I don't get it," she says after a time. "What do you get out of this mediation? Aren't you costing yourself twenty-five thousand or thereabouts in legal fees?"

"Yes, but I could take fifteen or sixteen other clients through mediation during the time I would have spent on discovery and motions for you. Believe me, I'll make just as much." He shakes his head. "Never fear, I'm not about to go around cutting my own income." Bianchi pauses. "Besides, I get much more kick helping bring about a happy settlement than fighting it out in court. Some of my court winners wind up bitter people—and as for losing, no thanks, ma'am."

Rosemary ponders this new idea. "It takes some getting used to. I sure don't like sitting around the same room with Steve."

"You're only together part of the time. The mediator spends a lot of time alone with each side. . . . By the way, who's Stephen's lawyer?"

"Peter Cavanaugh. A nice enough guy."

"I don't know him, but I've heard of him." Mark explains that he first must persuade Cavanaugh and his client to try the mediation route. "That may not be easy. We may have to file our complaint to soften them up. Of course, if they refuse mediation, we could urge arbitration." He describes the process by which both sides submit their case to a neutral arbitrator for a final and binding decision.

"And if they say no again, we'll have no alternative but to go ahead with a lawsuit."

But if Stephen does agree to mediation, Mark says, the process should not take more than a day or two. If Rosemary is not satisfied with Stephen's last offer, she can break off the negotiations and go ahead with regular courthouse litigation.

"You lose nothing by trying," he advises. "A law associate and I will prepare for mediation by a thorough review of the law and by putting our case in order. I'd guess twenty to thirty hours at the most. The mediator charges one hundred and fifty dollars an hour, split between the two parties."

"How long does this take altogether?"

"If it works, you should have your agreement in six or seven weeks. That contrasts with more than two years if you go the lawsuit route."

"I don't know." Rosemary came here for action. "I think I'd rather have my day in court."

"No question you're entitled." Mark grins. "It's the right of every American. But remember, in your case, it may be a thirty-thousand dollar day—with no assurance that you'll win. You might come out of court empty-handed after all those months of hassle."

"It's not fair," says Rosemary with a flash of anger. "I've been done out of my job for the crime of increasing business and I have to wait more than two years to do anything about it."

"No, you can do something about it within a few weeks." Mark squares the legal pad before him. "If we go to mediation, you'll have a satisfactory settlement promptly. And if you don't, we go to court and fight for your rights."

They discuss the matter for another ten minutes. Rosemary shies from the thought of bargaining with Stephen. Bianchi assures her that he'll do the talking, will be at her elbow throughout mediation, will support her fully, and will not permit her to bend to an agreement that does not fully serve her interests.

"All right," she says at last with a sigh. "Let's go ahead and give it a try. You're a persuasive man, Mark."

"It's just experience talking. All twenty-seven of my clients who reached an agreement at mediation felt they got a fair shake—and some of them even became friendly again with their opponents."

Rosemary throws up an arm in mock defense. "Oh God, friendly with that damn Stephen? Not a chance."

"Stranger things have happened at mediations." Mark makes small talk for a few minutes, then takes Rosemary's elbow as he walks her to the door. "I'll let you know what develops after I talk to Peter Cavanaugh. One route or another, Rosemary, we'll get satisfaction for you."

Rosemary Wofford leaves after two hours with her attorney. She's headed toward mediation and she's spent $300.

Mediation

5

New York
May 9

Part Two: *Huddle with Enemy Agent*

Mediation Agreement

Bill Hutchinson and most other lawyers would approve of Mark Bianchi's opening move in his campaign to gain monetary and emotional satisfaction for his client, Rosemary Wofford, discharged by her brother after she had increased his profits.

Attorney Bianchi fires off a letter to the brother, demanding that Stephen Holloway pay his sister $750,000, including nearly three years' pay on a broken contract, bonuses she probably would have earned, recompense for injury to her career, and punitive damages the law allows to punish the offender. Actually the letter is written by Douglas McGinness, a young associate in the firm of Archer, Gonzalez and Bianchi, who earned his degree the previous year from Ohio State University's College of Law. Bianchi sketches the Rosemary Wofford matter for McGinness and later edits the letter with the fledgling attorney at his elbow.

A week later a contentious letter arrives from Peter Cavanaugh of the Manhattan firm of Sturgis, Diamond, Cavanaugh and Heinrich. Cavanaugh, representing Stephen Holloway, brushes off the demand for money, says Holloway owes his sister nothing, and warns that should Rosemary Wofford press her claims in a lawsuit, Stephen Holloway will countersue, charging breach of contract, slander, and heavy damage to his business.

At this point, custom decrees that Mark Bianchi summon his client and law associate and start preparing the formal complaint that would be filed in court to touch off the lawsuit. Instead Bianchi telephones Peter Cavanaugh.

"We don't know each other," he says after the amenities, "but I'd like to buy you a lunch and talk over this Holloway brother and sister thing."

"You don't know me," Cavanaugh replies, "but I know you. I heard you give a talk on mediation at the University Club last year."

"Well, good. This Holloway matter is just the sort of case that adapts itself easily to mediation."

"Look," says Cavanaugh, "if you want to talk settlement by having Stephen pay good money to your client, we're wasting each other's time. My client has nothing to settle. His sister didn't work out and he let her go. That's all that happened. There's no lawsuit here, Mark."

"You'll think differently when you read our complaint. But come on, Peter, what have you got to lose? There are some things you ought to know before we tee off on you. Make it the Côte Basque. They serve a good quenelle." After more backing and filling, Cavanaugh agrees to lunch. Meeting at the appointed hour the next day at the East Fifty-fifth Street restaurant, both men order a drink while awaiting the quenelle, a delicate fish mousse. Mark has a chance to appraise the other lawyer while sipping a Scotch and soda. Peter Cavanaugh is a large, genial, heavy-shouldered man with a hearty laugh, broken nose, Boston brogue, and cynical world view. Mark surmises that he once played football and it turns out that Cavanaugh earned his varsity letter as a defensive tackle at Notre Dame after attending a Jesuit-run school in Boston. He's a product of the Notre Dame Law School.

"I thought you did the best job possible with that mediation talk at the University Club," he says, "but frankly I'm not sold on the process. One of my partners has tried it twice with so-so results. Once they failed to reach agreement and on the other case, he thought his client insisted on settling for less than he could have gotten in court."

"Including costs and your firm's fees?"

"Well, no." Cavanaugh frowns. "I guess Jake wasn't figuring in the costs."

"But of course," says Mark in his soft voice, "that's half the point, isn't it?"

"Hey, man, what are you up to?" Cavanaugh feigns alarm with a laugh. "You trying to do us out of our day's wages? You want the repossession man to come and get the big-screen TV, the Ferrari, and the wife's sapphire?"

"Not quite. I've done a lot of mediation in the last three years and my income has actually gone up."

"Hard to believe. Sounds to me like shitting in your own nest." Cavanaugh lets go with his rolling laugh again.

"Can I tell you a couple of my experiences with mediation, just to give you an idea?"

"Be my guest—since I'm yours." He beckons to a waiter. "One more of the same while I listen to this rug merchant."

Mark Bianchi, who decides he likes the man, tells the story of three mechanics who built a highly successful car repair service, then got into a fight that broke up the company. Each man hired a lawyer, one suit and two countersuits were filed, and pairs of accountant investigators made a shambles of the offices during the discovery process. At the end of a year, the case had still not come to trial, the owners had spent more than $80,000 on legal fees and expenses, and were farther from a fair division of the assets than they were the day the company fell apart. Bianchi met one of the men at a political fund-raiser, listened to his tale of woe, and suggested that they try mediation with him.

"They each came to our office with an attorney," Bianchi relates, "and the first morning sounded like a boiler room—everybody blowing off steam. One guy walked out and had to be hauled back by his lawyer. But in the afternoon, I got them to talking dollars and shares and who deserved what. I spent an hour alone with each of the three that afternoon and then the next morning I had two more individual meetings, followed by another joint session and still more time with individuals. Anyway, it took five days over a couple of weeks, but at the end we had a signed agreement that two partners actually praised and the remaining guy said he could live with. It shows you what can be done."

"How much did it cost them?" Cavanaugh, stirring his drink, appears skeptical.

"My fee at a hundred fifty an hour came to four thousand three hundred and fifty dollars—twenty-nine hours spread through those five days. With a few extras, duplicating, lunches sent in, that sort of thing, it came to a little over forty-five hundred. They split it, fifteen hundred apiece, and I swallowed the remaining few bucks."

"Magnanimous of you, Mark." Cavanaugh toasts him with his drink. "So how are they doing today?"

"All prospering. . . . Listen, Pete, in case you think this was a fluke, it wasn't. I've mediated twenty-three cases and got agreements all but twice."

"What happened to them?"

"Both went on to litigation. No results in yet on either of them. . . . I've also taken thirty-five of my own clients to mediation in the last three years. Good agreements in all but eight cases. And the big thing is my people generally like the agreements they help make. I've only had one real dissenter and he's the kind of guy who bitches at everything."

Bianchi describes two quite similar cases of his in which contractors made major mistakes in constructing comparable buildings. One structure, more than an inch out of kilter, suffered cracked ceilings and walls in the first year. In the other, the basement flooded and a leaking roof ruined the top floor. Bianchi estimated needed repairs of $290,000 in one instance and $305,000 in the other. In the first case, the contractor's bonding company agreed to mediate and five weeks later the owner had a check for $245,000. In the second case, the bonding company insisted on litigation.

"That one is still dragging on two years later," says Bianchi. "No trial date in sight and each side has racked up more than twenty-five thousand in fees and costs. Since we're still into discovery, my guess is that it'll cost my client another ten grand before we get into court."

"Yeah, but he stands to collect four or five hundred thousand with damages, doesn't he?" asks Cavanaugh with a yawn. His interest is less than total.

Bianchi shakes his head. "One chance in twenty. You know all the things that can happen to us, Pete. The judge pressures us into a settlement, or their expert witness romances the jury, or my client dies—he's an old guy—or his accountant messes up on the stand. Come on, don't make me run through all the possibilities. The point is, we've got just as much chance of losing as we have of winning.

"Compare that with the other owner I told you about. He banked his money two years ago, made his repairs, and has been collecting top-dollar rents for more than a year. I ask you, who's better off?"

Cavanaugh shrugs off an answer. "You just don't like to litigate, Mark. Sure, it's a gamble, but you take risks every day you get out of bed. I'll tell you one thing. I'd never go into mediation if it meant foreclosing my right to take our case to court."

"You don't have to give up anything." Bianchi leans forward on the table. "Anytime you think your client's getting a bad deal in mediation, you can call it quits and walk out."

"So give me a blueprint of the action." Cavanaugh's skepticism surrounds him like smoke. "I know how mediation works, but review the ground rules for me."

"Two parties can go out and hire a mediator, but I prefer to go through the American Arbitration Association. They do all the administrative work, setting the date, calling the two sides, providing the room. They also have a panel of mediators here in New York. If you went the mediation route, I'm sure we could agree on somebody on the panel. They're predominantly attorneys. The triple-A fee for the arrangements and meeting room is around six hundred dollars for each side."

"Okay, suppose both sides agree to mediate?" Cavanaugh expresses mild interest now. "Then what? Who sits in on this thing?"

"Just the principals, their attorneys, and the mediator. Everything is confidential. In case of a bust, nothing said or done in the sessions can be used in litigation. Each party agrees to be open and candid, but also reserves its right to break off negotiations at any time and pursue the matter elsewhere."

"And the mediator? How does he operate?"

"Each one has a different style. When I mediate I spend a half hour with everybody assembled in the room." Bianchi, a doodler, sketches on the back of an envelope. "I explain the setup, how we'll proceed, some simple ground rules. Then I sit down with the plaintiff and his lawyer, find out precisely what bugs them and what they want. Then ditto with the other party. Before long I'm shuttling between the two sides, carrying offers, explaining positions, maybe suggesting some course neither side has thought of."

Bianchi goes into detail on some of the mechanisms, says that when an agreement is reached, "I ask the attorneys to draw up a settlement agreement. Then I ask them if they want to appoint me as their arbitrator. If so, I sign the agreement as arbitrator and either one can then take it to court and make it a judgment. The court will enforce it."

"Okay, fine," says Cavanaugh, "but I don't see where this suit of clothes fits my client."

"The stronger the relationship between the parties, the better the chance of success in mediation. Here you have a brother and sister. Now, no matter how frosty they may be toward each other at the moment, they're going to have some kind of dealings or connection all their lives. They can't avoid it. They're family."

"You're a persuasive guy, Mark. You got that missionary zeal." Peter Cavanaugh tilts his head in approbation. "But I come back to Square One. My client has nothing to mediate—or litigate for that matter. He let his sister go when she violated policy. It's as simple as that. It happens every day and he has nothing to answer for."

"Oh, come on, Pete." Bianchi's smile is as soft as his speech. "You know Rosemary Wofford had a valid contract with her brother. And he broke that contract when he fired her. You know the law as well as I do."

"He didn't break the contract, she did." Cavanaugh polishes off his drink. "She had a clear obligation to maintain Holloway Interiors as an elite, prestige establishment. She reneged on that obligation. Now what she's saying about Stephen Holloway in the trade amounts to slander and believe me, if she persists in this matter, we're prepared to prove she's trying to ruin him."

The quenelle arrives and both men retreat from talk for a few minutes, savoring the fish mousse. "Damn good," says Cavanaugh. "A couple more lunches like this, and I might buy mediation."

Bianchi takes up the argument again. "I doubt my client has slandered anyone. She's not the type. Actually, we'll be able to show that Stephen's remarks about her in the trade are hurting her. She'll have a hard time finding a job after the way he's talking."

"Did you know your Rosemary had an affair with another employee?" Cavanaugh doesn't wait for an answer. "That made for more bad feeling in the company. I'll tell you, when her behavior at Holloway Interiors is spread on the record, she won't look so good."

"Maybe, maybe not. Pete, none of that kind of gossipy stuff in this family fight belongs in the open courtroom. That's the type of thing we can toss around in the privacy of mediation and then get down to the gut issues—was it a valid contract that was broken and what's the legal definition of profits? Pete, you should look at two things. First, the contract. The presumption is that it's valid, so you know we've at least got standing to avoid summary judgment in court. We've got a case for sure. Whether or not it's a winner is another matter. Second, does your client want his remarks about his sister—or hers about him, for that matter—spread on the public record? Does he really want all that dirty laundry hung up in Foley Square?"

"You want my guess or a one-word answer?" Cavanaugh lifts a forkful of the quenelle. "No."

"There you have it." Bianchi's voice is still soft, low-pitched. "Pete, this is a perfect case for mediation. This is a brother and sister, like it or not, who'll have to relate to each other over the years. A bad court case means bitter times ahead for them. A good mediation might even bring them together again."

"The chances of my client agreeing to pay a compromise of several hundred thousand bucks is nil." Cavanaugh shakes his head. "I mean it, Mark."

"A good mediator can come up with all kinds of innovative suggestions. He or she might even propose something that doesn't involve money at all. Who knows? The field's wide open."

"Well, I got to admit that you might get something out of Steve Holloway in litigation." Cavanaugh pauses, fork in hand. "I may think you haven't much of a case, but I'm not a jury."

"Mediation makes sense, Pete. Give it some more thought and phone me tomorrow."

"I'll go this far. I'll take it up with Holloway and try to give him a candid estimate of what he faces in court."

"Which isn't all good," says Bianchi.

"And isn't all bad either," says Cavanaugh sharply.

Late the next afternoon Cavanaugh calls Bianchi. The attorney says he has talked to Holloway and the home furnishings chief agreed to mediation "because he didn't want to drag family matters through the courts." Bianchi translates this to mean that Cavanaugh has warned Holloway that he might get stuck for considerable money by a jury and that if mediation could settle the matter, he'd save time, money, and mental turmoil.

Two days later the two lawyers meet at the West Fifty-first Street offices of the American Arbitration Association, a national nonprofit organization dedicated to short-circuiting the complicated court system by the simpler means of arbitration or the even swifter and leaner mediation. Here an administrator describes the process and offers them a list of names from a panel of 200 mediators. After mulling over many recognized names, Cavanaugh and Bianchi agree on Seymour F. Weinstein, a corporate attorney whom they both know and respect. Weinstein is a senior member of the New York bar, now all but retired from active practice. After a phone call to him, the date for the mediation is set three weeks away on a Monday.

Cavanaugh declines to go to binding arbitration, should the mediation fail, reserving his right to go to court. Bianchi reserves the same right when they sign the formal agreement to mediate. They then establish their own ground rules. Each attorney is to prepare a paper, setting out his client's position, and send it to the opposing lawyer and the mediator within ten days. Each man then prepares an answer, which he mails to the other attorney and the mediator within five days.

Cavanaugh doesn't look happy. "I don't know. This seems like fixing to sign a peace treaty while you're still stacking the ammunition."

"Exactly." Bianchi grins. "Trouble is, Peter, neither of us knows how much ammo the other guy has, do we?"

The Costs

Counting ninety minutes spent on the letter to Holloway, the calls to Cavanaugh and Rosemary Wofford, and his two-hour quenelle conference with Cavanaugh, Bianchi has added four hours to his total spent on Rosemary's case. Together with the three hours that Doug McGinness ($75 an hour) spent on preliminary legal research and the letter to Holloway, the law firm has added $825 to Rosemary's bill, which now stands at $1,125.

Mediation

6

Part Three: *Preparing to Talk*

The Mediation Position Paper

Rosemary comes to Mark Bianchi's office to help him draft their position paper. With the mediation date set, both Bianchi and Cavanaugh are giving the Wofford–Holloway case priority, although neither can promise complete attention. Lawyers who juggle eight and ten cases at once often have to seek delays or switch rapidly from one battleground to another.

"We'll be in good hands with Seymour Weinstein," says Bianchi of the mediator after greeting his client. "He's highly respected, a man who turned down several judgeships in his time. We couldn't ask for a fairer guy to facilitate these sessions."

"I'm glad." Rosemary seats herself and smoothes out her skirt. "When he hears the facts, I know he'll rule for us."

"No, no." Bianchi holds up his palms. "This isn't a judicial hearing, Rosemary. This is a mediation. You and I will work out the agreement with your brother and Cavanaugh. Weinstein will merely facilitate matters, shuttle back and forth with offers, keep things on rails."

"I still don't like the idea of sitting around and bargaining with Stephen." She makes a sour mouth, shakes her head. "He really shafted me, you know. You can't trust the bastard. I learned the hard way."

"I understand how you feel." Bianchi leans forward across the desk. "On the other hand, the fact is that you're sister and brother, and like it or not, you're going to continue to have some kind of relationship for many years to come."

"As distant as possible, I hope."

"Could be, but you never know. At any rate, Rosemary, we want our position paper to be as strong as possible. We have to justify these demands we're making, present a good concrete foundation so that any reasonable person would recognize the merits of your case. I've been through a lot of these mediations and I think it's vital to impress the mediator. If he starts out viewing you as a competent, reliable, and reasonable woman who apparently has been badly mistreated, we're that much ahead. It's true that a good mediator doesn't prejudge a case, but believe me, he can spot bogus or extravagant demands in a minute."

"Do you think I'm being unreasonable in asking seven hundred and fifty thousand dollars?" Rosemary frowns as she studies her lawyer.

Mark Bianchi doesn't answer for a moment. Instead he strolls to the window and stands for a moment looking down at the sidewalk, heaped high with plastic trash bundles that haven't been collected in several days. The sky is overcast and the city looks gray and dowdy today.

"Unreasonable? That's hard to say." He returns and sits down at his desk again. "But frankly, Rosemary, I think we'd be on firmer ground if we scaled that down some. Let's look at it from a neutral's standpoint, someone like Weinstein. You're a very capable businesswoman in the prime of life. You have plenty of zip, ideas, and know-how. You're quite able to make a good salary. So, a neutral would say, it's unlikely that your discharge by your brother will make much dent in your career."

"What figure would you suggest?"

"Remember my estimate that first day that if you went to trial, you'd probably wind up with something in the neighborhood of two hundred thousand—minus some thirty thousand for legal expenses? Well, I'd like to get you more than that, fifty or sixty thousand more. To do that, I'd like to take a good commonsense approach all through the negotiations. So yes, I think seven hundred and fifty thousand is out of the ballpark as a starting figure.

"I'd like us to to put the figure at five hundred thousand in our position paper. We can easily justify that what with your three years of lost salary, loss of the expected bonuses, injury to your career, and our request for punitive damages. We can build a strong case around five hundred grand. How does that strike you?"

"Okay, if you think best." Her smile is a wry one. "Even if that's a long way from the millions that juries seem to hand out." It's obvious that Bianchi has gained Rosemary Wofford's trust.

"You can forget about the millions. Now if Stephen had thrown acid in your face or run you down with his car, crippling you for life, we'd have a different story." Mark Bianchi leans forward again. "Rosemary, before we get to work on the position paper, I'd like to take some time here and talk a little more about your relationship with your brother."

"More? What kind of thing do you mean?"

"Your feelings about each other over the years."

"So my lawyer's playing shrink now?" She laughs. "You want to know did we sneak into each other's beds when we were kids?"

He joins the laughter. "Sure, if it's still an emotional thing with you." He pauses. "Seriously, I'd like to understand the feeling between you and your brother before you went to work for him. Mediation is a lot different from adjudication. A trial considers only the narrow point at issue between contending parties. Mediation is wide open and often when it's truly successful, it deals with the entire relationship of the parties. Mediation has the power to heal wounds that go a lot deeper than the issue on the surface."

"Well, I don't mind talking about Stephen, but if you think mediation can do any healing, forget it. What that man did to me, my worst enemy couldn't have been any meaner. Look, Stephen and I had a lot of fun as kids. When he was little, he was proud of his older sister—I'm the senior by two years—and he used to tell other kids, 'Hey, call Rosie. I'll bet she can do it.' He always called me Rosie then. But as he grew older, he had a hard time with that age difference."

"In what ways?"

"Envy. Because of those two years, I could play softball on a par with him, outfish him, hold my own in one-on-one basketball, and beat the hell out of him in indoor games like checkers, Monopoly, rummy. And you know, a funny thing. I don't think he ever got over it."

"Just the two of you kids in the family?"

"Right."

"What does he call you now?"

"When he stoops to speak to me? . . . Rosemary."

"You think he still resents you?"

"Yes, I do. Oh, he'd never admit it, not proud, starchy, oh so correct Stephen, But he's never gotten over those early years when I, not Stevie, was the prize kid. You see, our friends all picked up on it and used to tease him about being the kid brother. He was overjoyed when I went off to college.

"And then that summer vacation when he was a senior in high school and drinking up a storm to prove how macho he was. I lied for him then, bailed him out with our parents. Instead of being grateful, he took the incident as showing his inferiority."

"Did the two of you ever talk about his resentment—in later years, I mean?"

"No, we were raised in a family that never aired its differences, just swallowed our anger and pretended all was well."

Bianchi, cocking his head, pays close attention. He is a rapt listener. "Didn't that underlying feeling affect your business deal? I'm wondering why, if he had such a carryover resentment of you, he ever offered you a job?"

"You know, so did I at the time. At first, I thought it was a matter of family duty. Stephen adheres to the conventions and much as he may have despised me, he would have thought he was obliged by birth to help his to-be-divorced sister. But later, I decided no, it was his way of getting even with me."

"Getting even?" Bianchi shows his surprise.

"Yes. I'm sure now that he thought I would fail, that I not only wouldn't increase the business of the Princeton store, rating the bonus, but that I'd strike out, maybe even run the business there into the ground. It was a tough situation and he'd been on the point of dumping the Princeton outlet several times."

"What kind of evidence of that did you pick up?" Bianchi is intrigued.

"Oh, nothing definite, nothing he said or wrote or anything like that. It was just the way he acted, you know. I swear he would have been delighted if I'd messed up as manager."

"Tell me this. Do you love your brother?"

"No, I don't." She bites off the words. "I did once, made allowances for his feelings of inferiority, but he's managed to kill my love for him."

"What if, by some miracle, he apologized, admitted he'd pulled a rotten trick and asked your forgiveness?"

Rosemary Wofford reacts as though struck in the face. "No way. Never in this world would you catch grand Mr. Holloway admitting that he acted like a heel. And if he did, I wouldn't believe him. Mark, I feel nothing but negatives for the man."

But reading her body clues as closely as he listens to her words, Attorney Bianchi doubts what she says. Her voice quivers, she appears to be on the verge of tears, and she twists her ringless ring finger as she talks. He decides that she loves her brother very much.

"That's too bad. You're going to be brother and sister for a lot of years yet."

She nods and he has the impression that if she says a single word, she'll fall into weeping. Bianchi files the impression for future reference. Almost all clients have hidden agendas, often concealed from themselves as well. Rosemary Wofford, he concludes, is no exception. At the risk of finding himself mistaken, he sizes up her current feeling this way: On the surface, she wants to make her brother cough up enough money to make him hurt. But deep down, what she wants most is a reconciliation with the kid who used to call her Rosie.

"All right," says Bianchi, "let's get to work on this position paper. Doug McGinness will do the actual drafting, so I'm going to get him in here. The three of us can rough out just what happened, what we're prepared to prove if we're forced to go to trial, and just what we want from Holloway."

He phones McGinness and soon the young lawyer appears carrying a yellow legal pad. He's short with a crew cut, has a quick, eager manner, and bears the mark of ambition.

As Bianchi questions Rosemary with occasional assists from McGinness, the threesome plots the outline of the position paper: family relationship, the origin and validity of the contract, Rosemary's understanding of her job via Stephen's instructions, her dedication to work, her long hours, necessary changes she made in the furnishings line for the Princeton store, the rationale for firing Sam Mortensen, the veteran employee, how she increased the store's profit, her plans for future growth, her bewilderment and chagrin when her brother dismissed her without warning and, finally, evidence of the damage done her in the home furnishings business by her dismissal.

"We're taking the position, Doug," says Bianchi, "that she did nothing whatsoever to provoke the summary firing by Stephen Holloway in direct violation of their contract. On the contrary, she expanded the business and increased profits. Her dismissal hit her like a surprise bolt of lightning on a clear day."

"What about our legal attack?" McGinness was schooled to think in bellicose terms.

"I'm coming to that." Bianchi nods. "I want you to research the law of ambiguity. We have the matter of the meaning of net profits and also this contract, as I read it, says nothing about Mrs. Wofford's obligation to maintain the Social Register nature of Holloway Interiors' business. It merely states that H. I. serves an 'exclusive clientele,' to use Stephen's words. So we want case law on ambiguity that supports our position. Second, we want a good solid treatment of the law of anticipatory repudiation and total breach. Did Rosemary actually breach the contract by putting in a lower-priced line or did she merely make a reasonable change in the store's operations? Of course, we hold that she made a perfectly sensible and logical alteration."

They talk some more and when Rosemary leaves a half hour later, Bianchi and McGinness again go over the legal core of the presentation and discuss the format for the rest of the material.

McGinness spends two days researching the law and writing the ten-page position paper, Bianchi takes another hour to edit the document, and a secretary then types up clear copies that are mailed to Rosemary, Attorney Peter Cavanaugh, and the American Arbitration Association for transmittal to Seymour Weinstein, the mediator.

The next day's mail brings the position paper from Stephen Holloway and Cavanaugh. It runs to twelve pages and contains about what Bianchi expected. Holloway takes the stance that he entered a strictly business arrangement with Rosemary after her separation, employing her under contract to run his Princeton store, and that she totally breached the contract. How? By disregarding a flow of warnings from Stephen that the integrity of his quality line of home furnishings must not be marred by the sale of inferior goods, by hurting the chain's image as the "Tiffany" of home interiors, by discharging a veteran employee, thus undermining employee morale, and by alienating the large number of wealthy customers who traded at Holloway Interiors precisely because of its elite reputation and moneyed clientele.

On the legal issue, Holloway takes the position that since his sister breached the contract, he owes her nothing. On the contrary, she owes him $200,000 due to the expense of restoration changes in the Princeton store and a 5 percent slump in revenues suffered by the Southampton and Palm Beach stores.

Holloway attributes that slump directly to the tarnished image resulting from Rosemary's actions in the Princeton store. "Word travels swiftly in the small social world from which Holloway Interiors draws its best customers," says the paper. "The least rumor of a lowering of standards in the salesrooms has its impact on the balance sheet."

Holloway accuses his sister of misrepresenting the facts since she left his employ and says that some of her remarks in the trade about his business practices amount to "slander." This point, however, carries no elaboration and Bianchi surmises that Cavanaugh threw it in merely to fatten his list of charges.

The paper holds only one surprise. Holloway contends that his sister had an affair with an employee of the Princeton store, a man ten years her junior, and that this liaison not only damaged the morale of the nine other employees of the establishment, but became a matter of unfavorable gossip among some of the store's best customers, a set of women "representing the town's old money families."

After Rosemary receives her copy, Mark Bianchi discusses the paper with her on the telephone. She explodes when he asks her about the romantic reference and its impact.

"Affair! I went out with Torrey exactly twice. Once we danced at the Nassau Inn and another night we had dinner in New Hope across the Delaware and made a couple of the town's night spots afterward. If I'd gone to bed with him, it was nobody's business but ours, but as it so happens, I did not.

"I like Torrey, but I have no romantic interest in him, really, and I told him that for the sake of relationships in the store, it was best that we had no more dates. He agreed and that was that. Where Stephen heard that limp piece of gossip, God only knows."

"Forget it." Bianchi chuckles. "Actually, I heard it myself. I should have told you that Cavanaugh mentioned an affair at our meeting over lunch. I'm afraid it didn't make much impression."

"That's just like Stephen, though," adds Rosemary. "Ever since he quit carousing around as a young man, he's been insufferably puritanical, strict with his own kids and quite censorious of other people."

Bianchi switches the subject. "What about their charge of slander? Have you done any running down of Holloway Interiors since you were fired?"

"Oh, I've told plenty of people about my shock at the way Stephen got rid of me, but I've never talked about store policy or the quality of the Holloway furnishings, which, by the way, I still think lead the market in style and craftsmanship."

Bianchi makes a note. "How about any obnoxious personal remarks about your brother?"

"Other than that he acted like a perfect shit, nothing." Her voice rises. "And I'll tell him that to his face."

"Their paper indicates that you were warned a number of times not to lower the quality of merchandise. What are the facts about that?"

"Stephen spoke to me only once on the subject," says Rosemary quickly, "and that hardly qualified as a warning. He came down to the store from New York for his annual inspection just a couple of weeks after the close of that fiscal year when I racked up that big increase in profits and got the bonus. As we walked through the place, he stopped occasionally to finger various materials, some of which he found to be 'below our quality standards,' as he put it. So we had a discussion. He wanted me to return several textiles, but I told him I'd already sold some of them to our best customers, names he knew. He didn't like it, but he didn't order me to stop. Stephen never complained about making more money, I can assure you."

"So his recollection has betrayed him badly?"

"And how! . . . And that malarkey about the Southampton and Palm Beach shops having a slump in sales because I'd 'tarnished the image' of Holloway Interiors. That's a laugh. Those two stores were off because of the general economy. I must say Stephen and his lawyer have fertile imaginations."

They talk some more and then Bianchi puts McGinness on the phone. The young lawyer quizzes Rosemary on all charges contained in her brother's position papers. After they hang up, he drafts the reply to the Holloway brief, spending six hours this time.

The exchange of replies throws no new light on the dispute and Rosemary hears nothing from Bianchi for a few days. The Friday before the scheduled Monday 10 A.M. mediation, he calls his client and asks her to meet him in his office Monday at nine o'clock.

Rosemary appears wearing a somewhat severe business suit and a taut expression. She's obviously anxious as she approaches the session with her brother.

"Easy does it," Bianchi says after their good mornings. "Relax, Rosemary, there's nothing ahead to worry about." He chats with her a few minutes in an effort to get her loosened up.

"Only three things to remember about this morning," he concludes. "One, talk as freely as you wish with the mediator. Two, be honest with him as well as open and relaxed. Don't worry, he'll guard what you say in confidence. Third, the decisions are yours, always. I'll be there to advise you and speak to the legal issues, but it's your show."

They drink some coffee from the law firm's coffee maker and shortly after nine-thirty they stroll three blocks over to the tall building on Fifty-first Street, between Sixth and Seventh Avenues, that houses the ninth- and tenth-floor offices of the American Arbitration Association.

The Costs

In preparing his client for mediation, including his work on the position paper and reply, together with his talks with Rosemary, Mark Bianchi has spent four hours at a cost to her of $600. Young Mc-

Ginness, who's billed at $75 an hour, has spent twenty-one hours on the matter. Total of both lawyers, $2,175. Added to the previous charges, Rosemary Wofford's bill with the law firm of Archer, Gonzalez and Bianchi now stands at $3,300.

Rosemary walks to the mediation conference exactly six weeks and three days after the day she first called on Mark Bianchi and told him of her bitter complaint against her brother.

The Lawsuit

7

Los Angeles
May 20

Part Two: *Initial Letter, Response, and Pleading*

Back in Los Angeles, Oretta Long's prospective lawsuit against the Long brothers who fired her is just getting under way.

On this date, ten days after Lawyer Bill Hutchinson edited and mailed a letter to the Long brothers, demanding more than a million dollars in commissions and damages for Oretta, an answering letter arrives from Martin I. Novack of the firm of Henderson, Shapiro, Novack & Kawagami, prominent Los Angeles attorneys in the field of business and contract law.

Novack, who had served on a bar committee with Hutchinson some years earlier, flatly rejects Oretta Long's demands. On the contrary, he says on behalf of Arthur and Wendell Long that Oretta Long had failed to perform her duties properly, that customers complained of her lack of diligence in servicing accounts, and that many of her calls had been made by unqualified, inexperienced sales assistants. In addition, the letter charges, she had run up lavish "totally unreasonable" expense account bills, had violated instructions in opening an East Coast market, and had refused to follow "company operating procedures" despite repeated warnings by top management. Her services had been dispensed with only after she ignored those warnings.

In light of these facts, says Novack, Oretta Long has no cause for action against the brothers. The shoe, he says, is on the other foot. Arthur and Wendell Long are contemplating a suit against Oretta, seeking justifiable damages for the loss of business she caused and for the cost of restructuring the East Coast market. Also they will demand reimbursement for her expense account extravagances.

Oretta becomes angry when Bill reads her the letter over the phone. Just like the half brothers, she says when she calms down, not a word of truth in the allegations. There had been no "warnings," she had serviced all her customers as she always did, her two assistant saleswomen were both experienced and capable, and the "restructuring" of the East Coast market was garbage talk. The brothers had done nothing new except to ship to the outlets she had opened. As for the expense account, her spending squared with normal practices of other quality houses.

"Oretta," says Bill, "I happen to know their lawyer, a Martin Novack. Despite his stonewalling language, he may call soon to see if there's any room for settlement. What are your feelings on negotiations at this stage?"

"Absolutely not." Oretta's temper flares on the line. "Didn't you tell me I had a good case?"

"No question. Nothing has changed there."

"Bill, I want to get those bastards. They're going to pay for firing me. I mean it. And as far as them suing me, don't buy that sludge for a minute. I know Wendell's wife and I know she couldn't stand the trauma of a lawsuit. She goes all to pieces under pressure."

"That's a point worth noting. . . . All right then, Oretta, we'll go ahead and prepare the complaint for filing. I'll get to it this afternoon with Susan Pennington."

Bill's hunch proves right. Martin Novack calls him soon after lunch just as he begins his conference with Susan on the pleadings.

"Hey, Bill." Novack comes across with the heartiness of the casual acquaintance. "Long time no see. I guess the last time was when I ran into you at Chasen's. . . . About your client on this ladies' sportswear hassle. Any point in talking? Any give in her position?"

"Not an inch, Marty. Why? Are your people in a mood to talk?"

"No, no. Frankly, your letter just raised their hackles. They think your client is trying to take them to the cleaners and they're having no part of it. They want action. No, I was just doing some routine exploring, see where we stood, Bill."

"We talked over your letter, Marty, and my client's more determined than ever."

"So we're heading toward court then?"

"That's about the size of it."

The two lawyers, as congenial as their clients are embittered, sign off after a round of banter. Marty is a Dodgers fan, whereas Bill likes the Angels, but neither team has the look of a pennant winner this year.

Bill turns to his law assistant as he hangs up the phone. "Susan, we have to turn out the complaint as fast as possible. As I see our position, we have to get the upper hand by suing first. We must be perceived as the wronged party by any judge who'll hear our motions or sit at a trial. Oretta must be perceived as so wronged that she's justified in being the aggressor at law, trying to obtain only what's rightfully hers."

Susan hitches up her chair. "I'm cleared to work the rest of the day on it."

"Okay. We're going to take a very strong position in this pleading." Bill places his hands on the desk. "I want to sue the Long brothers personally as well as in their corporate roles."

"Why?" She looks puzzled. "Weren't these corporate acts that Mrs. Long is complaining about?"

"There's definitely a personal case to be made." Bill's tone carries a touch of reproof. "Remember the theory of ultra vires acts?"

"Oh, right." She nods in recognition. "Their actions went beyond what Bluebird's charter permits. What they did stems from a personal desire to hurt Oretta and has nothing to do with the corporation's purposes."

"That's it." His smile is one of approval for his young assistant. "Think you can build that case and find legal authority for it?"

Susan assures him that she'll handle the assignment, then apologizes for not remembering "the theoretical basis for suing the Long brothers personally."

Bill grins. "I never forget what one of my law professors told me: 'If you look long enough and hard enough, you'll always be able to find authority for any position.' As a starter, Oretta is ready to sign an affidavit stating that Arthur and Wendell commingled funds. She knows of a couple of instances where they mixed corporate moneys with their own accounts. So work on her a bit and try to pin her down."

As Susan makes notes, Bill continues: "Let's go through the complaint material and let me tell you what I envision. First, an historical paragraph showing that the brothers didn't build the business. Rather it was the child of Frank and Oretta Long with Frank running production and finances and Oretta marketing the new sports togs line for women. That will make Oretta feel good, but also it will put Marty Novack on notice that we have some solid emotional ammunition for use with a jury."

"How do you want me to phrase that?"

"We want to imply that we're ready to go into the whole corporate background, highlighting Oretta's major contribution. Our theme is that 'they used her until she was costing too much, then they tossed her aside.' "

Bill walks to the window and looks down on the stream of traffic on Wilshire Boulevard. "I hear that Marty Novack doesn't like to try cases in front of a jury. If he thinks we have strong emotional material, we may scare him into thinking a jury might award punitive damages."

"Aren't we in danger of overstating our case?" This is new ground for Susan.

"Not really. You'll be surprised what Oretta will remember when we start questioning her about the early days of Bluebird Sportswear. But even if it sounds exaggerated, it's best to roll out the heavy guns and hope to frighten the other side. We want to state our case in the most unequivocal fashion possible."

Susan picks up Bill's momentum. "Playing the devil's advocate, isn't there a real question under terms of their agreement whether she had to be paid fifteen percent commission outside the western states? Also can she really justify flying first class all over?"

Bill strolls back to his desk and swings back and forth in his swivel chair before replying. "Susan, that's the job of Marty Novack. He's the one to dig into their agreement and show when and to what degree Oretta exceeded its terms." His smile has a paternal touch. "Our job is to represent our client by positioning her in the most favorable light possible. That, after all, is what the advocacy system is all about."

Bill draws a legal pad to him, Susan places her black tailored suit jacket on the back of her chair, and together the two lawyers begin going point-by-point through an outline of the complaint that Susan will draft for Bill's editing and then file in court to begin the lawsuit against the Long brothers. . . . "Comes now the plaintiff above-named, by and through her attorneys undersigned, and for complaint against defendants alleges and avers . . ."

"I see a seven- or eight-point complaint," says Bill, "but all contributions are welcome."

They start with the first count, alleging breach of contract. In addition to describing the business and the agreement, this count includes "John and Mary Doe," identities and real names unknown, as defendants along with Arthur and Wendell Long and Bluebird Sportswear, Inc. Bill explains to Susan that Oretta believes that the Longs have formed a special marketing firm with unknown parties for the purpose of servicing her old customers.

"We want to be positioned to nail these people if discovery bears out Oretta's theory," he says. "Now in Count Two, Susan, we charge Oretta's wrongful dismissal and we want to say this was done maliciously with intent to harm our client. So we ask punitive damages of a million dollars." Bill frowns in thought. "No, make that a million five. I keep forgetting the inflation factor."

They decide on a third count of "negligent mismanagement," including shipment of defective goods.

"Since Oretta is a woman," says Susan, "why don't I draft a count that alleges employment discrimination on the basis of sex and violation of Oretta's civil rights?"

"Hmm. I'm not sure we even have an employment contract here." Bill looks out the window as he ponders. "But I like your thinking, Susan—and you can bet Oretta will like it too. Pleasing the client, remember, is part of the game. All right, let's make that our fourth count."

The fifth count alleges accounting fraud and conversion of moneys from Oretta to the brothers. "Let's throw an emotional scare in here," says Bill. "When Marty tells the brothers that conversion means stealing, Oretta will get her money's worth right there."

Count Six charges interference with contractual relations through the machinations of the now infamous John and Mary Doe. Count Seven strikes at "unfair and deceptive trade practices," and the final eighth count charges the defendants with conspiring to "fraudulently convert from Plaintiff moneys due her under the employment agreement."

"It's always good to throw in a conspiracy count," says Bill. "It gives us flexibility, room to maneuver in. The conspiracy, let's make it, wrongfully terminated her position and defrauded her of future commissions and thus did 'injure and damage Plaintiff's good name and reputation in business and in the community.' "

Summing up, the complaint will demand an accounting of gross sales and ask damages, reimbursements, costs, attorneys' fees, and punitive damages totaling some $4,500,000.

"See if you can't have that back to me by Thursday," says Bill. "That gives you three days. You might have to put in a few late hours. And Susan, I want a legal memo researching and supporting each of those counts."

Susan spends twenty-five hours drafting the thirteen-page complaint and the supporting legal memos and brings them to Bill's office early Thursday. He spends a half hour editing the complaint and another forty-five minutes on the phone with Oretta describing the contents, allaying her qualms, and preparing the embattled widow for the forays ahead.

"I must say that complaint reads much tougher than I'd expected." Like many clients, Oretta is surprised at how fierce her own accusations appear when mirrored in the rolling profundities of legalese.

"To win the case and get you the damages you deserve, we've got to jump out on offense, be aggressive." This is not the first time that Bill has encountered client stage fright. "Oretta, this might be a good time to prepare you for what lies ahead in the four years or so before we get to trial."

"Four years?" Oretta is astonished.

"I'm afraid so. Actually, here in Los Angeles County we're running closer to five years on the average. Our courts have one of the worst jam-ups in the country."

"My goodness." She feels suddenly dispirited. "I might not be around that long."

Bill laughs. "Oh, you're one of my healthiest clients. . . . Anyway, there are going to be long periods in which nothing is happening and we won't talk much. Don't let that worry you. Don't think your case has languished. It's just the way the system works."

"But I can always find out the status of the suit, can't I?" For the first time since her anger settled, Oretta begins to worry about the length of the process to which she has committed herself.

"Of course, and we'll talk occasionally on the phone during those quiet spells. Then, Oretta, there will be very tense periods." Hutchinson's voice quickens. "These will be times when you'll have to devote substantial time and energy to your case.

"I'll want you to work closely with Susan and me to prepare the interrogatories and the depositions for the Long brothers, employees, and experts for the other side."

When Oretta asks just what he means, Bill explains that much of their evidence for trial will be obtained through the questioning of the Longs and others under oath in private sessions with a reporter making a verbatim record.

"Then we'll want to prepare your answers for the interrogatories and depositions that Martin Novack has the right to demand. Also you'll have to read their depositions so you can come up with further points to follow up as the discovery process goes along."

"Sounds like a lot of work." Far more than she had counted on, Oretta thinks. Actually she had imagined that once she hired Lawyer Hutchinson, the work would be largely his, not hers.

"At times, yes. We'll have to hire some experts—accountants and industry specialists—and you'll work with them on how you managed your end of the Bluebird business, projection of profits, that kind of thing." Hutchinson pauses, then speaks in measured tones. "So there'll come periods when we'll ask you to drop everything else and devote your full time and talents to the case."

"I'll be ready." Under Bill's forceful guidance, Oretta feels a new spurt of desire for combat. "Just let me know in time."

"Good. Thorough preparation can be tough on all of us, but it can also mean the difference between winning and losing. There'll be stressful days, Oretta, but you, Susan, and I, backed up by our firm's paralegals and some outside experts, can make a formidable winning team. How does that sound to you?"

"Count on me, I'm used to hard work." Oretta means it. She's ready for the fight—even though she had never expected the law to require such arduous labors on her part. It dawns on her that perhaps she has committed herself to a long and alien endeavor on unfamiliar terrain. A small faint voice in her head asks whether she may have made a mistake. She ignores it, bends herself to the task ahead.

A law firm secretary types the complaint and early the next morning a messenger takes it to the Los Angeles Superior Court and pays the $99 filing fee that marks Oretta's complaint as the official launching of the civil lawsuit against Arthur and Wendell Long.

But the battle has yet to be joined for Martin Novack must first read, ponder, and analyze the complaint on behalf of his clients, the Long brothers, confer with them, and then draft and file their response and countercomplaint, an act several weeks down the road yet.

This is the 48,743rd civil complaint filed this year in Los Angeles County where the courts are inundated with more than 230,000 civil actions annually, including some 85,000 lawsuits. Oretta Long's grievance takes its place in line on a docket so crowded with conflicts that considerably more than four years probably will pass before her case can come to trial. For most of this century lawsuits in Los Angeles County came to trial within a reasonable period, but beginning in 1970 the time span widened, steadily increasing until in the eighties the median case has taken fifty-nine months to get to trial. Although Los Angeles courts are among the most congested in the nation, there are not many U.S. counties where Oretta's grievances could be aired in less than two years.

Although quite a routine complaint in the eyes of lawyers and the legal establishment, Oretta Long's pleading would amaze associates of the Long brothers and shock those friends who know Arthur and Wendell as amiable, if rather colorless, characters who treat their employees with the customary civility, play golf for small wagers, and pursue placid domestic lives with the usual amounts of boredom, love, generosity, titillation, and hypocrisy.

From two quite ordinary businessmen whose only connections with the police and law-breaking have been citations for overtime parking

and one speeding arrest, Arthur and Wendell Long have been transformed into monsters who have cheated, lied, stolen, defrauded, and
sacked an innocent woman.

But for those who might think the Long brothers have been overly
blackened and defamed for a quite routine act—discharging an employee—wait until they read what becomes of the fair Oretta under
the inventive pen of Martin Novack, attorney for the brothers. Would
you believe a hard, ruthless, extravagant, money-hungry, scheming
yet ever slothful liar, cheat, and thief?

The Costs

Oretta Long's billing timesheet now looks like this:

Initial Conference with Client:	
Att. Hutchinson (2 hrs.)	$300.00
Att. Pennington (1 hr.)	75.00
Letter to Long Brothers:	
Drafting, Pennington (2 hrs.)	150.00
Editing, Hutchinson (10 min.)	25.00
Phone Conversation with Client:	
Hutchinson (15 min.)	37.50
Conference on Pleading:	
Hutchinson (2 hrs.)	300.00
Pennington (2 hrs.)	150.00
Pleading:	
Drafting, Pennington (25 hrs.)	1,875.00
Editing, Hutchinson (30 min.)	75.00
Phone Call to Client:	
Hutchinson (45 min.)	112.50
Duplicating Documents	14.75
Filing Fee	99.00
Total to Date:	$3,213.75

The Lawsuit

8

Los Angeles
June 10

Part Three: *Answer, Counterclaim, and Response*

Two weeks after Hutchinson's firm filed its lawsuit, painting the Long brothers as double-dealing conspirators whose acts caused an innocent woman $4,500,000 worth of pain and suffering, the brothers' lawyer filed a formal answer in court denying all allegations except their names, occupation, and address.

Attorney Martin I. Novack also filed a counterclaim on their behalf, accusing Oretta Long of a multitude of contract violations and malefactions, including intentional "fraud, misrepresentation, duress, and conversion." Novack therefore asked the court to throw out Oretta's charges, make her pay costs and attorneys' fees, and set up a trial to assess what she should pay in "general and special damages."

Not to be outdone in the realm of high finance, the brothers' lawyer asked that Oretta be forced to pay "punitive damages" of $5 million to his clients.

Stakes in the legal struggle now have escalated far beyond the issue of a discharged saleswoman's aborted contract, and when she reads through a copy of the answer and counterclaim, Oretta experiences pangs of alarm. She calls Bill Hutchinson at once and he says he'll make time for her the following morning after Susan Pennington does an analysis of the documents filed by the firm of Henderson, Shapiro, Novack and Kawagami.

When Oretta appears in Hutchinson's Wilshire Boulevard office this time, her original combative mood has given way to one of baffled indignation and concern.

"Good Lord," she says. "They want five million dollars on top of costs and some other stuff. I couldn't pay anything like that if I lived to be a hundred."

"Oh, that's picked out of the air." Hutchinson dismisses the sum with a flick of his hand. "We asked four point five million, so they had to go us one better."

"But some of the things they accuse me of in this thing! You'd think I was a common criminal."

"Actually, there's nothing to worry about." Bill's tone seeks to placate. "They threw nothing at us that we didn't anticipate." He aims a comforting smile her way. "You mustn't take it personally, Oretta."

"Oh, but I do." Her retort is sharp. "It's me they're talking about, you know."

"They just tossed in a lot of the usual boilerplate. . . . Here, pull up your chair. First, let's go through their answer. They pretty much deny everything. Are there some points you don't understand?"

"Yes, Point Three on page five." Oretta reads the paragraph aloud. " 'The conduct of Plaintiff herein was such as to constitute waiver, estoppel, laches and/or unclean hands as to the claims set forth in the Verified Complaint, and Plaintiff is therefore barred from recovering any part thereof from Defendants.' Does that mean if I went to court, I couldn't get anything?"

Hutchinson laughs. "Oh, that's just lawyer talk. Don't concern yourself. The language refers to legal theories that really don't have any application here."

"So why did they put it in?"

"If facts developing later should make one of the theories applicable, and Marty Novack hadn't included it, he could be sued for malpractice. So, to be on the safe side, lawyers often throw in the kitchen sink along with the dirty dishes."

"What a strange game. If this wasn't so important to me, I'd be laughing my head off." Instead, Oretta looks worried, points to Paragraph 2 under a section headed "affirmative defenses."

"The claims of Plaintiff," it reads, "have been discharged by payment, accord and satisfaction, and/or compromise and settlement."

"What in heaven's name are they talking about?" she asks. "The only thing I got paid was my last salary check and expense money. They owe me more than five years' salary on the contract."

"I know. They're just saying in another way that they don't owe you a thing."

"How about Number Seven that says my claims are 'barred by Statutes of Limitations.' God, it hasn't been two months yet."

"Number Seven is definitely not applicable." Bill shrugs. "Just more of Novack trying to cover the waterfront."

"And look at this!" She rattles the paper. "In Point Eleven they accuse me of 'duress, fraud, illegality of contract.' What's illegal about a contract that Wendell typed up himself? And fraud!" She laughs bitterly. "You'd think I'd stolen money from them. I think this whole thing is outrageous."

Oretta tosses the paper aside. She's clearly baffled and frustrated by the legal bluffmanship and has the look of a woman who wonders if she made a mistake in starting all this.

Bill Hutchinson has seen this reaction before. The same people who want to sue and bash the enemy, regardless of cost, sometimes lose their lust for blood the moment the opposition fires its first volley. Bill has seen dejection and depression at this point and regards it as a stage that some clients must pass through.

"They end the answer by asking the court to dismiss the complaint and make me pay their lawyer fees and court costs." Oretta is puzzled. "Can they get away with something like that?"

Bill shakes his head. "Not a chance in a thousand. If the Longs try to move for summary judgment, the judge will deny the motion. This is a factual issue to be decided by a jury."

He reviews the answer, dismissing its main points as routine maneuvering that has little bearing on Oretta's demands. He speaks in a calm voice, seeking to quiet her fears. He closes their conference on a light note, hoping to lift his client's spirits.

"We'll let Susan Pennington take over now. She has to go through the Longs' counterclaim with you so that she can do a draft of our answer."

"Answer?" Oretta is confused again. "What answer?"

"Oh, we have to file an answer to their counterclaim. That's part of the machinery. Don't worry. Susan's very good at drafting answers."

Oretta accompanies Susan to the law firm's conference room and the two women seat themselves at the end of a long table. The counterclaim charges that Oretta Long failed to properly perform her duties for Bluebird Sportswear, "lacked diligence in servicing her customers, employed inexperienced and unqualified assistants, violated proper and necessary instructions, refused to follow company operating procedures, breached her fiduciary duties, misrepresented facts, converted monies and acted to benefit interests in competition with the interests of Defendant Bluebird Sportswear, Inc."

Susan ticks off some of the counts of the counterclaim. "Let's go to Count Five, Number Twenty-five. They say you entered into dealings with competing businesses. Is there any truth to that at all? Did you work for anybody outside Bluebird?"

Oretta taps and lights a cigarette. "Yes, I did handle a small line of women's beachwear. It didn't compete at all with Bluebird's items."

"Oh." Susan looks surprised. "Why didn't you tell us about that at our first meeting?"

"I just didn't think it was involved at all. It was a completely different line and I only sold it to southern California outlets. It earned me only a few thousand a year. The half brothers knew all about it. They never complained. In fact, they never mentioned it, so far as I recall."

"They'll undoubtedly use it in court. Suppose they say they asked you not to handle the other line?"

"They'd be lying. No way can they say that if they tell the truth." The possibility rekindles Oretta's smoldering anger.

Susan thinks a moment. "Of course, you never misrepresented the situation to the Long brothers, did you? As a matter of fact, didn't the beachwear actually complement your Bluebird line?"

Grateful for the assist, Oretta nods emphatically. "Yes. Actually, one store in La Jolla increased its Bluebird orders after I introduced the beachwear to them."

"So in reality, the beachwear line at all times served in a complementary role. And isn't it true that the beachwear they now complain about actually enhanced the sale of Bluebird's clothes and accessories?"

"Yes, it did." Oretta's smile is one of gratitude. She has a new appreciation of Susan's advocacy talents.

"That's fine for our answer. But it might be well to search your memory now for other examples, just to fix them in mind. You can forget a lot in the years before we get into court."

Susan moves to Count Six of the counterclaim, reading it aloud. It accuses Oretta of making untrue allegations about her employers, "in writing and orally, to customers and prospective customers of Defendants, maliciously, without a valid purpose, business or otherwise." Therefore Oretta has "committed acts constituting libel and slander as against Defendants" and should be required to pay "general, special, and punitive" damages.

"What kinds of statements could they be referring to here?" Susan asks.

"Wow! Talk about making mountains out of molehills." Oretta inhales and blows a tumbling cloud of smoke. "Once I wrote a letter to a store in Oregon that had returned some badly stitched tennis sweaters. I just said that a quality control problem was being straightened out and no need for future worry. I had to say something to keep the account. It was a big one."

"Were those your words, 'quality control problem'? Could you possibly have used more colorful language?"

"No, no. I remember. Those were the words I used. I was trying to be as vague as possible, you know."

"Did you make any similar statements on invoices, bills, sales notes, or anything else?"

Oretta gazes upward as she thinks. "I'm not sure. I have a dim recollection of writing something to a customer who complained about . . . oh, I don't know, some item."

"Can't think who it might have been or what the circumstances were?"

"No. I think it was a department store buyer in Seattle, but I can't be sure."

"Oretta, I know this is a drag, but I think you'd better bring in all copies of your business correspondence over the years. We don't want to be surprised by Novack and his people."

"I don't have any copies."

"You mean you never kept carbons?" Susan is astonished.

"Yes, my secretary kept carbons, but when the half brothers fired me, I just cleared out of the office and left everything in the file cabinets."

"Oh, that's not so good." Susan makes a note on her legal pad. "We'll have to do our best to locate them during discovery."

Seeing Susan's frown, Oretta becomes alarmed again. "Does this mean I could lose the case?"

"Not to worry. While there are no guarantees, Oretta, I think you've got a very good case and just as important, you've got Bill Hutchinson."

The legal assistant goes to two points under Count Seven of the Long brothers' counterclaim. One charges that Oretta "has been using confidential information, such as customer lists and pricing policies, for her own benefit and for the benefit of Defendant's competitors." The other accuses her of continuing to use confidential Bluebird information since her dismissal.

"Any truth to that, Oretta?"

"Well, I do have a customer list at home, but I haven't even looked at it since they fired me."

"Are these customers you procured or were they brought in by someone else in the company?"

"Ninety-five percent of them are people I worked up and made the original sales to. A handful, no more, came from the half brothers and a couple of other people at headquarters."

"Of course," says Susan, "you had no intention of using the list to sell competing lines, did you?"

Oretta actually had considered doing just that should she decide to take over sales for a rival women's sportswear company. She senses, however, what her proper conduct should be in light of the lawsuit.

"I haven't contacted any other firm in the field, no."

"And it's true, isn't it, that the only reason you have the list is that you used to make calls from your home and you just forgot to mail it back to Bluebird offices?"

"I did use to make a lot of calls from home, yes. That's why I had the list there."

"And you never made any copy of the list nor did you intend to. Isn't that correct?"

Oretta, not as certain of her past intentions as Susan, thinks for a moment. "I haven't made any copy of the list, no."

They work on a few more clauses of the Longs' counterclaim allegations, all of which infuriate Oretta, then take a break while Oretta goes to the ladies' room. When she returns, Oretta again brings up the matter of the customer list.

"Susan, suppose I did use that customer list someday? It contains the names of somewhat more than three-hundred outlets. Figuring conservatively, I'd say I personally contacted two hundred and ninety of them. I'm the person who did the cultivation and I'm the one who put their names on the list. I've always regarded it as my list. Now could the half brothers sue me if I used those names while working for another women's sportswear house?"

"They could bring an action, yes. In fact, that's just what they're doing here in Paragraphs Thirty-one and Thirty-two. But that they could stop you legally from calling on all those customers is highly improbable."

"But it's possible, huh?"

"Anything's possible in a lawsuit," Susan replies. "So, to be on the safe side, you should make no use of that list. You say you never looked at it since you were discharged?"

Oretta nods her head. "Right. The last time was a couple of nights before I was fired when I looked up the phone number of a shop in Santa Cruz."

Susan makes a note, then remembers the CYA principle. In the student bull sessions at law school they often discussed the first rule in staying out of trouble after you start practice, CYA—Cover Your Ass. She glances at her watch and writes: "3:17 p.m. Instructed client not to make any use of the list of Bluebird customers which she has at home. Will send her confirming letter."

"Good," says Susan. "We'll just let that list gather dust in the drawer, Oretta."

Another hour passes before the two women finish their work. They have gone through the Long brothers' counterclaim and Susan has made copious notes for her draft of Oretta's answer. It has not been a pleasant experience for Oretta. She finds that the struggle will be more difficult than she imagined, that the attack, counterattack, and second strike leave her more confused than embattled, and that she is much more vulnerable in combat than she had thought when she walked into Hutchinson's office three weeks ago.

As she leaves, Oretta feels unsettled and on edge. It appears to her that this case has become a warlike chess game between opposing lawyers and that she is in danger of becoming a pawn of their legal tactics. How much of this, she wonders, directly concerns her lost job and the missing salary checks?

"I'll mail you a copy of the draft Monday," says Susan as they part, "and then we can talk on the phone. I want you to check it for factual error."

Oretta walks out with a firm stride. She's not happy over the day, but she's still resolute. The half brothers must be made to pay for their cavalier firing of the woman who had as much to do with the success of Bluebird Sportswear as either of them.

The Costs

The bill Oretta will receive will show that she spent a half hour today with Bill Hutchinson ($75) and an hour and a half with Susan Pennington ($112.50). It takes Susan four hours ($300) to draft the answer and fifteen minutes ($37.50) for Bill to review it. Time spent on phone calls with Oretta come to $37.50 for Hutchinson and another $37.50 for Pennington. By the time a law firm messenger takes the answer to Los Angeles Superior Court for filing, Oretta's bill has grown by another $600 and now stands at $3,813.75.

The battle has just begun.

Mediation

9

New York
June 20

Part Four: *Action*

The Mediation Hearing

Across the continent in Manhattan, Stephen Holloway and his law-yer, Peter Cavanaugh, are waiting in the reception area of the American Arbitration Association offices as Mark Bianchi and his client, Rosemary Wofford, arrive for the scheduled mediation.

Holloway nods to his sister with a thin compressed smile as he says his good morning. Sizing him up, Bianchi sees a tall, lean man, dressed in a three-piece dark blue suit, obviously custom tailored and expensive. He wears a figured silk tie, tightly knotted, with a matching maroon handkerchief peeping from his breast pocket. With his air of quiet elegance, Stephen Holloway is the kind of man who, in another era, would have worn a carnation in his buttonhole.

Rosemary does not return her brother's smile, merely acknowledges his presence with a small nod. She stands stiffly while Bianchi and Cavanaugh go through the introductions. Cavanaugh's geniality expands to cover the absence of warmth, his laugh sounding louder and brassier than usual.

The mediator walks in a moment later. Seymour F. Weinstein is a large friendly man with a craggy face that no one would call handsome. A toucher, he uses both hands in greeting, holding the handshake just a bit longer than customary. Unlike the dapper chief of Holloway Interiors, Weinstein has a rumpled air about him.

"Well," he says after the amenities, "we have a nice zippy day for our talks." He beams a smile. "Let's hope we can do as well as the weather."

"Terrific day," echoes Cavanaugh. And indeed it is one of those rare June days in New York, cool and fresh with the morning sunlight splashing the tall buildings and tossing long bright ribbons along the shadowed streets.

A young assistant in the AAA offices ushers the group to the Harry De Jur Commercial Mediation Center on the eleventh floor and leads them to the room where the mediation will take place. Large, with fluorescent lighting and wall-to-wall carpeting, the room has a conference table and comfortable chairs. Weinstein shucks his jacket, hangs it over the chair at the end of the table, and gestures toward the seats on either side of him. "No protocol here. Let's have Mr. Holloway on one side with his lawyer and Mrs. Wofford and her attorney on the other. Take your pick."

When the contending pairs have seated themselves after some hesitation over location, Weinstein begins. "First, about myself, since all you know about me is what you've read in that biographical sheet that was sent you." The profile had touched his career highlights: New York University, Harvard Law School, forty-one years with a prestigious Wall Street firm, an expert in antitrust and securities law, member of the American Bar Association special committee on dispute resolution, and recently an arbitrator for the New York Stock Exchange as well as the AAA.

"More important to our session today," he says, "I've had experience drafting and litigating employment contracts on both the corporate and employee side, so I think I can empathize with the viewpoints of both of you." He smiles toward Rosemary, then Stephen.

"Now as to the style here. Everything's informal. No taking of oaths, no rules of evidence, no testifying and cross-examination. None of that courtroom routine. In no way is this a trial. This is a discussion. . . . Unless you object, I'll use first names and please call me Seymour. It's a good Jewish name that anybody around this city ought to be familiar with. For that matter, you're welcome to use my nickname, Cy. . . . If you want to take off your coats, gentlemen, be my guest. Whatever you're comfortable with."

He addresses himself to Rosemary. "No doubt, you feel outgunned here on the gender front, one woman surrounded by four men, but I assure you, Rosemary, that I'll deal with you and your brother as fairly and evenhandedly as I can. If at any moment you feel I'm being insensitive to a feminine concern, please tell me so."

"Oh, I don't think we'll have any problems." Rosemary smiles for the first time. It's obvious that she likes Weinstein.

"We have only one rule here," Weinstein continues. "Nobody ever interrupts another person. Say anything you want, cuss if you must, talk as loud and as long as you wish. But never, never interrupt another person even if you think he or she is lying through the teeth. Is that okay with everyone here? I need assurances from each of you."

After all four participants agree to observe the single rule, the mediator lays down the procedure. After an hour or so all together, during which each side would lay out its position, Weinstein would meet separately with Rosemary Wofford and her attorney, then switch to Stephen Holloway and his counsel. Thereafter he'd caucus with one side or the other or hold joint sessions, depending on developments.

"Please don't think I'm showing favoritism if I spend extra time with the other party. I intend to be completely impartial. I have no prejudgment whatsoever about this case after reading your position papers and replies. However, circumstances may demand more time with the other party. Don't worry. I may be pleading your case for you."

Bianchi, following the mediator's example, takes off his coat and lays it on a nearby chair. As he relaxes, he notes that Cavanaugh glances sideways at his client, but since Holloway makes no move to remove his jacket, Cavanaugh doesn't either.

"Allow me to tell just one war story here," says Weinstein, "since I think it's apt." He launches into a tale about a bitter fight between two old friends who bought a building together and then fell out over the conversion of the rental units to condominiums. One wanted to convert, the other didn't. They accused each other of reneging on promises, grew increasingly distant, finally refused to talk to each other. One filed suit, charging breached contract and mismanagement. The other countersued and before long they had piled up a joint total of $30,000 in legal fees as they foraged through discovery and depositions.

"They'd heard about me and in desperation, they decided to let me arbitrate and render a decision. Instead, I persuaded them to mediate. Well, it took three days, but you know we wound up with Ed, the condo man, buying out Jake at a good profit and throwing in a free condo for his old partner. They left the last session together and went off and had a drink. Later Jake moved into the place himself along with his wife."

Weinstein looks slowly from person to person. "I can't promise that anything like that will happen here, but I can promise you this— I'm going to do my damnedest to help you folks arrive at a fair settlement you'll all feel good about."

He spends a few minutes in congratulating both sides for agreeing to mediate, emphasizes that this is not a win/lose situation but a forum for joint accommodation. He understands both sides after reading their position papers, feels he's sensitive to the issues. He must add though that each case appears to him to have weaknesses.

"All right," says Weinstein, "let's begin. Mark, you start off for the complainant. As I said, talk as long as you want, but please keep your wants to fifteen minutes." He grins. "We all know what's in your position paper."

Bianchi takes but five minutes to summarize Rosemary's case: fired in violation of her contract after increasing profits of the Princeton store by $140,000 the first year and earning herself a bonus of $15,000. He notes her disappointment that her bonus was not based on these before-tax profits. Rosemary, he says, was bewildered and disheartened when her brother fired her without warning and charged her with "cheapening the Holloway Interiors name" just because she'd sold a good, but less expensive, line of fabrics and furniture.

Bianchi then spends his remaining ten minutes seeking to refute Stephen Holloway's contention that he'd warned his sister about lowering the tone of the store. "Holloway discussed the matter only in general terms with his sister and never issued a single direct warning. The contract itself draws a general picture of the 'fine' quality of merchandise and the 'discriminating customers' of the chain, but nowhere is there an explicit order to Rosemary to cater *only* to the wealthy set."

Bianchi concludes by noting that his client has reduced her request for damages to $500,000, down from the original $750,000 as set out in the first letter to her brother. "We wanted to enter these talks in a spirit of cooperation." However, the new figure is completely justified, he contends, when one considers lost salary and bonuses of almost four years plus compensation for the severe injury done to Rosemary's professional career. The sum, he says, does not include any punitive damages that might be obtained in a court action.

"Thank you." Weinstein turns to Rosemary. "Do you have anything to add?"

"I certainly do. Mark says I was disheartened when Stephen fired me. Disheartened! I was crushed. I had worked ten and eleven hours a day in that store." She speaks with heat and color rises in her cheeks. "I spent plenty of damn Sundays in the place too. I gave that shop everything I had and I boosted profits when friends said it couldn't be done. And then to be fired out of hand, not a word of warning—"

"That's not true!" Holloway shouts it.

Weinstein raises a palm like a traffic policeman. "Hold it. Remember our rule. You'll have your turn. . . . Go ahead, Rosemary."

"No word of warning, no apology, no nothing. Just bang, not even a thank-you, ma'am. God, the way he treated me, you'd think we were back in the Middle Ages with master and serf or something."

"Anything else?"

"Yes. I'm here because Mark thought it might work. But I'm putting everyone on notice. If I don't get a decent settlement for what happened, I intend to sue."

"Both sides reserve the right to go to litigation," says Weinstein. "That's part of the agreement here. . . . All right, Peter, let's hear how you and your client look at this matter."

"Cy, we think Mrs. Wofford has no cause at all for action." Cavanaugh shrugs and throws open his hands, a gesture of gentle innocence rudely wronged. "Here's a sister who goes to work for her brother. She changes the chain's image, hurts sales in other stores and so she doesn't work out, and he lets her go. That's all there is to it. So what's the big deal? This kind of thing, as unfortunate as it may be for the person let out, happens thousands of times every day in this country. That's the commonsense view of this matter. As for the law, it's squarely on our side."

Cavanaugh cites several cases to buttress his contention that Rosemary invalidated the contract, breached it in fact, by her defiance of her brother's order that the top-drawer image of Holloway Interiors be maintained and that no goods in any way inferior to those of the finest quality be sold. Stephen Holloway informed his sister several times in no uncertain terms that she was not to alter the policy that had yielded Holloway Interiors its reputation for serving "the chic exclusive set that winters in Palm Beach and summers in Southampton."

"That's untrue!" declares Rosemary. "He never once laid down a definite policy."

"Please." Weinstein lays a hand on Rosemary's arm. "We have only one rule here and you agreed to observe it." He looks about the room. "Once again, everyone, no interruptions."

Cavanaugh then expands on his position paper's contention that far from owing his sister $750,000—"or the five hundred thousand they've so quickly come down to"—Holloway should be paid $200,000 to recompense him for the slump in revenues caused by Rosemary's damage to the chain's image. He concludes by reiterating the "surprise" item from the position paper, that Rosemary's dating of a younger male employee in the Princeton store hurt the morale of other employees and alienated some wealthy women customers. Rosemary punctuates this accusation with a disgusted "tsk," but does not interrupt again.

"All right, Peter," says Weinstein, "thank you. Do you have anything to add to that, Stephen?"

Holloway nods. "There have been denials here that I ever warned my sister in specific terms about lowering our standards." He is a man of manners who adjusts his coat sleeves and straightens his tie before speaking. His tone is dry, precise, emphatic. "I made it a point to consult my business diary before coming here." He places a sheet of paper before him and puts on rimless reading glasses. "In addition to the discussion the day that I walked through the Princeton store with Rosemary, I called her on February nineteenth and told her that her order of five bolts of Princess Charlotte drapery material, manufacturer's number 71853, put a cheaper item in our Princeton shop that did not come up to our standards." He peers at Weinstein over his glasses. "We do not, I repeat do not, offer the Princess Charlotte line or any other Bramhall & Sons product. Decidedly not our quality.

"I called her again March fourteenth and told her not to buy the Judith & Annette bedroom carpeting that she had planned to purchase on her Chicago trip. My sources told me that this new firm, Judith & Annette, while producing quite lovely materials, had also turned out some shoddy work. I told Rosemary best we wait until the company proved itself, that we could not afford to offer our kind of customers goods in any way inferior. She nevertheless went ahead and ordered a large amount of J & A beige bedroom carpeting for one of our best Princeton customers."

Stephen replaces his reading glasses in a leather case and tucks them into a side coat pocket. "In addition, Mr. Weinstein, let me say that even if there had been no specific orders on this matter to Rosemary—and there were, as I just pinpointed—my position on maintaining the status of Holloway Interiors as 'the Tiffany's of the home furnishings industry' was well known to Rosemary. Everyone in the trade knows about our high standards and our exclusive clientele, and you must remember that Rosemary worked for me for ten years before she left to marry and raise a family. She knew exactly what my goals for the chain were because she lived with them in the early years and we discussed the pros and cons of a 'carriage trade' business a number of times. . . . That's about all I have to add at this time, I think."

"One question before we take a short break." Weinstein addresses Holloway. "In those cases where you say Rosemary ignored your insistence that she not buy the Princess Charlotte and the Judith & Annette materials, did you order her to return them?"

"No, I did not. Both had been ordered for valued customers upon Rosemary's advice and I did not want to provoke a scene that would just make matters worse."

"Okay, I think I have the picture from both sides," says Weinstein. "Let's take a ten-minute break and then I'll caucus with the complainants. So Peter and Stephen, if you want to take a stroll, plan on being back here at eleven o'clock when I'll confer with you two."

Rosemary and Mark Bianchi make use of the lavatories, then chat for a few minutes until Seymour Weinstein beckons them back into the conference room. He asks them to sit on either side of him while he takes his seat at the end of the long oak table.

Weinstein opens with a request. "Do you mind," he asks Bianchi, "if I speak directly to Rosemary?"

"Not at all," Mark replies. "Thanks for asking, but no need to go through me. This is her show."

"Rosemary," says Weinstein, "I'd like to go into your family history a bit. I don't quite have a feel of your relationship with Stephen. We had a bad period like this in my family when I was a young man, still living at home in the Bronx. My uncle was living with us too. He didn't work nor did he make much effort to find work."

Weinstein tells the story at some length, obviously trying to put Rosemary at ease. He senses that she's still taut and uncomfortable at this session. The mediator tells about sharp scenes with his uncle Morris, how his father finally had to act as a peacemaker. But in the end Morris got a job and moved out. Later he and Seymour became good friends. "So conflict and a bit of shouting aren't necessarily bad. The point is, I guess, not to take hard ugly stances that prevent eventual reconciliation."

Under Weinstein's nudging, Rosemary tells of growing up in Albany in a household financed by the modest income of her father, a state civil service worker, and the sporadic supplements provided by her mother who sometimes worked as a caterer's assistant. She reiterates what she had told Bianchi about Stephen, two years younger, who first took great pride in her feats and called her Rosie, but who later came to resent her prowess at indoor and outdoor games when she consistently beat him. Again she tells about Stephen's drinking in high school and how she lied for him and took his part with their parents.

"What about the years when you worked for him before your marriage?" asks Weinstein. "Did you feel he still resented you or had that passed?"

"You know, I was just a clerical worker in the New York headquarters office then, handling accounts, dull housekeeping chores, mostly junk work. I was in my twenties and doing a lot of partying around town. I really didn't regard my work as a career or pay much attention to Stephen, and of course he was busy building Holloway Interiors and turning it into Snob Center. I guess you could say our feelings about each other never came up, although I always had that sneaky feeling that he'd be just as pleased if I made some big boo-boo so he'd have an excuse to fire me."

"How about during the years of your marriage?"

"Pleasant enough. He and his wife would join us on Thanksgivings and we'd take Christmas dinner with Stephen and Francine and their son Bruce. Of course, we weren't close. Francine is very social and I never cared to play that game."

Weinstein listens attentively, keeps his eyes on Rosemary. "And what about your relationship since you went back to work for him?"

She cocks her head and thinks for a moment. "I guess you could sum it up in the word 'correct.' While we weren't formal with each other, we weren't old pals either. It was always very clear that he was the head of the corporation and I was a store manager."

"Never called you Rosie, I take it?"

Her laugh is sardonic. "I haven't been Rosie to him since we were little kids."

"And he hasn't been Stevie to you either, has he?"

"No, he hasn't." She glances quickly at Weinstein. "I hadn't thought of that, but I guess it's true."

"Could you tell me exactly what took place when he dismissed you?"

"Yes, you ought to know that." She is eager to talk about the episode. "It'll tell you a great deal about Stephen. . . . I had just opened the store at nine-thirty on a Monday morning when he called from New York. He said—and I remember very clearly his first words—he said, 'Rosemary, it has become clear that we can no longer work together. I'm requesting that you leave our employ as of the close of business this Friday.'

"It was like being hit on the forehead with a mallet. I couldn't say a thing for a time, but when I got myself together, I asked him why and he said my actions had 'cheapened' the Holloway Interiors name and that my discharge of one of his old employees—that's in the position papers—had caused 'emotional shock waves' among both employees and customers.

"I was so shook, I wasn't even angry, just kind of numb. I couldn't figure it. I did say that we had a five-year contract, in case he'd forgotten. Oh, he knew about that, but he said I had 'breached' the contract by my actions in buying 'less than high-quality merchandise.' When he used the word 'breached,' I got the idea that he had talked to a lawyer before calling me.

"Of course, I was in a state of shock. I remember, Henrietta, my top assistant, came to the back office right after the call and asked me what she should do about an order for wrought-iron garden furniture that had never arrived. I said, 'Henny, do what you think best. I've just been fired.' Then I burst out crying and was a mess for the rest of the day. I remember that I called Stephen back about ten-thirty and asked him if he didn't have any more to say to me. I meant, you know, as family. After all, he had just fired his sister without so much as a single 'I'm sorry' or anything. He just said that our merchandising ideas were too far apart and that I did not share his goals for the company. Nothing personal, no apology, no sorry, just zap like that.

"Seymour, I've never been so hurt in my life. Not just the dismissal, but that my own brother would do it that way, cold and unfeeling. God, even in the big anonymous corporations, the personnel officer tries to be decent when he has to kick somebody out."

Weinstein takes a pocket-size notebook from his hip pocket and jots down a note. "I understand how you felt. I'm wondering now how you'd feel if your brother apologized at this late date for the manner, if not the reasons, for firing you?"

"I'd feel like he was putting me on—if he ever could bring himself to do it. Or I'd figure he was trying to get some advantage in these sessions here."

"What about those February and March phone calls from your brother. He says he admonished you not to buy goods he considered inferior. What's your recollection of those talks?"

"It's true that he said roughly what he told us today. But he conveniently forgot what I said." She shakes her head, a gesture of disdain. "I told him that both orders involved high-quality materials and the customer thought so too. If those were the warnings he's talking about, his case falls apart. No way could they be classed as warnings. They were just simple disagreements between one executive and her superior. Any sharp with-it outfit has a dozen of those a week."

Weinstein draws her out some more on her family life before the separation from her husband, her relationship with her two sons, and her ideas about working in the future. They chat for some time and she concludes by voicing a fervent hope that she can get another challenging job in the home furnishings field where she wants to make a career for the next fifteen years or so.

"But of course after the way Stephen has been talking about me in the industry," she says, "that's going to be hard. Believe me, he's not giving his sister any ringing endorsement."

"What if we could get a pledge from him that he would not say anything belittling or disparaging about you from now on? Would that be a major point with you?"

She brightens. "Indeed it would."

"What if we could get him to write a good reference for you?"

"Oh, la-la, that'll be the day." She tosses her head with a mocking laugh. "You get that, Seymour, and I'll recommend you for sainthood."

"Nice idea, but wrong religion. Besides, I look strange enough without a halo. . . . Just two more questions, Rosemary, and remember that what we say in this room stays right here. How old are you?"

"Fifty-three."

"Lastly. If you could wave a fairy's wand and waft yourself into the best of all possible situations, what would it be? What would you consider an ideal life for yourself from now on?"

"Oh, I'd like a good long cozy romance, probably with marriage again." She tilts her head as she reflects. "As for work, I'd like my own home furnishings shop that I could run as I wish. I've got a lot of ideas and I think I could make a success of it, maybe build my own chain in a few years. And no snob appeal stuff, either." She laughs. "Well, not much, anyway."

Weinstein turns to Mark Bianchi on his left. "Mark, now that we've got most all the facts at hand, I'd like to explore your client's position with you. Let me think out loud here just a bit. You check me if I misstate anywhere."

"Shoot."

The mediator takes ten minutes to sum up the highlights of the case, stressing the contract and dismissal, the argument over the meaning of "net profits," the degree to which Holloway Interiors suffered a tarnishing of its image, and how much harm had been done to Rosemary's career by her discharge.

"To start with, Mark, I can't see five hundred thousand dollar damages here. Oh, sure, you might get one jury out of a hundred to go up that much, but looking at the average jury, no. You're way too high. And let me tell you why I think so." He glances at Rosemary as well as her attorney.

"First off, age is a factor here. Rosemary, you have about fifteen good career years ahead of you, maybe one or two more. Now unfortunately, as attractive and as healthy as you appear, you are at that stage of life where things can happen to you, although not as much as at my age, thank God. So, even if we concede that the discharge injured your career, it's not as though you had thirty working years ahead of you.

"Second, Mark, has Mrs. Wofford's career in home furnishings actually been hurt all that much? We don't really know, do we, because she hasn't returned to the job market yet? My guess is that a woman with her credentials and background—she boosted earnings in a difficult situation—would get a job with relative ease."

"But one of comparative executive responsibility?" asks Bianchi quickly. "That's the question here."

"I realize that." Weinstein nods. "But we haven't tested that, have we? So we just have to take the commonsense view that in today's employment picture, an attractive capable woman with know-how and friends in the industry could make a fairly decent connection for herself." He hesitates. "What's the big grin for, Mark?"

"Your comment," the lawyer replies. "Cy, in one sentence, you've just stated what in litigation would require reams of case citations and pretrial statements and hours of argument without ever arriving at a definite conclusion."

"That's why I like mediation. You don't have to endlessly document what can never be conclusively proven but which everyone knows anyway." Weinstein talks some more about Rosemary's current economic situation. "What I'm getting around to is this," he says at last. "What if I could get a pledge out of Holloway, one that would be written into any final agreement, that henceforth he would say nothing disparaging about his sister?"

"Of course, that would be a big step forward," says Bianchi. "Wouldn't you agree, Rosemary?"

"Oh, yes. That would help. Definitely."

"But in money terms? If I could get you a nondisparagement pledge, would you be willing to reduce your demands?"

"I could recommend that, assuming it was a straight good-faith promise without any cute hedging. What's your reaction, Rosemary?"

"I'm inclined to follow your advice. Sure, if Stephen made an honest promise like that, I'd be willing to cut down on the money."

"How much? Would you authorize me to tell the other side that you'd drop to four hundred thousand with that kind of promise?"

Bianchi looks questioningly at Rosemary.

"What do you think?" she asks in response.

"I'd say yes, provided we approve the proposed wording."

"Okay then, on that condition." Rosemary nods. "I want to see just what he'd promise."

Weinstein grasps the edge of the table. "All right, that'll permit me to take something concrete to the caucus with the other side. If we can get a comparable measure of movement from them, I'd say we'd done a good morning's work. We'll see. . . . And Rosemary, I'm going to try for that letter of recommendation."

"Good luck." She shakes her head. "As I said, that'll put you up there with the other workers of miracles."

In the caucus with Stephen Holloway and his attorney, Weinstein repeats the seating arrangement, placing Stephen on his right and Peter Cavanaugh on his left. He starts off in a cheerful, upbeat manner.

"I'm happy to tell you that we already have some major yielding from the other side, provided they can get a promise from you people, a quite reasonable promise in my view."

"What do they want?" Cavanaugh is promptly suspicious.

"A simple pledge from your client that he would not at any time disparage or comment negatively on Rosemary Wofford's abilities as a home furnishings executive."

"And what's the major yielding?" asks Cavanaugh.

"They'll reduce their demands to four hundred thousand dollars. In short you're getting a hundred thousand for a promise not to do what you probably wouldn't do anyway. I call that a bargain."

"I'm certainly willing to make that promise," Holloway says quickly.

"Good, that's our first movement." Weinstein plucks at his shirt sleeves. "Now I'd like to get to know something about you, Stephen." He turns to Holloway. "Rosemary was good enough to tell me something of your family life up in Albany when you were children. I'd like to get your slant on those early years too. Do you mind?"

"Well, I guess not." But Stephen looks uncomfortable. "Just what do you want to know?"

"Oh, just tell me what you remember about growing up with Rosemary, how you got along with her, what kind of games you played, that kind of thing."

"Is this really necessary?"

"Nothing is mandatory here." Weinstein slides down into a slouch. He knows this won't be easy. "But Stephen, in an informal process like this one, I can help you and Rosemary much better to come to some kind of agreement if I have the feel of you both as persons. I want the human side of this equation."

"Well, if you insist. . . . I suppose it was a quite ordinary childhood in an average middle-class family of limited finances." Stephen begins slowly, reluctantly. He describes the frame house he grew up in, the neighborhood on Mercer Street, and Rosemary as he first remembered her, "a jumping-jack kind of girl with a wild mop of hair." She was a tomboy who could outrun and outclimb many of the boys she played with. "Frankly, I kind of admired her when I was five and six. She was two years older and I thought there wasn't much she couldn't do."

"What did you call each other?"

"Oh, let's see. She was Rosie." He looks startled as if the memory had taken him by surprise. "And she called me Stevie. My, that's a long time ago.

"Later we weren't so close." Stephen recounts a number of anecdotes about growing up, but none of them mention the defeats at Rosemary's hands that she had described. Instead he stresses their varying paths as the boy and girl grew into teenagers.

"Did you ever take each other's parts against your parents?"

"Yes, I often sided with Rosemary. Then once, let's see. . . ." He hesitates as if trapped in a painful memory. "I drank too much in high school and I remember she lied for me a few times, said I was okay when I was falling down drunk."

"Did that play a part in your hiring of her two years ago, a sense that you owed her one?" Weinstein is sunk deep in his chair, his hands folded beneath his chin, as he studies Holloway.

"Not really. I did it because she was family. I believe that family members owe certain obligations to one another."

Holloway talks some more about his maturing years, unbending slightly as he does so, then tells of college at Amherst where he was a good student, a textile design course in New York, and two years working for Bamberger's furnishings division before he started his own shop.

"I've always admired the sense of excellence one gets in the Holloway stores," says Weinstein. "Sarah and I have become fairly good customers in the last few years. Frankly, I don't mind paying the price when I know we're getting the best in materials and advice. I wonder, just how did you arrive at your formula?"

Holloway responds with some eagerness and soon he's rattling on about his business. Weinstein does not interrupt. As Stephen, absorbed, talks with less and less self-consciousness, a new side of the man begins to emerge. A stranger walking into the room might mistake him for an artist or musician talking quite passionately about his art.

It is a good fifteen minutes before he finishes and Weinstein turns to Cavanaugh for a discussion of legal points. After a few exchanges, Weinstein says that he thinks their request for $200,000 damages from Rosemary "just doesn't belong in this ballpark."

"My hunch is, Peter, that you just tossed that in as an extra bargaining chip," says Weinstein. "Could we start off by disposing of that? You must realize that under the circumstances—a quite valid contract broken, for one thing—no court in the country would ask Rosemary to pay you a dollar, let alone two hundred thousand of them."

Cavanaugh chews on his lip. "In light of the other side's full-scale retreat from their original asking price, I think I can recommend to Stephen that we not insist on that figure. Stephen?"

"You're in charge of the dollars and cents, Peter. You're the expert, not me."

Cavanaugh beams as he spreads his arms. "Now Cy, what more could a lawyer ask of his client?" He bows to Holloway. "I'm putting you up for the Wise-Man-of-the-Year Award."

"May I take it then that you've withdrawn the request?" asks Weinstein.

"Subject to reactivation should we go to litigation, of course."

"Of course. That's always understood here." Weinstein leans across the table. "All right, now let's talk real money. If I could guarantee prompt acceptance, what would you offer Rosemary at this moment? What'll you pay to walk out of here right now with an agreement in your pocket?"

Cavanaugh nods with a grin. "I figured you'd ask that, Cy, at just about this time." He glances at his wristwatch. "Eleven forty-five A.M. And in just about that way. As a matter of fact, Stephen and I discussed the situation last night." He lists the expenses they'd face if they prepared for trial, legal and auxiliary costs, charges against the business for Stephen's lost time and energy, the embarrassment of sister fighting brother, the risk of Holloway Interiors being damaged by some unforeseen testimony.

"In light of everything," Cavanaugh concludes, "and not for an instant admitting any blame on our part, but solely to get rid of a nuisance complaint that has some unsavory potential to it, we are willing to make a walk-away offer of fifty thousand dollars."

"Would that include a written pledge not to denigrate Rosemary in any way?"

"From my standpoint, yes." Cavanaugh looks at Holloway. "Stephen?"

"Absolutely." Holloway nods emphatically.

"What about a letter of recommendation for Rosemary?"

Holloway shakes his head just as emphatically. "Absolutely not."

Weinstein sighs. "That may cause problems." He rises, looks from Cavanaugh to Holloway, then stretches. "Still, I think we're making progress." He's in a good mood as he puts on his jacket. "Let's get the others in here for a minute."

Weinstein summons Wofford and Bianchi and they all stand in the conference room. "I just want to tell all of you that our work is paying off. Stephen Holloway has put a solid fifty thousand dollar offer on the table along with a promise to give a written pledge not to disparage Rosemary Wofford in any way. He has also withdrawn his demand for two hundred thousand. Mrs. Wofford, on her part, has reduced her asking sum to four hundred from five hundred thousand. So after three hours' work, we've squeezed the difference between you down to three hundred and fifty thousand—or just half of what it was when we walked in here."

He looks about the room. "So I consider that real headway. If we can do as well this afternoon, we might even wrap this thing up in a couple of days. So now let's break for lunch and be back here at one-fifteen."

After lunch Weinstein meets again with Rosemary Wofford and Mark Bianchi. "We're looking at progress," he says as they take their seats on either side of him. "I feel quite satisfied with the way things are going."

He reiterates that the parties have cut their money differences in half, that Holloway now is offering $50,000 to settle the case.

"Don't get the idea that I'm going to let him off that easy." Rosemary folds her hands in her lap, signaling patience in the face of frivolity.

"Nevertheless," says the mediator, "that represents a significant shift on their part. They came in here asking two hundred thousand from you. Now they're willing to *give* you fifty thousand and in addition Stephen promises a written pledge not to disparage you. That means, Rosemary, that he'll put no obstacles in the way of you finding another job."

"What about a letter of recommendation for me?"

"No, he's not willing to go that far, but many things could happen here to change his mind about that."

The mediator says that the next move is clearly up to Rosemary and her lawyer. The other side has yielded $250,000 since arriving in the morning, whereas Rosemary has reduced her demands by only $100,000.

"That's not so, Cy," Bianchi protests. "We started this action, asking seven hundred and fifty thousand. We've come down three hundred and fifty thousand dollars, more movement than they've shown."

"I was taking the situation as presented by both sides when we began this morning. At any rate, whatever the starting numbers, the ball's now in your court."

They parry and thrust for a half hour, circling about the same spot. "I can't go back to the other side without something to offer," says

Weinstein finally, opening his palms as if awaiting an offering.

Bianchi says he'd like to talk to his client in private, says they'll leave the room for a few minutes, but Weinstein offers to leave instead. He uses the few minutes to stroll about the mediation center and think out his strategy for the hours ahead. In disclosing his background to the battling siblings, the corporate lawyer neglected to reveal one significant aspect of his recent career. As a wise man, his essence contains a chunk of humility. He knows better than the next man how little he knows. However, he has learned that he's a good mediator and he's proud of his record: In the nine mediations he has done, he has never failed to guide the contesting parties into an agreement.

He does not want to fail on this, his tenth case, either. And while he sees movement and a willingness to make concessions on both sides, he also senses a stubborn streak in both brother and sister that spells danger. This one, he thinks, is by no means a sure thing and he decides to press forward with caution, being satisfied this first day with a narrowing of the issues and the focus.

When Weinstein returns, Rosemary says that after consulting with Mark she has decided to reduce her monetary demand by $25,000 and is now asking "only" $375,000. Weinstein is tempted to make a tart remark about her choice of the word "only," but he resists the urge.

"That isn't as much reduction as I'd hoped," he says. "I don't think either you or Mark has yet made a realistic forecast of what you could expect to get from a jury. From my experience with juries, only a rare, rare one would award you that much in this kind of case."

They discuss the figure for a good half hour before Bianchi says: "Of course, Cy, if Stephen Holloway will give his sister a good letter of recommendation, we would consider that equivalent to a bit of money."

"How much would the letter be worth? Is it a hundred thousand dollar letter?" Weinstein bores in.

"It might be." Bianchi eyes the ceiling. "All depends on what the letter says, how strong the recommendation is."

"Okay, I'll try the other side again now. Send in Stephen and Peter, please."

The mediator radiates confidence and pleasure as he greets the home furnishings executive and his lawyer. "Once more, I can report progress." He talks in broad generalities for a few minutes. "So, while their monetary concession is a modest one, twenty-five thousand, bringing their total demand down to three hundred and seventy-five thousand, they've also dropped an especially revealing hint." Weinstein has learned the value of suspense in his dealings.

"A hint?" Cavanaugh snaps at the bait. "What's the revealing hint?"

Weinstein leans forward, lowering his voice as if about to convey a secret: "I got the clear impression that one of Rosemary's major goals in these sessions is to come away with a strong letter of recommendation from you, Stephen. She wants to go back to work as a manager or executive in home furnishings and a letter from a person of your stature would be worth a great deal to her."

"Worth how much?" asks Cavanaugh quickly.

"No, no," says Stephen just as quickly. "I don't intend to trade a letter of recommendation for some reduction in her demands for money. It's a matter of integrity. She either deserves a recommendation or she doesn't and money doesn't enter the equation."

"All right then," says Weinstein, "doesn't she deserve a recommendation? She increased the profits of one of your stores by a hundred and forty thousand dollars her first year on the job."

"That was a hundred thousand after taxes." Stephen looks severe. "And making money by selling an inferior brand of merchandise is not difficult in a store with a Tiffany's reputation."

They discuss Rosemary's business talents and the possibilities of a letter of recommendation for a solid hour without nearing a consensus. It becomes apparent that Cavanaugh is quite willing to trade a letter for a substantial reduction in Rosemary's money demands, but his client adamantly refuses to let his sister "buy a recommendation from me." Weinstein, seeing that he has erred in placing a dollar sign on the letter, tries to advance the trade by casting it in other terms.

"I can't quite understand, Stephen," he says, "why you object to consideration of a letter of recommendation for your sister when you obviously think that she does have managerial talent."

"True, but there are so many minuses involved. She barges ahead on her own, refuses to take direction from a superior, and runs risks without checking with those who have the experience."

They discuss the letter for another extended period and finally Weinstein observes that "it seems that Stephen might consider giving a letter of recommendation if it were written in rather narrow terms that he felt would not violate the truth as he sees it."

"But," objects Stephen, "a letter written that carefully might do her more harm than good. The smart reader would get suspicious."

Weinstein looks at his wristwatch. A few minutes before five. He risks a shot.

"Look, we're right up against quitting time and I'm beginning to wonder just how much good faith bargaining we've got here. The other side made a modest concession this afternoon. You've made none at all. I'd like to ask a blunt question: Stephen, do you want an agreement to come out of these sessions?"

"Yes, I do." He says it with emphasis. "I do not want my company taken to court." He glances at Cavanaugh. "But that doesn't mean, on the other hand, that I'm willing to give away Holloway Interiors just to stay out of court. Oh no. I'll fight if I have to. Any agreement here has to be fair."

"Right." The mediator opens his palms once more. "But what are you giving me to take back to the other side? This afternoon you haven't budged an inch."

Holloway gets up and beckons Cavanaugh. "Pardon us, just a minute, Mr. Weinstein." The two men confer in whispers at the end of the table while the mediator reflects that Holloway is the only participant who has yet to call him "Seymour" or "Cy." He thinks that of the two disputants, he prefers Rosemary by a wide margin, but no sooner does he become conscious of the thought than he bans it. He knows from experience that he can never afford to take sides, that to do so might influence his behavior subsonsciously and thus hamper chances of an agreement.

"Cy," says Cavanaugh when the two men return to their places. "As a token of our hope to get an agreement, we've decided to raise our offer to sixty-five thousand."

"Good." It is much less than Weinstein expected, but at this late hour he'll take anything. "And how about a letter? Will you at least consider one, Stephen?"

Holloway pulls at his chin as he thinks. "I'll do this, I'll promise to think it over this evening. I want to review in my own mind just what her talents are."

Although Weinstein can picture Holloway bent over a "pro" and "con" sheet, laboring to strike a balance on his sister, the mediator reacts as if he'd just received news that he'd been named to the U.S. Supreme Court.

"Fine, fine." He rubs his hands as he goes to the door and summons Rosemary and her attorney who are in a room down the hall.

"Stephen has just told us that he is now offering sixty-five thousand dollars to settle this matter." Weinstein speaks to the four participants who are all standing now.

Bianchi shakes his head. "That, of course, is unacceptable."

Weinstein waves his hands, a gesture of erasing the number. "I assume that Stephen would be as astounded as I would if you had accepted his offer right off. But think about it overnight. That's good cash money, equal to a whole year's salary for Rosemary at the Princeton store. . . . In addition Stephen will give thought overnight to the possibility of writing a letter of recommendation for his sister. He does not promise a letter, but he does promise to give it serious consideration. So now we've narrowed the money gap to three hundred and ten thousand dollars. That may seem like a formidable figure to resolve, but remember it's only a number and any number can be changed. Besides, the progress is tremendous. When we walked in here this morning, you folks were seven hundred thousand apart. So you've squeezed almost four hundred thousand out of your differences."

He continues for several minutes in this optimistic vein, then sets the resumption of talks for ten o'clock the next morning.

The mediator's cheerful appraisal is not mirrored in the faces of brother and sister. Stephen looks grim. Rosemary shakes her head as if she has scant hopes for tomorrow. The two fighters leave without speaking to each other.

Mediation

10

New York
June 21

Part Five: *More Mediation*

The Mediation Hearing

Mediator Seymour Weinstein has a brisk businesslike air when the battling brother and sister and their lawyers meet him at 10 A.M. to begin the second day of mediation. He summarizes the situation in his customary optimistic vein, then faces Holloway.

"Can you tell us what you've decided about the letter of recommendation, Stephen?"

The president of Holloway Interiors, cool, controlled, and precise of speech, nods with a tight smile. Today he is wearing a different three-piece suit, this one of a pale blue summerweight material as elegantly tailored as yesterday's. "I've come to the conclusion that it would be a mistake to give a letter of recommendation priority here. My main concern is to clear the decks of Mrs. Wofford's totally unjustified claim for damages. I consider that claim outrageous in any amount. I dismissed her because she defied orders. No business can operate with that kind of insubordination."

"Stephen—" Mark Bianchi begins.

"No." Holloway cuts off Rosemary's lawyer. "Let me finish. We have offered sixty-five thousand dollars to get rid of this matter. Even that I feel is a kind of blackmail." His temper is rising. "She threatens to sue me and the only way I can protect myself is to shell out money to buy her off. That's the trouble with our legal system. The innocent get hauled into court and then have to pay blackmail or else spend weeks and months mired in a swamp of legal actions."

"Stephen!" Rosemary shouts. "Damn it, you broke a contract when you fired me."

Weinstein raises a hand. "Rosemary, please. You've given your word not to interrupt." He takes command. "Now I think it's unfortunate that we've slipped back into accusations. I thought you two got all of that out of your systems yesterday." He continues in similar vein, trying to pacify the combatants, for several minutes. "The fact is," he concludes, "that you've both told us in straightforward terms that you want to reach an agreement here. I believe that you do. So please, humor me by throwing all those angry charges overboard. We'll make good progress if you both keep your eyes on the goal—a written agreement that will dispose of this matter."

"My client made the last move here, Cy," says Peter Cavanaugh when the mediator finishes. "Last evening he offered sixty-five thousand to walk away from this. We'd like to know, does Mrs. Wofford accept?" The lawyer fixes his gaze on Rosemary.

"I most decidedly do not. Do you need an explanation?"

"We can skip that, Rosemary," says Weinstein. "Now I'd like to caucus with you and Mark. My last session was with Stephen. So could you two gentlemen please leave now. I'll get back to you in a half hour or so."

When seated with Mark Bianchi and Rosemary, Weinstein cautions them against discouragement. "My hunch is that a letter of recommendation is still possible. You'll note that Stephen used the word 'priority.' He won't give the letter 'priority' because he first wants to clear up the money question. But he stopped short of saying he'd never write a letter."

"He just reverted to type," says Rosemary caustically. "He started blowing his top again. He knows he's in the wrong and that's his way of defending himself."

Weinstein remains silent for a few moments while he toys with his notebook and fountain pen. "Rosemary, yesterday you gave a graphic description of the time your brother discharged you. I got the impression that it was the manner of the act, rather than the fact itself, that hurt you the most. Am I right about that?"

"Absolutely." She taps the table. "Oh, of course, I thought he had no reason on earth to fire me and I resented it—deeply. But it was the rude, really cruel way that he did it." Suddenly she is blinking back a tear and dabbing at her eyes with a handkerchief. "I just can't imagine me treating him that way. . . . Well, so much for family."

As the mediator jots something in his notebook, she asks: "Why do you ask, Seymour?"

"I'm just not sure myself." He pauses, gazes upward. "I just happened to think of what you said yesterday. I suppose it's that I find the road to an agreement is always smoother if I can get a good fix on the psychology and character of both parties. Businesspeople come in here to mediate money matters, but actually there are often personal differences that trouble them as much as the money. Cash becomes merely a measurement in settling a lot of other things."

"I find Stephen a difficult character to deal with," says Bianchi.

"Yes, he's a complex man," observes Seymour. "On the one hand, he fires his sister with about as much sensitivity as a toad and then on the other, he shows that he's a man of principle. Yesterday he refused to discuss money and the letter of recommendation in the same context. He wouldn't, in other words, sell the letter to you folks by trading it for a reduction in your demands. And then when he discussed his business, it was in the terms of imagination and elegance, not money. He sounded more like an artist than a businessman. . . . Curious man."

They talk some more about Stephen and then Weinstein says that he gave considerable thought the previous night to their $375,000 offer and concluded that in light of Stephen's increased offer of $65,000, "they could do much better." He takes some papers from the inner breast pocket of his jacket, which hangs on the chair behind him. "I happened to have these statistics from another contract mediation I did last month." He spreads the papers on the table and invites attention to them. "These are average and mean jury awards in contract disputes correlated on this graph here with the original demands of the plaintiffs."

As they study the scrawled numbers and inspect the graph, Seymour says that although the data are confusing, it would appear that the great bulk of jury awards for cases in which the plaintiffs asked damages in the range of Rosemary's demands fell far below the asking prices. "Of course, you get a few million-plus awards in there that throw the averages out of whack. But certainly, a look at these figures gives little hope that you'd get three seventy-five from a jury."

"Can I tell you something in confidence, Cy?" asks Bianchi.

"Of course. As I said at the outset, nothing said in confidence goes to the other party—at least not through me."

"I told Rosemary the day she brought her problem to me that I thought the case was worth in the neighborhood of two hundred thousand, that she'd get about that from a jury or a settlement on the eve of trial or at mediation, for that matter."

"Are you telling me that you'd take two hundred thousand to end this case?"

Bianchi laughs. "Hey, Cy, you close in as fast as a boxer. . . . Would we call it quits for two hundred thousand? I can't tell you that. Depends. We would promise utmost consideration. Now that's strictly between us."

"And for the record?" Weinstein cocks his head as he waits.

"Last evening before we quit, Stephen and Peter raised their offer to sixty-five thousand. Rosemary and I discussed the whole situation this morning at breakfast. We feel that their fifteen thousand dollar increase, while completely unsatisfactory—paltry stuff, really—does show intent to bridge the gap between us. In return, we're willing to reduce our demand for damages by fifty thousand. So Rosemary authorizes you to tell Stephen and Peter that we now ask only three hundred and twenty-five thousand."

The mediator nods and gets up quickly. "Thanks. Would you please send in the other side. I hope to keep this momentum going until there's no gap at all between you."

But Weinstein's hope founders shortly before noon. He tries many of the tools in the mediator's bag, but can fetch Stephen Holloway no higher than $75,000. This $10,000 increase arouses neither excitement nor gratitude in Rosemary and she refuses, under Bianchi's advice, to reduce her demand to less than $315,000. It is apparent to Weinstein now that Rosemary has a new game plan: She will match any offer her brother makes, but in no event will she exceed that amount. As for Stephen, Weinstein senses that the brother's sticking point is about $100,000.

Calling all four people together before the noon recess, Seymour tries to put the best face possible on the matter, even though he senses that they are near deadlock. "All right," he says with a gusto he does not feel, "we moved more slowly this morning, but we made real progress. When we arrived, brother and sister were three hundred and ten thousand dollars apart. Now the difference between you has been narrowed to two forty. In other words, you're within striking distance of each other. You're about at the point where a proposal to split the difference might be quite attractive."

"Go up another hundred and twenty thousand?" exclaims Cavanaugh. "Not on your life. Let's hang on to reality here, Cy."

"I'll echo that from our side," says Bianchi.

Seymour, dejected, plans to sneak off for lunch by himself. He is putting on his rumpled jacket when an idea strikes. God, why hadn't he thought of that before?

He turns to Bianchi and his client. "By the way, would you two mind if I lunched with Peter and Stephen? I've got a hunch that just might take us somewhere."

"Not at all," says Rosemary. "Actually, I didn't sleep much last night. I'm beat. I'm going to skip lunch and take a nap in one of these rooms."

"Okay with me, Cy," says Bianchi.

"Come on." Weinstein steps between Holloway and Cavanaugh and takes the arm of each man. "Be my guests. I know a nice cool place and I've got something I want to try out on you."

The trio saunters along the streets of mid-Manhattan on another of those fine June days when the air has a sparkle to it and the streaming crowds slow their restless pace to enjoy the warm sunlight. Sidewalk vendors hawk their gaudy wares and male office workers, lounging on steps and esplanades of buildings, admire the trim legs of brisk women walkers.

Seymour Weinstein, the big shambling mediator, walks along with

Stephen Holloway, the fastidious, correct, and humorless prince of home furnishings, on one side, and Peter Cavanaugh, Holloway's bluff irreverent attorney, on the other.

"So what is this, Cy?" asks Cavanaugh. "You shanghaiing us or what? I'm advising my client to go on red alert. The wily Weinstein is up to something that bodes no good for our side."

"You picked yourself one suspicious lawyer, Stephen." Weinstein enjoys the bantering. "I'm taking you both to lunch at a mystery location and I'm paying. An act of common courtesy. Now does that sound like a flimflam act, I ask you?"

"Don't answer that, Stephen." Cavanaugh laughs. "And keep your fingers crossed."

"Here we are." Weinstein steers his companions sharp left into one of the city's vest-pocket oases. This is the Samuel Paley Memorial Park, squeezed between two tall buildings on East Fifty-third Street between Fifth and Madison. It's crowded with white-collar workers eating lunch at garden tables beneath a small grove of honey locust trees. The feathery leaves tremble in a cool breeze stirred by a waterfall that tumbles down a back wall.

"We line up for sandwiches." Weinstein propels his guests toward a queue in front of a bricked enclosure where two women are taking snack orders. "You'll note I don't spring for a fancy lunch with wine. But you'll love the ambience here." He waves his arm toward the wide waterfall.

"I like your taste in settings, Seymour," says Stephen Holloway. "I sometimes walk over from my office and have lunch here when I have a problem to work out."

They wait in line, then take their soft drinks and snacks—a hamburger and two hot dogs—toward the waterfall. They sit on a bench against the wall, but soon a table opens beneath a honey locust tree. They chat for a while about city spaces, parks, and architecture and agree with Weinstein that "this two-by-four nook wouldn't make sense in a spacious city like Denver or Vancouver, but here it's a bit of heaven in the summer."

"Okay," says Cavanaugh after a time, "what did you want to try out on us?"

"Oh, just an ordinary bit from your old Pyschology 101 classes," Seymour replies. "You know, sometimes we tend to forget the obvious." He takes off on a circuitous route through the relationships of human beings, the failures in communications, the times when a person unintentionally hurts another, mixed and double signals, how vulnerable people are, the difficulty of making amends, in all a long slow ramble through the thicket of who does what to whom and why.

"I understand all that," says Stephen, "but what's the application . . . "

"Yeah," says Peter, "where's this train heading?"

"Let me ask you a direct question." Seymour levels a finger at Stephen, swings it toward Peter. "If, by making one single move—a move that wouldn't cost you a penny—you could get the kind of agreement in this mediation that would satisfy you completely, would you make that move?"

"Depends." Cavanaugh tilts an eyebrow. "If you want Stephen to slice off his thumbs or shoot his attorney, no."

"What move are you thinking of?" Stephen is intrigued.

Weinstein lays a hand on Stephen's arm. "You have the chance to wind up these negotiations and get the kind of settlement you want by performing one simple, but difficult act. Nobody has so indicated from the other side, but I'd stake my mediator's fee on it. You do the right thing and this case might just fall in your lap."

"And the right thing is?" Now Stephen's voice reflects some of Cavanaugh's skepticism.

"Apologize to your sister for the way you fired her."

Color flares in Stephen's face. "I'll be damned if—" he begins in anger.

"No. Hear me out." Weinstein holds up his hand. "This woman, your sister, hurts deep down inside her because of the manner in which you fired her. Not the business reasons, mind you. Those nicked her pride, but she can live with them. What came like a knife slash was the sudden peremptory and naked way you did it—"

Cavanaugh cuts in. "Cy, let me—"

"No," says Weinstein, "both of you listen now for a while. I'm trying to save you guys a couple of hundred grand, so let me finish. I've got a lot to say."

The mediator says he has come to the conclusion that the *manner* of Rosemary's discharge is the crux of the case, that although Rosemary probably doesn't know this herself, it becomes obvious to anyone who listens closely to her. "You heard her yesterday. She said she was 'crushed' after all her work to be fired out of hand, no warning."

Actually, Weinstein surmises aloud, if Stephen had broken the dismissal news to his sister gently, explained it with kindness in some detail and offered to help her get another job, she would never have gone to a lawyer and they wouldn't be here today. Weinstein says that Stephen has said nothing to cast the manner of firing in another light, so he assumes Rosemary's account is substantially correct.

"Am I right about that, Stephen?"

"Well, I intended to make it easy on her," he replies, "but it just didn't come out that way. I have, frankly, a very hard time with that sort of thing. I'm no good at applying, you know, social ointments, as it were."

"I know." Weinstein continues talking about the need for an apology, the difference in personality between brother and sister, how Rosemary talks fondly of the days when she was Rosie and he Stevie. This leads into a conversation about the old days of childhood and on one exchange Stephen denies that he ever wanted his sister to fail at her job so he'd have a chance to fire her in revenge for her little triumphs over him as a kid.

"I believe you," says Seymour. "You sound sincere to me, but you see, Rosemary thinks otherwise and she does so because you two have never talked honestly and deeply about your relationship, one of the most important you'll ever have in life." He shrugs. "I know I sound like a shrink, not a business mediator, but lots of times in a case like this, it's not the law we have to wrestle with, but the minds of contrary people."

They sit in silence for a time, then Seymour says: "Stephen, you said you 'intended to make it easy' on your sister that day you called her from the city. Does that mean you do regret the way you discharged her?"

"Well, yes, I wish I'd had the words to tell her in a different way. I told you how bad I am at that kind of thing."

"So if you do regret it, why not go the extra step and apologize to Rosemary for the way you did it?"

"You mean today?" The chief of Holloway Interiors looks stricken.

"Sure, why not? I can tell you one thing." Weinstein leans forward and focuses his gaze on Stephen. "If you can make a sincere apology to your sister—sincere now, no faking—it'll go a long way toward wrapping up this case the way you want. That woman is crying for a sign of your affection."

"That's hard to believe, Seymour." Stephen, frowning, shakes his head. "She's acted like an absolute bitch."

"Trust me. I know what I'm saying."

"Did she tell you that?" Cavanaugh, reentering the conversation, looks his most skeptical.

"No. She thinks the idea of her brother apologizing is so remote, it's not worth considering. So she says, but what she feels is a lot different. For that judgment I'm banking on my knowledge of human nature."

"I'm not sure I could do it." Stephen looks pained.

"Tell me this. If you had to do it over again, how would you fire her the second time?"

"With a lot more thought and, well, kindness, I suppose. Yes, as I think you said, kindness."

"And you truly feel that?"

"Yes, I do."

"Then, for God's sake, man, tell her so when we go back for this afternoon's session. Take her off in a side room and tell her you're sorry. Tell her just how you feel."

"Christ, facing her would be awful."

"Stephen, whatever happens to this case, Rosemary's going to be your sister forever. If you don't make this effort, as hard as it'll be on you for a few minutes, your refusal's going to nag at you for the rest of your life."

Holloway looks at Cavanaugh. "What do you think, Peter?"

"As a fellow guest at this chic hot dog luncheon, I shouldn't fault anything our host says. As your lawyer, I am attracted by Cy's prediction that if you apologize, you may get what you want out of this case. I have no idea whether he's right. But hell, what would you be risking? I don't see how you and Rosemary could make your relationship any worse than it is."

Stephen sits in quiet struggle, his thoughts of the trauma of confrontation written in his pained expression.

"Okay," he says at last. "I'll do it. You two go on together. I want to walk by myself and plan just what to say."

Weinstein and Cavanaugh forge ahead after the three men leave the park.

"You a gambler, Peter?" asks Seymour.

"I never go to Atlantic City. I like sure things."

"I've got a sure thing for you. Bet your apartment that we'll wind up this thing with an agreement everyone's happy with."

"You're mighty cocky. But don't bet your own apartment, Cy. I could always sabotage a settlement, you know."

"You're smart enough, Peter." He stops on the sidewalk and grasps the attorney's arm. "But you're not mean enough."

Weinstein and Cavanaugh find Mark Bianchi awaiting them in the AAA's suite of offices. He has a quizzical expression.

"What did you do to Holloway?" he asks.

"Why, what happened?" counters the mediator.

"He walks in here, takes Rosemary by the arm, and says, 'We have to talk,' then leads her down the corridor to the same room where she took her nap. Zap, they disappear."

"We might as well sit down and make ourselves comfortable," says Weinstein. "They'll be in there a few minutes. . . . Stephen's apologizing for the way he fired her."

"He's what?" Bianchi's astounded.

"He's apologizing. I suggested it might help matters."

"Suggested!" Cavanaugh exclaims. "Don't let him kid you. He lowered the boom on my client. Whopped him on the head with a load of Psychology 101. Are we paying this guy a hundred fifty bucks an hour to mediate a dispute or psychoanalyze our clients?"

Bianchi grins. "Great idea, Cy. Beautiful." He looks at his wristwatch. "One-oh-eight. Let's see how long they stay in there."

Cavanaugh points at each man, then himself. "Should we tell them the combined meter's running at about four hundred and fifty dollars an hour? That's quite a price for them to pay us to sit around and read magazines."

"Don't bother them." Weinstein is serious about this. "We want them to get into the talk they should have had thirty years ago."

"Okay by me." Cavanaugh shrugs and takes the day's *New York Times* from the coffee table. "People want to pay me to catch up on the Mets, City Hall, and the situation in Upper Volta, I'm their man every time." He folds the paper in half, then to quarter size.

"I see you ride the subway," Bianchi observes.

"Best deal in town—outside this we-pay-you-to-read library." Cavanaugh makes a sour mouth.

"I take it you're not a devoted fan of mediation?" Weinstein picks up a copy of the *National Geographic* with a soot-eyed giant panda on the cover.

"I'm giving it my best shot, Cy. But frankly, I'd rather earn my pay than sit around reading." Cavanaugh snaps the paper.

"Oh, come on, Peter," says Bianchi. "Think how much time you waste sitting around courtrooms during those long recesses waiting for the judge. My partner, Pepe Gonzalez, has just been through two months in court on a libel case. You should hear him talk about sitting around."

This provokes a discussion of misspent and idle hours during the practice of law. Weinstein tells of his last antitrust case, which lasted seven months in court after four years of preparation, maneuvering, motions, discovery, and depositions.

"Once," he says, "during one of those interminable recesses, I added up the total daily costs of that litigation and I came out at around twenty-five thousand dollars a day."

"That sounds high, Seymour," says Cavanaugh.

"Not at all. We had fourteen attorneys in that courtroom and five of them were from Houston, staying at the Plaza on expense account. Including the high-priced talent, hotel, and food bills, I figured a minimum of twenty thousand a day just for the lawyers. Now you add on the salaries of the judge and four court personnel, per diem for the jurors, wages of the custodian and cleaning women, law firm messengers and secretaries working on the case, phone bills, heat, light, and maintenance chargeable to that courtroom, and you're easily up to twenty-five thousand a day before you finish."

"Look at the bright side," says Cavanaugh. "Think of all those hustlers you're keeping off the streets."

"A terrible waste of the country's energies." Weinstein turns the levity aside. "And wouldn't you know, that case was eventually settled one night with a payment by the defendant corporation—you may have heard, Stricklin & Adler?—that was only two percentage points away from the offer they made three years earlier."

"One more horror exhibit in the halls of litigation," observes Bianchi. "No wonder mediation and arbitration are gaining."

"Oh, spare me the propaganda," Cavanaugh retorts.

"Peter," asks Weinstein, "didn't you tell me that your blood line is English?"

"Yeah, I grew up with the Boston Irish, but I'm part of that small but noble breed, a Catholic Brit."

"So you know all about John Bull as a symbol for Great Britain?"

"No, not much." Cavanaugh cocks his head. "He's the Englishman's Uncle Sam. What else?"

"He was created early in the seventeen hundreds," says Weinstein, "by John Arbuthnot who wrote a satire called *Law Is a Bottomless Pit.* John Bull was pictured as a hardy litigant involved in an interminable lawsuit. He was an honest bluff good-natured but terribly stubborn man who poured all the family resources into the lawsuit."

"So?"

Weinstein smiles. "Just wanted to polish off your legal education. I find it ironic that the cartoonist's symbol for Great Britain should be a guy who wasted the family's sustenance in litigation. What John Bull needed was a shot of mediation."

"Maybe, maybe not." Cavanaugh shakes his head. "I'm not even sure mediation is going to work in this dinksville case."

They fall silent and Cavanaugh picks up his folded *Times* again. Weinstein leafs through his magazine and Bianchi finds a copy of *Newsweek* on the table.

More time passes. Weinstein finishes looking at the *National Geographic* photographs, returns to the story about the giant panda in China's Min Mountains, and actually begins to read it. Bianchi looks at his watch and announces: "One-forty-nine. They've been in there almost three-quarters of an hour."

When Rosemary and Stephen finally appear, Bianchi clocks the entire dialogue at one hour two minutes. Brother and sister stand quietly with the three lawyers. Stephen wears an ambiguous smile, but seems no more relaxed than he did earlier. Rosemary may have been crying. Her eyes look strained and she holds a handkerchief in her hand.

"Well?" It is Weinstein who speaks but the other attorneys appear just as impatient for the news.

"I apologized to Rosemary for the brusque way I discharged her, she's forgiven me and we're ready to resume the mediation." Stephen apparently does not care to amplify.

When Seymour looks inquiringly at Rosemary, she says: "We didn't do any negotiating, if that's what you're wondering."

"All right then. Let's go back to work." The mediator leads the group up to the eleventh floor and back to the mediation room. They all take their original seats.

"Now," says Weinstein, "I'll need some more information on just where you two stand. We can't mediate blindfolded in total darkness. Without going into details, could one of you please outline what you discussed, decided, or whatever?"

Stephen nods to Rosemary. "You do it, will you?"

"Well, I'm not sure what to say." She looks down at her lap. "Stephen apologized to me in a very sweet way. I know it was hard for him, but he did it, saying that you had suggested it." She glances at Weinstein.

"Did you talk at all about the matter before us?" Weinstein asks.

Stephen answers this time. "Just that Rosemary said maybe our trouble was partially her fault because she never really liked the idea of aiming a business solely toward the affluent. I don't understand that attitude at all, but she does feel that way, so I guess it was a mistake for her to take the Princeton store in the first place."

Rosemary sighs. "Yeah, there were mistakes on both sides." She looks at Weinstein. "But that doesn't change the fact that I was bounced without cause and that my career has been damaged and that the law has been violated or at least bent the hell out of shape." She says this last sharply.

"All right then," says the mediator. "Can I assume two things then? One, that the emotional charge between you has been somewhat defused. Two, that otherwise the status of this case remains where it was when we adjourned for lunch."

Stephen nods. "Yes, I'd say that's a fair summation. Maybe I should add this though. If any of you have gotten the idea that I don't appreciate Rosemary's business talents, you're wrong. I think that she's very good at what she does and that with a different company with different goals, she'd make a fine executive."

"Thanks," says Rosemary. "Of course, there's never been any question about Stephen's ability. His success speaks for itself. . . . I won't quarrel with either of your assumptions, Seymour. You stated the situation just about right."

"Okay, and when we quit for lunch," says Weinstein, "we had collapsed the gap between the parties to two hundred and forty thousand dollars. That is, Stephen had offered seventy-five thousand to settle, but Rosemary was asking three hundred and fifteen thousand. . . . Now, going back to our regular mediation sessions, I'd like some time with Mark and Rosemary. So, Stephen, if you and your client could step outside for a few minutes, please."

"I think we can make some real headway now," says Weinstein when he again has placed Rosemary on his right and Mark on his left. "This morning Stephen flatly refused to write a recommendation for you, Rosemary, but in light of what he's said about your talents just now, I see no reason why he wouldn't change his mind. What do you think?"

"Yes, I think he might give me a decent letter now."

"All right then." A yellow pad rests in the center of the table and Weinstein draws the legal-size notepaper to him. "Let's draft a statement for him to sign that will be as strong as you want. I think it ought to admit the differences that led to your leaving Holloway Interiors—since everyone of any consequence in the trade knows it anyway—but otherwise give you a big send-off. Okay with you, Mark?"

Both Bianchi and his client agree, so the three set to work devising a recommendation. Each writes out several paragraphs, they discuss the differences, and then Mark draws up a draft that Rosemary approves. As perfected after some twenty minutes of work, it reads:

To Whom It May Concern:

I highly recommend Rosemary Wofford for an executive or managerial post in the field of home furnishings. She has exhibited extraordinary talent in our company, is ambitious, and plans to continue her career elsewhere.

While it is no secret in the industry that she has left Holloway Interiors, I want to say that our disagreement over policy in no way reflects on her wide-ranging abilities.

Sincerely,
STEPHEN HOLLOWAY
President, Holloway Interiors

"All right now," says Weinstein, "how much are you willing to give to get that letter? Is this a one hundred and fifty thousand dollar letter?"

"Not in my book." Bianchi shakes his head. "I'd be willing to make some concession, but come down to one sixty-five in our demand? No."

"I don't know, Mark." Rosemary frowns. "Why not come down that far? With that letter and a hundred and sixty-five thousand dollars, I'd be all set. I'd take me a good vacation and then hit the job market with lots of confidence."

"I'm thinking of our bargaining position," Mark replies. "Let's not come down so fast. I'd call it a hundred-grand letter. So we'd reduce our price to two hundred and fifteen thousand dollars."

"Why not round it off?" asks Weinstein quickly. "Tell 'em you want two hundred thousand and the letter."

"Fine with me," says Rosemary.

"Okay. I'll buy that," Mark adds.

Seymour folds the long yellow paper on which the letter has been written. "Good." He rises. "Please send the others in. I'll see what we can do with this. I'll get back to you in a half hour or so."

Weinstein waits until Holloway and Cavanaugh are seated, then hands Holloway the folded paper. "If you're willing to sign that, Stephen, it'll save you an awful lot of money."

Holloway slowly reads the letter, looks at the mediator, and taps his fingers on the table. "You know I told you this morning that I wasn't ready to give my sister a letter of recommendation."

"I didn't forget," Weinstein's eyes lock with Stephen's. "But everyone felt that circumstances had changed markedly since your talk with Rosemary. Haven't they?"

"Yes, they have." Stephen places the letter on the table, takes a ballpoint pen from the breast pocket of his jacket, and rapidly scrawls his name under "Sincerely." He says, "There," and starts to hand the paper to Weinstein. "Wait a minute." He scratches out "wide-ranging" in the last line and writes in "superior" so that the final phrase reads: ". . . I want to say that our disagreement over policy in no way reflects on her superior abilities."

"That should be all right with Rosemary," says Stephen. " 'Wide-ranging' doesn't sound like me. Let me keep this. I'll have it typed up on Holloway Interiors stationery and mail it to her."

"Hold it, not so fast." Attorney Cavanaugh raises a hand. "Let's find out first how much they'll come down in return for that letter."

Stephen inspects his coat sleeve, brushes a speck of lint from it. "I don't want this mixed up with money. Rosemary is entitled to the letter. She does have superior abilities and as her brother, I intend to say so."

"Damn it, man, as your attorney, I can't allow you to throw away a bargaining advantage like that. That's worth a lot of money."

"Allow me or not, as you please." Stephen's tone has frost on it. "The fact is, I've already agreed to it. I'm not going back on my word."

"Jesus," Cavanaugh shrugs.

After a few moments of silence, Weinstein says: "I hear you, Stephen. However, your sister also has already acted. She is now asking only two hundred thousand to settle this matter."

Again Stephen looks Weinstein full in the eyes. "And I'm offering only seventy-five thousand. On your next shuttle, please inform Rosemary and her lawyer that I won't budge from that position. My lawyer informs me that my sister, not I, broke the contract, so I'd be entirely within my rights to refuse to pay anything at all. I'm offering seventy-five thousand only to avoid the tedium of a court trial and the scandalous loss of time involved. I'm no workaholic, but I hate to fritter away valuable time." All this is said in a dry, precise manner.

Weinstein thinks a bit, then says slowly, stressing his words: "Stephen, we're at a critical point in this mediation. It's apparent to all of us, I'm sure, that a new mood of flexibility has entered this room. That being true, you can keep up the momentum by increasing your offer—if only by a small amount, say adding another twenty-five to your seventy-five thousand dollars. If, however, you remain adamant without a bit of give, we might run out of gas here within clear sight of the finish line."

Holloway nods. "I've given that some thought. Still, I have my rights and we have the law. I didn't break the contract. She did."

"Stephen, Stephen," Weinstein admonishes. "That contract is your weakest point under the law. It is very, very doubtful that any jury would conclude that Rosemary, rather than you, breached that written contract. You're standing on awfully slippery ground there. I'm sure your attorney will concur."

"I've told him that his legal grounds are not solid," says Cavanaugh, "and that juries tend to favor the subordinate in cases like this. I haven't changed my mind."

Weinstein again centers his eyes on Holloway. "Stephen?"

"I will not go a penny above seventy-five thousand." He clenches his jaws.

Weinstein slumps down in his chair, stares balefully at the executive and his attorney, then takes his pen and begins doodling on the yellow pad. There is such a long silence that Cavanaugh finally makes a business of clearing his throat. The sound has the impact of an earth mover striking rock.

"Yes?" Weinstein looks up.

"Cy, if you don't mind, I think it's over to the other side now." Cavanaugh for once speaks quietly, perhaps out of respect for a senior member of the bar whom, Cavanaugh recognizes, has stumbled on the apparent threshold of an agreement.

"I wouldn't have the gall to go back to them." Weinstein too speaks softly with the drip of discouragement in his tone. "Since this thing started, they've reduced their asking price a half million dollars. You've moved up only half that amount. Unless . . . "

"Hold it, Cy. They had a lot more air in their demands," Cavanaugh protests.

Weinstein nods wearily. "You could be right. However, unless you're willing to make some further concession, however small, as a sign of good faith, I'm afraid we're at the end of the road."

Cavanaugh looks at his client. "Stephen, let's . . . "

Holloway shakes his head. "No use talking further, Peter. My limit is seventy-five thousand dollars and that's that."

"You must realize," says Weinstein slowly, "what that means, Stephen. Your sister most certainly will file suit and your life for the next several years will be dominated and harassed by a legal action that will cost you a great deal of money and which, in the end, as your lawyer has indicated, you have little hope of winning outright."

"I'll take that risk. I will not pay a cent more." Holloway sets himself in granite. "I know I'm right."

"In that event . . . " Weinstein slaps the table and gets to his feet. He slips quickly into his jacket and pockets his ballpoint pen. "That's it, gentlemen, the end of the road." Although his expression is impassive, it's obvious that the mediator is seething inside. "You will, of course, honor your promise on the letter of recommendation, Stephen. Also Peter will draft a nondisparagement statement for you to sign as per your agreement."

"No, no," protests Cavanaugh. "The nondisparagement was dependent on a final agreement which we don't have."

"All right." Weinstein couldn't care less now. "If that's your reading of our talks. But on the letter of recommendation—"

"I've already signed that," Holloway interrupts. "Rosemary will have it on Interiors stationery day after tomorrow. I gave my word."

"If you gentlemen will stay here a moment," says Weinstein brusquely, "I'll fetch the others and we'll lay this thing to rest as quickly as we can."

The mediator strides purposefully to the door, but a slump to his shoulders betrays his dejection. The man who has achieved nine straight mediation agreements for the first time faces failure.

Mediation

11

Part Six: *Mediation Ends*

The Settlement

Thwarted, Weinstein stalks to the door, places his hand on the doorknob, pauses, straightens, stands immobile for a curiously long time, then suddenly whirls about toward the surprised pair.

"Well, I'll be damned!" He marches back to his chair, whips off his jacket, and hangs it on the back of his chair again. "Sit down, men." His craggy face has a glow. "Now why didn't I think of this an hour ago?"

Holloway and Cavanaugh ease back into their seats. At first baffled, they quickly surrender to curiosity. Cavanaugh, however, has a small smile as he tilts his head. What, he seems to be asking, is this shrewd old dude up to this time?

"How many ways to skin a cat?" asks Weinstein. "Is it nine? No, that's lives. There's more than one way to skin . . ." He talks with a rush of excitement. "Anyway, I got this flash at the doorway, what if . . . All right, slow down, Seymour, and let's backtrack here." He levels a finger at Holloway. "Stephen, am I not correct that you think highly of your sister's business abilities? You said so in the letter of recommendation and you also praised her talents to us. Right?"

"I wasn't just being generous," Stephen replies. "She's excellent at business. It's just that she and I . . ."

Weinstein ends the demurrer with a sweep of his arm. "And it's also true, as you know, that Rosemary is very anxious to get back to work. Indeed, she'd like to open her own shop and go after the business that's a price level or two below the one you aim at. Let me ask you, Stephen, is there any reason a home furnishings shop aimed at the upper middle class shouldn't make money if properly run?"

"None at all. It's not my bag, but lots of shops make good money targeting the economic slice below my customers."

"Do you think Rosemary could make good money doing that?"

"No question," says Stephen emphatically. "She's got the head for it and the necessary drive as well."

"How much profit should a store like that make?"

"On sales? I'd say twenty percent after taxes."

"Does Holloway Interiors make that much?"

"No. To maintain our reputation for excellence with elegance costs money. We net around twelve percent after taxes."

"How much in start-up costs to open a store aimed at the people we're talking about?"

Holloway reflects with a finger at his lips. "Depending on the location, I'd say between a million and a million-two, including everything. That's renting, not buying your floor space."

"Would you invest in a store like that?"

"That depends on who's running . . ." Holloway checks himself, looks at Weinstein with dawning recognition. "Oh, I see what you mean." He gathers his brows in concentration.

"And why not?" Weinstein spreads an expansive smile. "You and Rosemary are back on speaking terms. You admire her ability. She certainly admires yours. She borrows the money with your credit guaranteeing the loan. Maybe she puts up some money, whatever she has. You leave her alone to run her own show. You don't make your investment public. She expands the business as she goes along and you both get fat on the way. It's regular movie script stuff. Writes itself."

"Hey, Cy," says Cavanaugh. "Let the man catch his breath."

"Yes, I . . . Well, I never thought along those lines." Stephen pauses, frowns. "It takes a bit of getting used to."

"Take all day, the night too." Weinstein has caught fire with the idea. "We can recess the mediation while you think it over. This project has legs, Stephen. This time you get Cavanaugh and Bianchi to draw up a tight agreement between you and Rosemary. Lots of ways to go. You could make it a corporation with you owning most of the stock and Rosemary owning some and she taking a stipulated salary and a bonus arrangement. But she runs the thing. All you have to do is rake in the money and give Rosemary advice if she asks for it."

"It does have some attractive features." Stephen is pondering. "I would have to insist on at least eighty percent ownership. I don't know whether she'd—"

"Stephen," Cavanaugh interrupts, "are you sure you want to go into business with this lady? We have plenty of grief with her as it is."

"I'm thinking, Peter. Rosemary could reach a market that's been undercultivated."

"And now you and Rosemary are on a more normal footing." Seymour bulls ahead. "Oh sure, you're not pals, you're still keeping your distance, but you trust each other's ability and each other's drive to succeed. Those are often better trusting points for the long haul than affection. Also you know you're not going to cheat each other. It's not like doing business with a stranger."

"I'm listening." Stephen's mind, it's apparent, is also working at a fast clip. "What about this frightful case, Rosemary's demand for money?"

"In my thinking," says the mediator, "you'd wipe out everything but this new project. Nobody pays anybody anything. You don't write any letters or sign any statements. You two just agree to go into business together. Case closed."

"We kiss and make up and live happily ever after, huh?" says Stephen with a splash of acid.

"Forget your sibling feelings for a minute. Think about business." Weinstein leans closer to Holloway. "Why not let me put this up to Rosemary? Let me tell her that while you haven't said yes, you haven't said no either. Let's see if she has any liking for the deal."

"All right, let's find that out," says Stephen. "After all, if she isn't interested, there's no use us wasting time on it, is there?" But the possibility lights up his eyes.

"Done." Weinstein stands up. He's supercharged now. "Send in Rosemary and Mark, will you? Then I'll get back to you as soon as she gives me the word."

"What happened to Stephen?" asks Rosemary as she walks in. "He looks like somebody just handed him a million dollars."

"Maybe you did." Weinstein grins. He finds it hard to contain himself. "Or better yet, maybe you will—and get as much yourself."

"Okay, Cy," says Mark Bianchi. "No more suspense, please."

"Oh, but I love suspense." He waits until they're seated. "Rosemary, if you could get a million dollars worth of financing tomorrow, could you open up the kind of store you want to run?"

"Let's see. If I scratched, I might scrape up fifty or sixty thousand of my own." She sighs. "So, yes. A million is just about the size of the lottery I'd have to win."

"How about a bank loan?" Weinstein is enjoying this.

"With my collateral and track record? Let's not fantasize, Seymour."

"If I could get you the million, how soon could you get under way on the project?"

"First thing next week." She pauses. "Hey, what is this?" Suspecting, she asks: "For God's sake, Seymour, don't tell me that Stephen wants to back me in business now?"

Seymour glows with his project. "He didn't say yes and he didn't say no. What he did say was that I should find out first whether Rosemary would consider it."

"Well, of all the . . ." She sinks back in her chair. "I don't know. I have to give this some head power." She taps her temples.

"Was this your idea, Cy?" asks Bianchi.

"Yep. Hit me like a flash. Why are we in here fighting over who gives how much to whom, I thought, when these two fast-track business types can join forces and make themselves a pile?"

"And just what did Stephen say?"

"I told you. But I swear he's hot for the idea. He's willing to cosign for a million at the bank. You should see his eyes light up."

Rosemary raises a hand like a traffic cop. "Hold it. The caution light is on. He's thinking about control, I'll bet. No way would I do that. I worked for him once, remember."

"I don't think so." Weinstein shakes his head. "He didn't object when I said you ought to have control, he to advise only if you asked him. You'd get a fixed salary, but you'd both put the profits back into the business for a few years. I think I could get him to agree in writing to your control. Don't forget, Rosemary, your brother is a good businessman and he likes money. He knows how good you are and he knows how much you could make with stores aiming at the upper-middle folks."

"Stores?" Rosemary laughs with mock hysteria. "God, I haven't got one yet and the man is already multiplying me into a chain."

"Right. A chain it could become with Stephen's guarantee for a bank loan and your ideas, work, and talent."

"Phew. Things are moving fast." Rosemary has a touch of pink in her cheeks now. She's caught the fever.

"Let's look closely at this thing." Weinstein begins to digit-count, tapping a little finger. "Number One. Bianchi and Cavanaugh draft you a tight agreement where Stephen's money gets priority on the profits, but you're insulated so he can't control you and it's all your show. Two, you make provision for plowing the bulk of the profits back into the business so that you can expand and grow. Third, you agree not to talk about his investment so that your line of merchandise won't reflect on his 'Tiffany' image. Fourth, you both drop all demands connected with this case and forget you ever made them. Fifth, you agree to forget the past and start fresh in a new joint venture."

"And no letter of recommendation for me from Stephen?" she asks.

"Why would you need it? But say, do you know he signed one?" Weinstein tells of Stephen affixing his signature after changing the description of her abilities from "wide-ranging" to "superior," then adds: "And he refused to link his signing the letter to a money demand. He said you deserved it."

"Maybe he'll agree to let you frame it and keep it in your trophy room," says Bianchi.

There is a span of silence.

"No question, the proposal tempts me," says Rosemary. "Do you see any reason why not, Mark?"

"None in sight." The attorney shares Weinstein's enthusiasm. "We'll just make sure we have an unmistakable agreement on your sole control. Then we want to insist that Stephen spell out just how he sees the arrangement. No ambiguities this time around."

Like a batter before the pitch, Rosemary takes a deep breath. "All right. If Stephen gives the right answers, I'll go."

"Great. That's it then. . . . You two stay here and I'll call in the other side." Weinstein bows to Rosemary with a smile. "Pardon, your partner and his attorney."

Seats are shuffled as Holloway and Cavanaugh return to the room. Weinstein waits until everyone has the place he or she occupied when the first joint session began.

"Stephen," he says, "Rosemary is willing to start up a joint business venture with you, she borrowing roughly a million with you as the guarantor. But only on one important condition. Why don't you state it in your own words, Rosemary."

"Yes." She addresses her brother. "Stephen, I think this is an exciting idea that has a lot of promise for both of us. But I'm not interested unless I can run my own show. Are you willing to give me control?"

"Yes." He is serious, unsmiling. "I would want you to keep me informed at least on a monthly basis and I'd hope that if you needed advice, you'd feel free to call on me."

"Would you be willing to put that in writing?" She asks this gently, yet with insistence.

"Yes, of course. I assume all this and everything else connected with a deal would be put in careful legal language and that our lawyers would set up the necessary framework."

"I'm considering two agreements," says Weinstein. "One when we finish here today that seals the arrangement in plain but explicit English and then a second one in a few weeks in which Peter and Mark spell it all out in proper legal terms."

"Okay, if Stephen's willing, I am." She looks at her brother with a touch of shyness.

"I'm willing," Stephen responds.

"All right." Weinstein beams on brother and sister. "Could you please seal that with a handshake."

Stephen arises and puts out his hand. Rosemary, standing, reaches out and grasps it.

"It's a deal," he says as he shakes.

"Deal," she says.

As they retake their seats, Weinstein says they'd do well to agree on a few subsidiary matters. "For instance, let's have an understanding as to how much money you'll each put up."

Stephen nods. "Yes, I'll cosign for one million dollars when we're ready. If more is needed to start, I could go another two hundred thousand. That's my limit."

"I think I can put up sixty thousand," says Rosemary. "I'll have to go through my books tomorrow to make sure."

"Do you both agree to drop all pending demands in this matter?" Weinstein is making notes.

"Gladly," says Rosemary.

"Yes," says Stephen. "That's all erased now."

"Do you instruct Peter and Mark to draw up the proper papers and consult with you on whether it should be a stock corporation, a partnership, or just what?"

When they both assent, Weinstein says "the new partners" can do as they please for a half hour while he, Mark, and Peter draw up a short written agreement.

Thirty-five minutes later Stephen and Rosemary return and read through a statement handwritten by Weinstein on the long yellow paper. Headed *Settlement Agreement in Mediation*, it says that Rosemary and Stephen, resolving their dispute, agree to enter a "corporate or partnership" arrangement to sell home furnishings at retail and that Stephen will solicit a $1 million bank loan to fund the enterprise.

Two paragraphs provide the kernel of the agreement. "4. In consideration of the loan guarantee, Holloway shall have an 80% interest in the new enterprise and Wofford a 20% interest.

"5. Holloway agrees that Wofford shall have exclusive control over all decisions concerning the setup and operation of the new enterprise. Wofford agrees to present Holloway with monthly financial reports of operation."

The paper sets Rosemary's salary at $65,000 "plus minimal executive perks," provides that all profits should be reinvested in the business for five years, calls for lawyers to draft enabling documents, and releases each person from "any claims or demands, known or unknown" by the other one up to this date.

A final paragraph provides that "any disagreements regarding negotiations or operations" during the first year "shall be presented to Seymour F. Weinstein, Esq. for mediation."

"All right," says Rosemary. "I'll sign it." She accepts a pen from Seymour.

Stephen signs in turn, then hands the pen back to Weinstein.

"A good day's work," says the mediator. "I must say that at one point I thought this thing was doomed." He describes, for the benefit of Rosemary and Mark, going to the door to announce the end of mediation after Holloway declined to budge from a final offer of $75,000.

"So where did the idea come from?" asks Rosemary.

"Well, while I voiced the idea first, I think I got it by telepathy from you two. I think the plan was banging around inside your skulls and you just needed someone to bring it out."

"You're too generous, Cy." This is the first time Stephen has used the mediator's nickname. "Everybody knows who brought us to an agreement."

"Don't disown your own lovely child, Cy." Rosemary has a gay lilt to her voice.

Bianchi, the self-appointed timer, looks at his wristwatch. "Six-fifty-six. Cy, you wrapped this one up in slightly less than sixteen hours, including lunches."

The two lawyers talk about drafting the formal papers for the new enterprise, then Weinstein invites all hands for a celebratory drink. Brother and sister walk out together.

The Costs

In reaching an agreement with her brother, ending all existing legal differences between them, Rosemary Wofford has added a sixteen-hour bill from her attorney of $2,400. She must also pay $1,200, half of Weinstein's fee for the mediation. She must add another $650, the American Arbitration Association's charge per party for arranging the mediation and providing the meeting place. So her expenses have grown by $4,250 and now stand at $7,550.

Since the cost of drafting the legal agreement for the joint home furnishings venture will be charged against start-up costs, Rosemary Wofford has thus closed out the contract and discharge dispute with Stephen Holloway at a final cost to her of $7,550. It has been six weeks and four days since she walked into Lawyer Bianchi's office with intent to sue her brother for breach of contract.

The Lawsuit

12

Part Four: *Digging In for Trench Warfare*

Discovery, Interrogatories

In Los Angeles, Oretta Long's lawsuit over charges similar to those mediated in New York is just getting under way in earnest.

A week after the filing of Oretta's answer to the counterclaim of the Long brothers, which escalated a rather mundane business dispute into a multimillion-dollar confrontation, Oretta receives a phone call from Susan Pennington asking her to come to the law office to help prepare the interrogatories.

Long lists of questions probing matters set out in the complaints and counterclaims, interrogatories often open the intricate discovery process of a lawsuit. Opposing attorneys mail the inquiries to each other and then sit down with their clients to work out their responses.

At Lawyer Pennington's request, Oretta comes to the law offices of Devereaux, Goldstein, Hutchinson and Tong to help Susan prepare the interrogatories that Bill Hutchinson, the prime lawyer on the case, hopes will strike and explode ammunition buried in the enemy camp.

Oretta has a complaint and Bill Hutchinson chats briefly with her about it in his office before she goes to work with Susan.

"Susan says it will take me most of two days on these inter—these questions." Oretta looks put upon. "Frankly, Bill, I didn't realize I was expected to spend so much time on this suit. I thought that once you took over the case, you'd be the one doing the work."

"Oh, we have plenty to do." He speaks in a reassuring voice. "But remember I told you at the outset that there would be times when you'd have to devote considerable energy to the case. This is one of those times. It's vital that we find out just what the Longs base their claims on."

"I was hoping I could do my part over the phone."

"No, this requires a fairly detailed discussion between you and Susan." Hutchinson leans back in his chair. "Look, Oretta . . ." He pauses. "I often compare this stage of a lawsuit to the old trench warfare of the First World War. Both sides are dug in within sight of each other, but neither side is strong enough for a frontal attack. So they stay in their lines, sending out reconnaissance patrols to probe for signs of enemy weakness. Occasionally there are some firefights and artillery barrages—we call these 'motions'—but mostly it's a dull waiting game with lots of discomfort and anxiety."

Oretta isn't sure about the analogy, but she likes Hutchinson and his demeanor of cheerful patience, and she goes off to work with Susan. The two women are glad to see each other again.

"What we're trying to do here," says Susan, "is find out everything we possibly can about the way the Long brothers and Bluebird Sportswear acted on matters affecting you. For instance, you say that Wendell refused to pay you a commission on goods you'd sold but which the customer returned because of defects and shoddy workmanship."

"That's right." Oretta draws up a chair and lights a cigarette. "I did the work of selling and it wasn't my fault that some of the stitching was bad. They probably replaced the items, so I should get my commission on them."

"Okay, so then we want to send them questions that will reveal just how many pieces of defective goods came back to Bluebird Sportswear and how much they replaced." Susan squares the ever-present pad of legal-size yellow paper in front of her. She writes "Interrogatories" at the top and places a numeral, 1, at the left beneath it. "About how many times did customers return defective goods on which Wendell Long refused to pay you your commission?"

"Oh, goodness, I have no idea really." Oretta inhales sharply.

"Well, are we talking just once or twice or lots more than that?"

"Oh, much more."

"More or less than a hundred times, do you think?"

"More than a hundred." Oretta frowns. "Yes, almost every week there for a time shipments were coming back. I'd say a minimum of maybe a hundred and fifty. Lots of them were those tasseled tennis socks that the tassels came off of."

"Fine." The prolonged extent of the Long brothers' deficiencies pleases Susan. "That means we'll want to ask a great many questions on that subject. . . . Oh, by the way, do you have a good friend still at Bluebird?"

"Yes, Tina Jordan. She worked for me for a couple of weeks and then transferred to personnel. But I wouldn't want to put her on the spot on anything."

"Oh, no. But if we get in a jam for inside information, we might need her someday."

Susan continues to write as she talks. Susan says Bill Hutchinson will like this first section of the interrogatories almost as much as the Longs will despise them. In fact, she says, maybe the Longs won't want a public record to show just how much defective sportswear they did ship. "That's the kind of side effect you get from some interrogatories. In this case, Wendell Long might think seriously of settling instead of letting that kind of evidence be aired at a trial. It's certainly something he wouldn't want his competitors to know about."

Susan continues to talk and write and when she finishes in her open, highly legible handwriting, she hands the pad to Oretta.

1. State, for each calendar year, beginning in 1981 and including the present calendar year, whether any notices or complaints or returned goods were received from customers involving defective merchandise shipped by Bluebird.
    a. For each year for which an affirmative answer was given above, please state:

(1) The number of complaints received each year.

(2) The total number of written complaints.

(3) The total number of oral complaints.

(4) The total number of return shipments of defective goods.

b. For each year for which an affirmative answer was noted in Question 1 above, state the names and addresses of customers who complained or who returned defective goods.

(1) State the number of complaints or returned shipments by calendar year from each customer named above.

(2) State the nature of each complaint or returned shipment received from each customer.

(i) If you will do so without a Motion to Produce, please attach all written memoranda concerning all answers above.

"Goodness!" exclaims Oretta. "That's certainly thorough." Her face lights up. "I'd like to see Wendell and Arthur when they see all those questions. Do they have to answer?"

Susan nods. "It's one of the rules of law. We don't even have to get a court order to force them to reply. Of course, they'll try to weasel out of some of them."

"And how many questions will you send them?" There's a glint in Oretta's eye as she crushes out her cigarette stub. She's beginning to enjoy this.

"Oh, seventy-five to eighty probably, along with a lot of subsidiary inquiries under subheads. Don't worry. It'll keep them busy enough."

"How do they find the time to answer such a flock of questions?"

"It's a problem sometimes." Susan taps her pencil. "My first month here, I did a batch of interrogatories for Mr. Tong. They were so detailed and required the attention of so many executives of a big construction outfit, that they complained they couldn't get their daily work done. Actually their secretarial staff had to work nights and two weekends to gather all the stuff for them."

"I hope it ties up the half brothers for months. The way they behaved, they deserve to be badgered." There's a hard edge to Oretta's voice as if she's recalling assorted iniquities visited upon her. "Is there a limit on what can be asked?"

"Oh, Los Angeles County has lots of rules governing interrogato-

ries." Susan shrugs. "But most of them don't have teeth." She goes
to a shelf behind her desk and brings back a stapled sheaf of papers.
"Here are the rules on discovery in this county. I keep this handy
because that's a lot of what I do in the firm. Now, for instance, you
take the paragraph dealing with 'shotgun questions' that contain a lot
of subcategories." She leafs to a page. "The court merely says such
questions quote 'should be avoided' unquote. Same for 'boilerplate'
or standard questions that roam far afield of the subject." She reads:
" 'Counsel are reminded that the use of boilerplate interrogatories
should be avoided.' So the whole thing's fairly loose. You can get a
protective order and you can also petition the judge to impose sanctions on an attorney who buries you under an avalanche of silly questions. But sanctions are rare."

"So," says Oretta, "it sounds like you can ask just about anything
you want."

"That's about the size of it—if your questions are at all connected
with the matters of your suit."

Except for the noon hour, when the two women lunch in a patio
restaurant around the corner, Oretta and Susan spend the whole day
preparing the list of questions to be sent to Martin Novack dealing
with the business activities of his clients. A number of inquiries re-
plow the issue of the defective garments, demanding to know how
the complaints had been answered, by whom, when, and with what
customer satisfaction, if any. Similar multiplicity of auxiliary questions and detail attend all phases of the dispute: the employment contract, the definition of gross profits, when and where the Long brothers
"conspired" to discharge Oretta, the nature of the "restructuring" of
Bluebird's business, and the opening of the eastern market. Alleged
abuses of Oretta's expense account receive special attention, the inquiries seeking to put on the record policies and practices of travel
and entertainment expense incurred by others in the company.

Oretta's attention flags during much of this tedious stacking of detail, a chore about as engrossing as a computer's daily calculation of
compound interest, but she gets a renewed charge when the interrogatories narrow their focus to the mistress of Wendell Long who
first appeared on the payroll the previous year.

"I hear now that she's got my old job in all but title," says Oretta
with heat. "So it turns out my guess was right. I was kicked out to

make room for Wendell's woman. Old friends at the company tell me that her name's Mrs. Diana Kelbaugh and she's still married with three children, college age and beyond. And would you believe it, that horny hypocrite Wendell is a deacon or something at a Lutheran church in the Valley."

With Oretta's zestful help, Susan Pennington compiles a small library of information desired about Mrs. Kelbaugh who, Oretta has heard, has auburn hair and a certain suggestive way of walking. When, why, where, and for what purpose did she go to work for Bluebird, her duties, salary, commissions, overtime, promotions, and people to whom she reports, please? The subsidiary questions spill over page after page until an uninitiated reader might think that Mrs. Kelbaugh was the target of a criminal investigation.

Oretta anticipates the repercussions with relish. "I'd love to see Wendell's face when he reads those questions, but even more I'd love to see Grace—that's his wife—if and when she hears about them."

Susan outlines eighty-five questions in all, each with countless dangling allied inquiries that she will spend the next day putting into an orderly sequence that will cover 117 pages when typewritten by one of the firm's secretaries. She surmises, when Oretta asks, that the Longs and their assistants will have to spend a week or more in order to answer the questions properly.

While the sheer volume of this minutia perplexes Oretta, she nevertheless leaves that evening in good spirits. A major attack is being mounted. Even a brief encounter with Bill Hutchinson on her way out does not discourage her. He warns her to expect a packet of interrogatories from the opposition—"they have the same rights we do, you know"—but since her cause is just, she can't imagine how the Longs could injure her. If the half brothers thought for a moment that they could discharge her with impunity, they'll have a huge second think coming in a few days.

Oretta's taste for battle is further titillated three days later when Susan in a phone call informs her that Martin Novack has honored a request for a production of documents involving sales, expense accounts, shipments, salaries, and all other Bluebird Sportswear records involved in the lawsuit.

"We expect to come back with plenty of ammunition." Susan sounds happily bellicose. "We're rolling, Oretta."

Susan and a $40-an-hour paralegal spend a day and a half in Blue-bird's administrative offices on Sepulveda Boulevard. They comb the files, using Bluebird's copying machine, to amass stacks of duplicates. Their search disrupts the office routine and forces reluctant clerks to spend most of their time helping the invaders. About half the material is stored on computer disks rather than on paper, so that a printer chatters throughout the day, delivering the printouts.

In the following two days the paralegal and a $15-an-hour legal assistant, trained at a two-year community college, go through the mass of material and index it with cross references according to subject matter, person, and date. Housed in five cardboard boxes, this treasure of enemy indiscretions resides in a corner of Susan Pennington's office.

A delivery of the U.S. mails the next week snaps Oretta Long's jubilation and spins her into a mood of sad bewilderment. It is the mail that brings Bill Hutchinson the interrogatories prepared by Martin Novack as attorney for the Long brothers and directed at Oretta.

When Hutchinson reads her sample queries from the hated half brothers, Oretta's first response is one of indignation. The gall! This quickly swells into outrage as Bill reads a question, complete with a dozen dangling auxiliary inquiries, that seems to challenge her claim that her sales assistants were competent women. Auxiliary query 14-b-(7), for instance, asks Oretta to "state the formal and informal training received by each person noted above," whereas 14-b-(8) asks for the dates of the training.

"Training, for God's sake!" Oretta explodes. "Nobody at Bluebird ever got any training. You just started in and went to work. Really!"

"Don't let these interrogatories raise your blood pressure." Bill uses his best soothing tone. He's been through this before. "If there was no training anywhere at Bluebird, just make a point of that in your answers."

Oretta agrees to come in early the next day and go through the questions with Susan Pennington. Relatively calm when she arrives, Oretta soon becomes infuriated, then goes into a slow burn that lasts through the long, irksome day. She regards each question as hostile and intended to goad, degrade, or embarrass her. Susan tries in vain to get her client and new friend to look upon the long list of questions as just a normal development in the lawsuit.

No. Oretta sees the ninety-six questions, whose supplements and addenda cover 130 typewritten pages, as a personal insult designed for no other purpose than to denigrate the very business accomplishments in which she takes pride. The matter of her dealings with competing businesses especially vexes her. Question 54 asks her to give the names and addresses of all women's apparel "companies, stores or persons" whose merchandise she handled for sale while an employee of Bluebird. Question 54-c-(1) requests the dates of sale and 54-c-(2) demands a list of the products sold.

"Damn it!" Oretta lights a cigarette. "Like I told you, I handled only one line of beachwear to which neither Wendell nor Arthur ever objected. Now these questions are trying to make me out a double-dealer who's piled up a fortune on the side."

"No problem, Oretta." Susan tries to quiet her. "You just answer with the facts, whatever they are."

"But they're trying to ruin my business reputation. I can't understand why the law allows them that kind of leeway."

"They're merely defending themselves. Your suit has hit them where they're weak and now they're out on a hunting expedition, hoping to bag anything that will help them." Susan has been practicing law long enough to know that a calm, dispassionate client makes faster progress through the mine-strewn terrain of interrogatories than one fired up with resentment and thoughts of revenge. Oretta, however, runs an unrelieved high temperature.

A series of questions about her "written and oral" criticisms of Bluebird, designed to "defame" the company, provides Oretta with a funnel for her anger. She answers that she has a clear recollection of writing to only one customer, a sports shop in Portland, Oregon, that complained about poorly stitched tennis sweaters. She wrote the retailer, she said, that "a temporary quality control problem" had been straightened out and henceforth all tennis sweaters would be in A-1 condition. "At no time," she dictates to Susan as an addition to her answer, "have I defamed or slandered Bluebird Sportswear orally or in writing and I resent the implication of these questions."

"I think we'll just leave off the last remark about your resentment." Susan looks up from her writing. "The closer we can keep our answers to straight colorless fact, the less room we give them to trot about looking for things you're sensitive about."

As the long day trails off toward evening, Oretta's anger recedes into a sludge of discouragement. The interrogatories that so delighted her when aimed at the half brothers now seem, in their altered form and direction, to show the perversions of the law. Instead of protecting her rights as a responsible citizen, the law appears to disarm her and to leave her open to the ravages of predators. She can't understand why a court would permit these endless compound questions that seek to vilify her.

When she voices her dismay to Susan, the young lawyer senses the need for sage counsel from a more experienced hand. She calls Bill Hutchinson who asks Oretta to stop by his office before she leaves.

"I understand how you feel." Hutchinson holds out a chair for his client before retreating behind his desk. "I told you there'd be low points and high points in these years before we get to trial. This is one of the low days. But we've got to hang in there and do our homework carefully."

Oretta sighs. "I can understand the reason for some of the main questions, but all those little offshoots, the excruciating detail they ask for. Nobody but a memory wizard could possibly remember all that stuff. And then there's another thing. It's as though all the questions were set up to show how dumb I was, a stupid woman who never did a thing right like everyone else did."

"I know." Bill smiles sympathetically. "Interrogatories affect a lot of people that way." He leans back, clasping his hands behind his head. "Overall the law does well by all of us, protecting our rights and providing safeguards for a stable society. But in practicing under that law, we lawyers often fall victim to what I call the 'perfect tiger' syndrome."

Bill Hutchinson is no exception to the rule that lawyers do double duty as mini-philosophers of the law. "We ask our questions, whether addressed to the witness in court or in interrogatories, as if all human beings were perfect just as all tigers or chipmunks are perfect. We assume that there is an ideal person who does everything perfectly and that this ideal is found in many people. Our questions then measure the witness against the ideal, against perfection. This accounts for the dreadful minutiae of the interrogatories, wanting to know every bit and scrap of your behavior as if your brain automatically recorded each tiny act as you went along much as a computer tracks transactions in a stock exchange."

"Nobody's perfect," Oretta objects.

"Of course not, but with twenty–twenty hindsight we act and question as if everyone were a perfect tiger." Bill warms to one of his favorite topics. "Suppose you're questioning an executive about a contract provision he claims he was unaware of. He admits he signed it. What, he doesn't know what he signed? Is that his habit? Didn't he read the sales contract on his house? Does he consider himself responsible for what he signs? On and on you go, question after question."

"I guess even big executives don't read the fine print," observes Oretta. "Not many people do."

"You're right again. Everybody knows that. The judge knows it. The jury knows it. Still, we taunt the witness with his failure to go through the contract word by word. The assumption is that such admissions of failure do tend to cut a formidable witness down to size. Anyway, Oretta, you'll spare yourself a lot of anguish if you remember that nobody except Marty Novack expects you to be perfect. We're all fallible. There are perfect tigers, doing what comes naturally, but no perfect human beings."

The soothing theme buoys Oretta only briefly. As she leaves the law firm for the day, drives the city streets, and then noses her homeward-bound Le Baron into the glut of traffic on the Santa Monica Freeway, she realizes that she feels about the way Los Angeles looks this evening. Smog, marked by poisonous yellow blotches, shrouds the city and blots out the surrounding hills. Tall buildings only a few blocks off the freeway stand like ghostly sentinels, their bodies wrapped in haze. The acidic air stings her eyes despite the car's air-conditioning.

Oretta sinks into depression, a rare state for her. She wonders just what she let herself in for the day seven weeks ago when she walked into Bill Hutchinson's office and told him she wanted to sue the half brothers. True, Bill Hutchinson had warned her against these low days, but never did she imagine this kind of distress. First the Long brothers fire her and then their lawyer comes along and makes her out to be a stupid broad whom no employer would keep on the payroll longer than he could help.

"Oh, shit." The slow-moving traffic grinds to a halt and the car behind her pings her bumper. She lights a cigarette, turns on the radio, and gazes out gloomily at the smog-wrapped city. One of those days.

The interrogatories that so depress Oretta are part of the longest and most expensive phase of litigation. In the discovery segment attorneys and their assistants labor like prospectors, picking up a scrap here and a nugget there, as they toil away in the pits of the law. Laypeople, who tend to think of the legal system as primarily trials and negotiations, usually know little about discovery, but it is here that lawyers spend the bulk of their time and where the expensive exploration often accounts for a major portion of a lawsuit's total cost.

Discovery has a number of facets—interrogatories, the searching of documents, physical exams, depositions of witnesses taken under oath—and it has grown in recent decades faster than explorations of outer space. A number of elderly attorneys and judges remember their early days of law practice when lawyers took their clients to trial after a factual investigation of short duration. Even in important cases the amount of pretrial exploration was minimal. Complaints of inadequate preparation led to adoption of federal rules of civil procedure in 1938, and state judicial systems followed with similar rules. These triggered an explosion of the time and energy spent on discovery of facts deemed vital to a lawsuit, and in ensuing years the costs of these extensive explorations mounted ever higher. More recently a reaction has set in and now many courts place limits on the range of discovery, sometimes imposing sanctions on attorneys who violate the boundaries.

Discovery in its various forms continues, however, to consume enormous amounts of time and money. Lawyers bent on harassing the opposition with frivolous and costly demands for information find few legal obstacles to deter them. Even the calls for facts and documentation that are deemed legitimate under today's practices can add greatly to a lawsuit's cost. In some large corporate suits, millions of dollars may be expended on discovery, whereas in relatively small suits like Oretta Long's, discovery can add thousands of dollars to the bill, often with questionable impact.

* * *

Oretta's blue mood lasts only a few days. She's a woman of spirit who wearies of depression before it wearies her. Soon she begins to anticipate the answers of the Long brothers to her interrogatories. She's especially anxious to see how they answer the questions about Mrs. Diana Kelbaugh, the rumored mistress of Wendell Long who reportedly has taken over Oretta's old job.

When a week goes by with no word from the law firm, Oretta phones Susan Pennington who turns her call over to Bill Hutchinson.

"I was just about to call you," he says. "I've agreed to give Martin Novack a thirty-day extension on answering our interrogatories. He's jammed up on another case in Japan and needs the time over there. I don't like the delay, but it's a courtesy he'd do for us, so I could hardly say no."

A month passes and Susan calls Oretta one day to say that Hutchinson had granted another thirty-day delay to Novack who had called from Tokyo where he faced new problems on behalf of his California clients.

"But why does this case in Japan take precedence over ours?" asks Oretta. For a woman of action, things are beginning to drag.

"It wouldn't if we were facing a trial date," Susan answers. "But remember we can't get to trial for about four years yet, so both Bill and Novack know there's no pressure of time now. Never mind, Oretta. It's just the law taking its usual sluggish course."

Although the young lawyer does not elaborate, the normal course of civil litigation in the United States is sluggish in the sense that a snail's advance through a pan of glue might be so described. In addition to the widely noted congestion in the courts, due largely to the complexity of lawsuits in recent years, the course is impeded by the individual nature of the legal profession and the gentlemanly code of the people who make their living from the law.

Because a lawsuit is usually directed by a single attorney, if a relative of the lawyer dies, the case waits while he or she attends the funeral. If a judge is indisposed, the pending motion in the case must await a hearing another day. If one lawyer finds that he or she is torn between two cases nearing a climax at the same time, one of the friendly enemy lawyers will oblige with a consent to postponement.

Delays, extensions, postponements, suspensions, and deferrals cluster like barnacles on the average lawsuit, their causes ranging from death to hangovers, from unexpected paperwork to weak bladders. Often a trial recesses so that the judge may attend to aspects of other lawsuits. Judges may absent themselves without explanation for half an hour while attorneys, plaintiffs, defendants, expert witnesses, and court functionaries—in all representing thousands of dollars an hour of talent—lounge about and make small talk. During one courtroom recess of a five-year-old antitrust suit, an attorney was asked how long he'd been on the case. He replied with a shrug: "Since I was a small boy."

It isn't that lawyers and judges don't work hard. They work as hard or harder than other professionals, but the system permits so many interruptions that a lawsuit rarely reaches fruition without suffering a number of deadline extensions.

In this matter of Oretta versus Arthur and Wendell Long, Martin Novack got two extensions, totaling sixty days, from Hutchinson with no questions raised. One might guess that the Tokyo contract muddle involved much more money than the Long case, but since Hutchinson, guided by the gentlemanly code, didn't ask, the facts remain a matter of conjecture.

Several days before the expiration of the second extension on answering the interrogatories, Novack calls again from Tokyo.

"Bill," he says, "I hate to do this, but could you give me another twenty days in that Long contract matter? We've struck an unexpected snag with the Japanese."

"All right, Marty, but that's the last one. Okay? We both know we've got lots of time, but my client doesn't understand why there's no action. So one last time. Twenty days."

"Thanks, Bill. You know I'll be flexible when you get in a jam."

This time Bill takes a good ten minutes on the telephone to allay Oretta's qualms and to reassure her that her case is still a strong one on which action will begin again shortly.

The Long brothers' answers to Oretta's interrogatories do arrive three weeks later. It is now early September, four months after Oretta brought her complaint to Bill Hutchinson.

The Costs

Previous Balance	$3,813.75
Phone Calls:	
Hutchinson (2 hrs., 20 mins.)	350.00
Pennington (1 hr., 40 mins.)	125.00
Hutchinson Talk with Client (15 mins.)	37.50
Interrogatories:	
Pennington (16 hrs.)	1,200.00
Hutchinson review (1 hr.)	150.00
Production of Documents:	
Pennington (12 hrs.)	900.00
Paralegal (12 hrs.)	480.00
Bluebird copying charges	85.00
Indexing Documents:	
Paralegal (16 hrs.)	640.00
Legal assistant (16 hrs.)	290.00
Answering Interrogatories:	
Pennington (12 hrs.)	900.00
Total	$8,971.25

The Lawsuit

13

Part Five: *Skirmishes, Patrols, and Land Mines*

Discovery, Depositions

A week after Attorney Martin Novack returns from Japan, his clients' answers to Oretta Long's interrogatories reach the law firm of Devereaux, Goldstein, Hutchinson & Tong. The sheaf of answers, running to 178 pages, joins the growing mass of documents in Susan Pennington's office.

Bill Hutchinson, in glancing through the papers, sees that the Long brothers have failed to answer questions asking for customer lists and pricing information. Instead Novack has appended a Motion for Protective Order which has been filed in Los Angeles Superior Court and bears an official notation that Judge Stewart Otterbein will hear arguments on the motion on a Tuesday morning two weeks hence.

Novack contends that Bluebird Sportswear's customer and pricing data are confidential commercial information that Oretta Long, as a potential competitor, could use to her advantage, possibly causing irreparable injury to Bluebird. Novack implies that Oretta wants to steal the data and the customers as well. Between the lines of the legalese, a reader might gather that Oretta is a common crook who's using a lawsuit to camouflage her larceny.

Novack therefore petitions the court to issue an order protecting his client's right to withhold the customer lists and pricing methods.

On the appointed hearing day in early October, Hutchinson and Novack remain in their offices working on other cases. In their places they send young law associates to argue the motion, Susan Pennington appearing for Hutchinson's firm and Philip R. Dumont, a lean, loose, and handsome black from Virginia via Yale Law School, appearing for Novack's firm. They join several dozen lawyers in the corridor outside Judge Otterbein's courtroom. All are waiting to argue this or that motion. Since this turns the corridor into a gossip parlor for young attorneys, Susan and Phil use the time to get acquainted.

When their courtroom turns come, they each intend to use the full five minutes allotted to a side. However, Judge Otterbein, whose black robe covers a multitude of diet fiascos, cuts each off after a minute or two. He summons them to his chamber where he says he's settling the dispute by refusing the protective order and ordering the answers to be provided to Pennington's firm with the stipulation that they will not be revealed to Oretta Long. In short, Lawyer Pennington, who argued that she needed the material to prepare plaintiff's case, can have the customer and pricing information for that sole purpose, but Oretta Long cannot use it as ammunition to compete against Bluebird.

With the judge leading the way, they return to the courtroom where the ruling is put on the record. Susan is to prepare an order framing Judge Otterbein's decision. His clerk calls the next motion. Justice is being dispensed at a fast clip today.

Susan and Phil have coffee together to celebrate their split decision. They find they're attracted to each other and before long they agree that in addition to the judge's ruling, they'll share a Saturday night dinner at Scandia.

Bill Hutchinson calls Oretta and tells her in a prideful voice of Judge Otterbein's decision, which he labels a victory. "Marty Novack was not at all happy. He had no doubt that he'd get the protective order. I have to credit Susan. Her research and argument paid off for us."

"That's nice." Oretta, who has been fretting over delays, has trouble generating enthusiasm for what seems to her a minor peripheral score. "But it doesn't seem to have a whole lot to do with the court making the half brothers pay damages for breaking my contract."

"Still, we don't like to lose motions." This is one of those times when a client's failure to appreciate litigation niceties taxes Bill's patience.

Months go by without visible action in the case of Oretta versus Arthur and Wendell Long. Oretta hears only occasionally from Bill Hutchinson or Susan Pennington.

Oretta gets bored. With her daughter Amy gone off to college at the University of Chicago, she takes a cruise through the Panama Canal, continues the shipboard romance with a dentist from Santa Barbara, and begins driving about, inspecting the merchandise in women's sportswear shops and flirting with the idea of going back to work soon.

Meanwhile Susan spends several days analyzing the Long brothers' answers to the interrogatories and the copies of documents which she had obtained at Bluebird headquarters. As highlights she notes that Bluebird's quality control problems had extended over three years and that the cost of returned defective merchandise apparently amounted to about $200,000. She marks for special attention letters to and from Diana Kelbaugh regarding new marketing concepts while Oretta was still on the job. Many questions about the new marketing program had gone unanswered, being objected to on grounds of ambiguity or irrelevancy.

In January of the second year, Bill Hutchinson sends Oretta a status report based largely on a memorandum from Susan following her analysis of the answers and documents. "Your position in our action against the Long brothers is improving," he writes. He bases his judgment on three main points: that Bluebird lost many customers because of sending out shoddy sports clothing rather than through Oretta's actions, that the bad merchandise had a value of $200,000, and that Wendell Long apparently made a verbal marketing arrangement with Diana Kelbaugh, Inc. while Oretta was still on the job under contract.

"We're entering another stage now," he says. "Novack and I have agreed to take depositions the week of January twenty-second. This will be a period when I'll want you to devote full time to the case."

Oretta becomes edgy when she learns that this means testifying under oath in Martin Novack's law office, but she's happy that action on her case has begun again. Although she had planned to spend the week at Lake Tahoe, she gladly postpones the trip.

Preparing for next week's taking of depositions by both sides, Hutchinson and Pennington spend Friday morning in a strategy conference. The general and his lieutenant decide to focus on Wendell Long's relationship with Diana Kelbaugh on the premise that this will prove to be the opposition's most vulnerable flank.

With Oretta's permission, Hutchinson has hired a private investigator, Pat McManus, to probe the relationship, and McManus's report reveals some interesting facts. Wendell, a deacon at a Lutheran church, and Mrs. Kelbaugh have had semimonthly trysts at the Pompton Arms Motel near Redondo Beach. Records of the Pompton Arms, a plush establishment catering to daytime dalliance, show that on many Thursdays over the past two years a guest named Hugo Angell has registered and listed the license plate of his cream-colored Oldsmobile. McManus's research at the department of motor vehicles established that the license plates belonged to a Wendell Long of Sherman Oaks, same street address as Bluebird's president. The motel's manager, primed by two fifty-dollar bills, told McManus that "Mrs. Angell" invariably arrived separately in a Honda Accord, the license of which he'd once taken the trouble to note. Upon investigation by McManus, it turned out—no surprise—to belong to Mrs. Diana Kelbaugh of Westwood.

Other reliable sources told McManus, an expensive but doggedly competent investigator, that Grace Long, wife of Wendell, had no idea of her husband's motel affair. A retiring woman who detested notoriety, Grace Long led a quiet conventional life symbolized by her regular Sunday appearance at church on the arm of her husband, the deacon.

Other inquiries by McManus fleshed out the intimate nature of the relationship, which apparently flourished during a number of three-day excursions by Wendell Long and Diana Kelbaugh to such places as Borrego Springs and Mendocino in California and Cabo San Lucas in Baja California.

Oretta is ecstatic when Hutchinson tells her of the pay dirt Mc-
Manus struck in his explorations.

"Oh, that's terrific." Her eyes shine. "Won't that win us a nice big
settlement? I can't imagine Wendell letting that be spread all over a
courtroom for Grace to hear."

"Could be." Bill Hutchinson has a note of caution in his agreement. "Remember, we're not sure how much of McManus's stuff
will be admissible. Also we don't know what surprise they may spring
on us. But it's certainly a big plus for our side, no doubt about it.
We intend to fire some big rounds when we depose Wendell."

The battle of the depositions opens at ten o'clock Monday morning
in Bill Hutchinson's law office on Wilshire Boulevard. Oretta and
Hutchinson meet the first witness, Fred Isingham, vice president of
operations for Bluebird Sportswear, who is accompanied by Bluebird's attorney, Martin Novack. Together with a court reporter, they
move to the law firm's conference room and take seats at a long oak
table ringed by shelf upon shelf of law books.

This is Oretta's first meeting with Novack and she has a quick
impression of a snappish fox terrier. The lawyer is short, dapper,
nervous, and wary and he keeps licking his thumb as he leafs through
his stack of papers.

Isingham, a small dark-complected man with a shoulder twitch, is
sworn to tell the truth by the court reporter. Questioned by Hutchinson for more than an hour, he admits that Bluebird shipped some
defective sportswear to customers, but says the quality control problem was remedied within a year. He says Oretta Long violated orders,
failed to service her customers diligently, and employed some ama-
teurish assistants who hurt sales.

However, when Hutchinson asks for specific times, places, and
deeds, the vice president fails to nail down his general charges, admitting he got his information from Wendell Long. Oretta thinks he
does not help Bluebird's case. Further, she finds much of his testimony repetitious and boring, causing her to yawn occasionally.

Depositions, Oretta has found via Hutchinson's explanations, occupy a curious place in litigation. Although not confidential, they
are rarely made available to the press or the public before a trial.
They are often filed as court documents and used to support a pretrial
motion, but sometimes are not even produced in typewritten form.

Yet all testimony is taken under oath by a court reporter and is usually transcribed for one or more of the attorneys at a cost of $2.50 and up a page. A typical deposition may fill several hundred pages and provide a valuable research document for the lawyer preparing for trial. People involved in a lawsuit must appear for testimony and other witnesses may be subpoenaed against their will. Judges uniformly reject appeals that seek to protect a witness from legitimate questioning.

In essence, depositions permit lawyers to stage a shadow trial of the case. After hearing major witnesses, an attorney has a much better idea of how his or her version of the facts will fly before a jury. Depositions trigger many settlements, although the final agreement may not come until sometime later, because rereading depositions frequently persuades one side, and sometimes both, that its case has serious flaws.

On this day Arlene Fields, vice president for finance, becomes the second Bluebird witness. She is a mellow gray-haired woman with an easy handle on numbers and no wish to harm either her employer or Oretta who urged her late husband to hire Mrs. Fields many years ago. Her testimony amounts to little more than factual documentation of dates and figures.

Oretta stiffens when Arthur Long shows up as the first witness after lunch. Paunchy and jowly, Arthur slouches in his chair and regards both Oretta and Hutchinson with suspicion. He answers questions reluctantly and acts as though Oretta brought her lawsuit on the flimsiest of pretexts with the sole purpose of harassing him and his brother. He belittles Oretta's contribution to the company in its formative years and says he and Wendell made a mistake out of a sense of obligation when they hired their newly widowed in-law.

Arthur admits under interrogation that he has little firsthand knowledge of Oretta's activities with the company. He's the brother in charge of producing the female sports clothing that Wendell's in charge of selling. Wendell is also the financial man.

Arthur does know about the defective ready-to-wear that the company shipped and he spends the better part of the afternoon dueling with Hutchinson over the extent and significance of the deficiencies. He ridicules Hutchinson's estimate of $200,000 worth of shoddily made sportswear shipped over three years, but then confirms lot after numbered lot when Hutchinson laboriously reads off the shipments that were returned by dismayed customers. When Hutchinson dismisses him at the end of a tedious afternoon, Arthur has made a piecemeal acknowledgment of what he first sweepingly refuted.

The next morning an air of tension pervades the law firm's conference room as Wendell Long appears and takes a seat at the conference table opposite Bill Hutchinson and Oretta. The court reporter sits at the end of the table with his stenographic machine while Martin Novack has a chair beside his client. Oretta and Bill feel that Wendell holds the key to the case and Novack has caught their vibrations. Oretta senses that Novack does not quite know what to expect and she sees him waiting, terrierlike, ready to snap and growl at the first sign of danger.

Wendell is taller and less flabby than his brother, but he has that slack face and posture of so many business executives who make deals over high-calorie lunches and dinners and who ride carts rather than walk around a golf course. A man of about fifty, he exudes an air of confidence and authority.

The deposition begins slowly—dates, times, places,—and seems to meander like a trail through the woods of biographical incidentals. Yes, he once was on the UCLA wrestling team. Yes, he belongs to Rotary, serves on the board of several wildlife preservation societies, and has a sloop moored at Marina del Rey. And yes, he is a deacon. Then the wandering forest trail suddenly opens on a rocky gorge and the dwelling of a mysterious woman named Diana Kelbaugh.

"Now did you," asks Bill Hutchinson, "during the course of Oretta Long's employment have occasion to hire a Mrs. Diana Kelbaugh?"

"No, I did not." The big man shifts in his chair. Oretta, watching closely, sees a puzzled look slip into Wendell's domain of confidence.

"Did you sign a contract with an entity named Diana Kelbaugh, Inc., on November twelfth of that year?"

"Yes,"

"And did not that corporation belong to the same Diana Kelbaugh who's now under contract to Bluebird Sportswear?"

"That's right."

"Now what services did Diana Kelbaugh, Inc. provide for Bluebird?"

"Auxiliary sales. It had lined up a number of women's apparel retail outlets in New Mexico and West Texas as customers for sportswear. It agreed to sell them Bluebird products exclusively."

"You say 'it.' Didn't Diana Kelbaugh sign the contract for the corporation and didn't she personally do the selling?"

"Yes."

Hutchinson studies the papers before him for a moment. "Now, Mr. Long, what was the monetary arrangement with Diana Kelbaugh, Inc.?"

"She was paid twelve percent of her gross sales."

"You mean 'it' was paid twelve percent?"

"Yes." Wendell Long glares at Hutchinson.

"Was that the standard commission in your company?"

"No. Oretta Long was paid fifteen percent." Wendell Long preens himself as if in self-congratulation for this good business deal and Oretta wonders why Bill would ask such a question.

"Was Mrs. Long informed of this arrangement with Diana Kelbaugh, Inc.?"

"I don't know about informed. I assume she knew about it."

"Did you personally inform Mrs. Long at any time of the arrangement with Diana Kelbaugh?"

Oretta admires her lawyer's casual but unwavering approach, never raising his voice or changing his tone, yet never veering from the line of target.

"No," Wendell replies. "There was no reason to."

"Did not Mrs. Long have an exclusive contract to market Bluebird's output in the western states?"

"Exclusive in four western states. They did not include New Mexico and West Texas."

Hutchinson digs out a manila folder from his pile of papers and withdraws a single sheet. "I'm reading now from a copy of your contract with Mrs. Long: . . . 'and shall have exclusive rights to sell the company's wares in the western states.' Isn't that what the contract said, Mr. Long?"

"Yes, but in company practice 'western states' meant only Washington, Oregon, California, and Arizona."

"Don't you think the citizens of Idaho would be surprised to hear that they do not reside in a western state?"

"Well, I don't know about—"

"Oh, come on, Bill," Novack cuts in. "Do we have to fill up the record with your little jokes?"

"Okay, I'll withdraw the Idaho question." Hutchinson smiles. "Mr. Long, if New Mexico is not a western state, what region does it belong to?"

"Southwest." Wendell's prompt answer comes with a glow of triumph.

"And West Texas?"

"Same. The Southwest."

"Was Bluebird's definition of 'western states' written down anywhere?"

"I think so."

"Could you give me a citation?"

Wendell thinks for a time. "Not at the moment."

"At any rate, even though Oretta Long had a contract for exclusive sales representation in the western states, you did not feel obligated to tell her that you'd contracted for another sales representative in New Mexico and West Texas?"

"The subject just never came up. No obligation, no."

Bill pauses, searches for a note on his pad. "Yesterday your brother Arthur said that you and he originally hired Oretta Long out of a sense of obligation to a widow. Did that feeling of obligation soon run out then?"

"You can't go forever on obligation."

"Did you feel any obligation to inform Oretta Long in her status as your sister-in-law and as a person instrumental in launching Bluebird with her late husband Frank Long."

"No, she'd sold out her interest to Arthur and me. She got a lot of money, nine-hundred thousand dollars."

"Do you think that just as a matter of common courtesy, you should have told the widow of the company's founder?"

"No." Wendell looks put upon. "This was strictly business."

The questioning goes on in this vein for half an hour as Hutchinson pokes, prods, and pries into the business relationship of Bluebird and Diana Kelbaugh. Oretta sits fascinated, awaiting the moment when her skillful attorney will strike. Bill Hutchinson eases up to the moment.

"Mr. Long," asks Bill in a quiet voice, "was and is your relationship with Diana Kelbaugh a purely business one?"

"Yes." He hesitates. "Of course, we're on friendly terms. She's a valued member of the team."

"So if I characterized the relationship as one of a friendly business nature, I would be correct?"

"Yes." Wendell is wary.

"By the way, Diana Kelbaugh is married, isn't she?"

"I believe so, yes."

"Mr. Long, did you have marketing conferences with Diana Kelbaugh?" The question seems a mere afterthought following extensive discussion of the woman.

"Oh yes, many."

"How often were they held, would you estimate?"

"Oh, about once a month, sometimes more."

"Always at company headquarters here in Los Angeles?"

Wendell frowns. "Well, almost always. There may have been one or two discussions over lunch, something like that."

"Did you ever meet Diana Kelbaugh for a marketing conference at 10134 Ocean Surf Drive near Redondo Beach?"

Hutchinson asks the question quite casually, but the effect in the room is electric. Oretta and Wendell both tense and Martin Novack goes instantly on the alert, his eyes drilling Bill.

"I don't recognize the address," says Wendell slowly. He hitches forward in his chair.

"All right. I'll ask the question in another form. Did you ever meet Diana Kelbaugh for a marketing conference at the Pompton Arms near Redondo Beach?"

"I . . ." Wendell flashes an angry look at Hutchinson. A bead of sweat appears above the executive's upper lip. He hesitates, then turns and whispers to his attorney.

"Going off the record," says Martin Novack. "We'd like a recess for a few minutes."

"Sure," says Bill. He's expansive, filled with goodwill.

When the court reporter also excuses himself and follows lawyer and client out of the room, Oretta bursts out: "Bill. You did it. You stuck it to the son of a bitch." She's exultant with the throb of vengeance in her voice.

Bill holds up a clutch of papers. "We're well primed with dates and times, thanks to Pat McManus."

"What do you think they're doing out there?" She points over her shoulder.

"I think Marty's hearing Wendell's confession and I think he's instructing his client not to answer."

Oretta shows alarm. "Doesn't he have to?"

Hutchinson nods. "Eventually. I can't imagine that the court won't order him to reply."

Novack and Long return several minutes later. Long has lost his air of confidence, but Novack is his normal, brisk, wary self. After they're all seated again with the court reporter, Hutchinson repeats his question.

"Mr. Long, did you ever meet Diana Kelbaugh for a marketing conference at the Pompton Arms, a motel near Redondo Beach?"

"I instruct my client not to answer that question," says Novack.

"You're objecting to the question on what grounds?" asks Hutchinson.

"It's immaterial and irrelevant and will not lead to evidence admissible at trial. Many of your questions have gone far afield today, but this one totally exceeds the bounds of relevancy."

"Now, Marty, you know very well I can get an order to compel." Bill puts on an easy smile. "No way can you stop this line of questioning."

"Until I know the direction, I shall instruct my client to decline to answer."

"We intend to show that Wendell Long had a romantic relationship with Mrs. Diana Kelbaugh and that the relationship directly caused Bluebird's discharge of my client."

"That's not enough, Bill." Novack had a dogged air now. "If you're not showing the relevancy, I'll object."

"You go ahead and object and I'll go ahead and ask the questions."

Oretta watches this sparring like a front-row fight fan up for the kill while Wendell suddenly seems to have shrunk. He's huddled back in his chair. Bill, on the other hand, sympathizes with Marty Novack. Bill has been in that corner himself, trying to protect his client from the impact of a surprise revelation that the client neglected to confide to his attorney.

Still there's work to do. Bill fishes a slip of paper from his open folder and peers at it. "Now, Mr. Long, did you ever register at the Pompton Arms motel near Redondo Beach under the name 'Hugo Angell'?"

"Objection!" snaps Novack. "I instruct my client not to answer that question."

"Did you ever register in your handwriting at the Pompton Arms as 'Mr. and Mrs. Hugo Angell'?"

"Objection. Instructing my client not to answer."

"Did you make a habit of driving to the Pompton Arms on Thursdays and parking your Oldsmobile there?"

"Objection." Novack taps a pencil without looking up. "Don't answer that."

"To your knowledge, did Mrs. Kelbaugh make a regular Thursday practice of driving to and parking her Honda Accord at the Pompton Arms?"

"Objection. Don't answer."

Wendell Long, slumped back, rests his elbows on the arms of his chair and makes a chapel of his fingers, over which he peers balefully at Hutchinson as though the lawyer were a vandal accused of trashing a church.

"Did you and Mrs. Kelbaugh occupy the same room at the Pompton Arms on a total of forty-six Thursdays since January of last year up to and including Thursday a week ago?"

Novack intones his response and Wendell continues to stare at his tormentor.

"Did you and Mrs. Kelbaugh customarily hold your Thursday meetings at the Pompton Arms between the hours of eleven A.M. and two P.M.?"

"Objection. Don't answer." Novack looks across the table at Hutchinson. "Now Bill, how long is this charade going to go on? Mr. Long is not going to answer any further questions about meetings at the Pompton Arms. You're just wasting everyone's time."

"Marty, you know very well that you and Mr. Long will be sitting in those same chairs several weeks from now, answering the very same questions. The only difference will be that I'll hold in my hands an order from the court compelling him to answer. So why waste everyone's valuable time?"

"We don't know what the court will do. In the meantime, spare your breath. My client is not answering."

Hutchinson sighs, stretches, leafs through his folder, and soon begins a line of questioning far away from motels and trysts. He wants to know the details of the discussion between the brothers when they decided to discharge their sister-in-law. From that he goes to finances, customer lists, pricing information, the broad area of employment discrimination—whether Mrs. Long was fired because of being female—to Oretta's opening of an East Coast market.

The questioning drones on for the remainder of the day and throughout the following day. Wendell now answers as he might a police detective interrogating him on suspicion of murder. The executive is by turns belligerent, reluctant, explosive, laconic, and argumentative. Several times Novack is forced to call a recess and Hutchinson suspects that the lawyer takes the time to lecture his client, probably reminding him to answer the questions as economically and as calmly as possible.

Before ending his three-day deposing of Bluebird executives, Hutchinson instructs Susan Pennington to prepare a motion to compel Wendell Long to answer questions about his relationship to Mrs. Diana Kelbaugh. A law firm messenger takes the motion to Superior Court where it is filed while Wendell Long is undergoing his second day of quizzing.

A court clerk sets a hearing on the motion for a Wednesday morning in the second week in February, a date three weeks away. Judge Stewart Otterbein, who rejected Novack's motion for a protective order, will hear oral arguments.

Although this means another delay, Oretta Long is in a euphoric mood. Hutchinson assures her that Judge Otterbein most certainly will order Wendell Long to answer the questions that will put his affair with Diana Kelbaugh on the record. And this, both lawyer and client agree, will place Oretta in a dominant position in the case. At this point, nine months after calling on Bill Hutchinson to begin her lawsuit, Oretta is sure she's a winner and that the half brothers will have to cough up a great deal of money.

The Costs

Balance to Date (Paid)	$8,971.25
Hutchinson	
Phone calls (Novack, Long, 1½ hrs.)	225.00
Analyzing, preparing case (6 hrs.)	900.00
Conferences with Pennington (2 hrs.)	300.00
Conference Mrs. Long (1 hr.)	150.00
Attendance depositions (24 hrs.)	3,600.00
Pennington	
Analyzing interrogatories (10 hrs.)	750.00
Analyzing produced documents (12 hrs.)	900.00
Preparing, arguing motion (5 hrs.)	375.00
Conferences with Hutchinson (2 hrs.)	150.00
Patrick McManus Investigation	
135 hrs. ($40 per hr.)	5,400.00
Expenses (incl. cash payments)	630.00
Bluebird Exec. Depositions	
Hutchinson–Pennington strategy conference	
(3 hrs.)	675.00
Transcript (714 pages)	
Sealed court original ($2.50 page)	1,785.00
Working copy ($1.25 page)	892.00
Court Fee	10.00
Total	$25,713.25

Although Oretta pays $75.00 an hour for Susan Pennington's services, Susan does not receive $75.00 an hour. As a novice lawyer, less than two years out of Duke Law School, Susan is paid a flat salary of $35,000 a year which, on the customary basis of 2,200 hours a year, would mean that she earns about $16 an hour.

What with overhead and expenses, it costs the seven-man law firm of Devereaux, Goldstein, Hutchinson & Tong about $50,000 to $60,000 a year to employ Ms. Pennington. Since the billings for her services bring the law firm about $165,000 annually, the firm makes more than $100,000 each on Susan and other young lawyers in their employ. This goes into the pot of profits that the seven partners split at the end of the year.

Although Oretta doesn't know of this specific arrangement, the general practice is common knowledge. Susan Pennington doesn't mind particularly. She knows that when she becomes a partner, she'll share in the money the firm makes off the sweat of the young attorneys to come.

Mediation

14

New York Area
February 12
The Next Year

Part Seven: *Rosemary's Venture*

Eight months after the mediated close of her heated dispute with her brother, Rosemary Wofford opens ROSEMARY'S PLACE, her new home furnishings store in Hopewell, New Jersey, a town with an 1890s atmosphere located about fifty miles from New York City. A converted warehouse gives the owner almost an acre of floor space on which to display the modish furniture, drapes, and carpetings that she has priced for sale to middle-class buyers.

More than a thousand people, attracted by cake, champagne, and several thousand dollars worth of door prizes, attend the gala opening. To her surprise, Rosemary actually sells furniture on opening night, enough in fact to pay for the festivities.

She calls her brother, Stephen Holloway, the next morning to report on the successful launching. Stephen, reconciled with his sister since the mediation, is Rosemary's silent backer, the major stockholder in Rosemary Furnishings, Inc. He cosigned for the million-dollar bank loan that his sister negotiated for the new enterprise's capital.

Rosemary is riding high. Her store promises to be a success and she hasn't felt so healthy and energetic in years.

The Lawsuit

15

Los Angeles
February 12
Second Year

Part Six: *Intelligence Snafu Leads to Sneak Attack*

Discovery, Depositions

Nine months and $25,000 after initiating legal action against her late husband's half brothers, Oretta Long is spinning along in a zesty mood. The lawsuit, after languishing for some months, is active once again.

On this date, two days before Valentine's Day, she visits the law and motions courtroom in the civil Superior Court building in the downtown Los Angeles Civic Center. There Bill Hutchinson will duel Marty Novack, the brisk, nervous lawyer for the well-loathed half brothers who bounced Oretta out of her job in violation of a signed contract.

A skirmish on the flank of the main battle, today's action nevertheless has crucial implications for Oretta. Judge Stewart Otterbein, one of the motions judges, is to decide whether or not Wendell Long must answer questions about his relationship with Mrs. Diana Kelbaugh, the woman who, Oretta believes, caused her discharge from Bluebird Sportswear.

While Susan Pennington argued a previous motion, Bill Hutchinson has come himself this time to demand that Wendell Long be ordered by the court to answer the questions. Novack also has come in person rather than entrust a young law assistant.

Ready for drama, Oretta is disappointed. The big courtroom is nearly empty. Only the judge sits on the judicial dais with a sallow bored court functionary nearby. A half-dozen lawyers, waiting to argue other motions, lounge about the last two rows of the pewlike benches. There is but one spectator, an elderly woman in a flowing floor-length dress and a soiled picture hat that looks as if it went to its last garden party in the days of silent films. She sneezes and coughs as she paws the contents of a swollen handbag.

As a further downer, Oretta can't hear the proceedings when Hutchinson and Novack speak their pieces in front of the judge. Because they talk at a conversational level without microphones at the other end of the room, Oretta catches only an occasional sentence or phrase. Each man speaks about five minutes, then Judge Otterbein leans down toward the two men with more subdued talk. Once again Oretta has the uneasy feeling that she has experienced several times since the lawsuit began, a sense of being excluded while the insiders of the law discuss her fate in private.

But the mood soon passes, for Bill Hutchinson comes striding back from the bench, a happy smile on his face. Novack, with a bad-weather look, turns aside to talk to another lawyer.

"We won easy," says Hutchinson. "I'm to draft the order to compel for Judge Otterbein to sign. Wendell Long must answer the questions about his meetings with Diana Kelbaugh. It's central to our case."

Now Oretta is certain of victory in the lawsuit itself and for a time she forgets that the day of vindication in the courtroom is still some three to four years away.

The next week Wendell Long's deposition takes up just where it left off in the conference room of Hutchinson's law firm. While Wendell no longer has the aura of chief-executive-in-full-command, which surrounded him at the start of the questioning, he has regained some of the air of self-importance that Oretta finds so annoying.

"And so," says Bill after a few preliminary questions, "we come back to the matter of Diana Kelbaugh. A month ago in this room, you said your relationship with Mrs. Kelbaugh was one of a friendly business nature. Is that how you'd still characterize the connection?"

"Yes, it is." Wendell's tone is firm.

"Mr. Long, did you ever meet Diana Kelbaugh at the Pompton Arms Motel near Redondo Beach?"

"Yes."

"Did you meet her there more than once?"

"Yes, I did."

"Would you say you met Mrs. Kelbaugh at the Pompton Arms as many as forty-six Thursdays over a period of more than a year?"

"I may have. I don't know the exact number of times."

"And what was the purpose of these meetings?"

"We discussed the marketing problems facing Bluebird Sportswear. Mrs. Kelbaugh was and is a top salesperson for us." Wendell's tone is dry, matter-of-fact. He might be discussing invoices.

Oretta is amazed. Although Bill Hutchinson had predicted that Wendell would try to bluff it through, transforming a series of assignations into ordinary business sessions, Oretta never bought that view. She always pictured the proud Wendell dissolving in a pitiable heap that the artful Hutchinson would scoop up and feed to the lions. Now the reality of Wendell's denial outrages her.

"Did you ever discuss marketing and sales matters with other executives or employees of Bluebird?"

"Yes, of course."

"With about how many individuals?"

"I couldn't say for sure. Eight or ten, I guess."

"Did you ever confer with any of these eight or ten people at the Pompton Arms?"

"No."

"Diana Kelbaugh was the only person connected with Bluebird Sportswear with whom you conferred at the Pompton Arms?"

"Yes."

Hutchinson pauses, refers to his notes. "Mr. Long, did you ever use one of the motel bedrooms for your conference with Mrs. Kelbaugh?"

"Oh, yes, all the time." Wendell offers a bland smile. "We needed a private room to do our work properly."

Oretta hoots in derision, then slaps a hand over her mouth.

"Bill," says Martin Novack, "please caution your client about the rules here."

"I apologize." Oretta bows her head, but inwardly the mocking laughter skitters about.

"Mr. Long," Bill continues, "did you ever register at the Pompton Arms as 'Mr. and Mrs. Hugo Angell'?"

"Yes."

"And was Mrs. Angell actually Mrs. Kelbaugh?"

"Yes."

"What was the reason for the assumed names?"

"Business competition. We decided we ought to keep our marketing sessions confidential. Rivalry can be cutthroat in the female sportswear field."

"I don't quite understand. You mean you feared a rival might eavesdrop at the keyhole of your room if you registered as Wendell Long and Diana Kelbaugh?"

"No, but—"

"Just a minute, Bill." Martin Novack leans over and whispers to his client. They turn their backs to the table while they talk for a minute in whispers.

"Okay," says Novack. "Go ahead."

"Please repeat the question, Mr. Reporter."

The legal stenographer reads back the inquiry.

"I just decided as a general policy," Long replies, "to keep our marketing conferences confidential. It made good business sense. In addition to rivals, there was the matter of employee relations in our own company. It just doesn't do to post all your meetings on the bulletin board."

"Then you did not fear eavesdropping at the motel room keyhole?"

"No, sir." Wendell looks neither aggrieved nor embarrassed.

Oretta, growing more angry with each exchange, concludes that Wendell decided several weeks ago to stonewall everything connected with the Pompton Arms and Diana Kelbaugh. She knows Wendell's remarkable talent for self-deception and surmises that once having decided on the marketing fiction, he found it quite easy to pass it off as truth.

The little morality play continues throughout the morning. Bill Hutchinson's questions frame the Pompton Arms meetings in every conceivable racy form smacking of assignation and matinee sex. Wendell, slack, sleek, and composed, turns each inquiry into another weighty conference on tennis frocks.

When Hutchinson dismisses the Bluebird co-owner just before the noon recess, Oretta stares at her former in-law in disbelief. As she and her lawyer walk to a combination bookstore and soup-and-salad bar a block off Wilshire, she's as downcast as he is upbeat.

"Why are you so damn cheerful?" she asks Bill over her cucumber soup and carrot salad. "I just can't understand the law, letting an old hypocrite like Wendell get away with that pack of lies."

"I'm in good spirits because we got just what I wanted out of your old friend Wendell." Bill spoons into his clam chowder. "It all went according to the book."

"How can you say that?" For the first time Oretta is openly testy with her lawyer. "He got away with murder, the bastard." She slaps the pepper shaker down on the table. This whole lawsuit has been an emotional roller coaster for Oretta and right now she's in one of the big stomach-churning dips.

"Oretta, he hasn't gotten away with a thing." Bill puts a calming hand on her sleeve. "Remember, we're taking this case to a jury trial and not one juror in a thousand would ever believe the outlandish scenario that Wendell concocted. The jury will know unanimously that he's lying, that he went to the Pompton Arms to crawl into bed with the woman to whom he gave your job."

"Oh, Bill, that's all three or four years off. We'll be lucky if we're still alive then." With no action in the offing, she can't shake her despondency.

"Short of a confession, I couldn't have asked for better answers from Wendell." Bill, caught up in the litigation game, is proud that he outpointed Marty Novack this morning. "That testimony will sound ludicrous before a jury and if Wendell tries to shift ground, we'll trap him with the deposition."

"I've got an idea." Oretta brightens. "What if I call Wendell and say if he doesn't come through with a big settlement, I'll mail his testimony to his wife, Grace."

"No, no." Bill raises a stopping hand. "That could get us tangled up in a charge of extortion. You're talking blackmail, Oretta."

"Well, what if I just leak the facts to a friend who goes to Wendell's church?" Oretta craves some kind of action. "She could start the gossip going at the church. That might bring Wendell around."

"No, best by far to just let the law take its course." Bill is his most persuasive self now. "If you go off on a tangent like that, no telling what might develop. The case gets out of our control. Listen, Oretta, don't fret. Your position is looking good and I still think a jury will find for us or you'll get an acceptable settlement. After this morning's feeble attempt at covering up a series of rendezvouses with the woman who got your job, Wendell is all but finished. So just be patient."

Oretta sighs. "That's one thing you need a lot of when you get into a lawsuit."

"Cheer up." Bill's tone is bouncy once more. "This afternoon we have Diana Kelbaugh to give us her version of the bedroom marketing talks at the Pompton Arms."

The appearance of Diana Kelbaugh in the afternoon so upsets Bill Hutchinson that he loses his place in his notes and does not fully recover his interrogation cadence for several minutes. Oretta Long too cannot quite credit what she sees.

Having anticipated a sultry temptress, Bill is confounded to meet a plump little woman who resembles the grandmother who used to bake him cookies when he was a kid. Oretta is equally nonplussed. Diana resembles her vision only in the auburn hair that Oretta had heard about, but the "suggestive walk" turns out to be a sway caused by excess weight. Diana Kelbaugh has a doughy face, creased by a passive smile, and about as much sexual charge as a nursery rhyme.

She answers Bill's questions readily with an air of candor. Yes, she grew up in West Los Angeles. Yes, she has three children, now grown and living in homes of their own.

After going through her job, contract terms, and other Bluebird business matters, Bill gets around to the case's Topic A. "And would you please describe your relationship with Wendell Long, the president of Bluebird Sportswear?"

"Well, he's my boss, you know." Diana, Oretta notes, has a dimple on one cheek. "So we're pretty much business, although friendly enough."

"Now did you have occasion to meet Wendell Long at the Pompton Arms near Redondo Beach?"

"Oh, yes. On lots and lots of Thursdays. We used to have our marketing conferences at the motel. He'd hire a room and we'd discuss our sales tactics." Her smile goes in and out like the sun on a cloudy day.

"It's true, is it not, that you came in separate cars and then registered in the same room as 'Mr. and Mrs. Hugo Angell'?"

"Oh, yes." Diana brushes at her closely set brown hair. "I know it probably looks funny to you, Mr. Hutchinson, but Wendell is a bit paranoid about security, if you ask me."

Bill decides that Diana is either stupid and incredibly naive or she's a brilliant liar. "There was no romantic or sexual interest between you and Mr. Long?"

"Oh, no. Mr. Hutchinson, I'm a happily married woman. Oh, no. None at all." She smiles demurely. "You've certainly got the wrong idea."

"A frank question, Mrs. Kelbaugh. Did you ever engage in sexual intercourse with Wendell Long in a room at the Pompton Arms?"

"I object!" Novack comes to life with a shout. "The subject's totally irrelevant to this case."

"On the contrary, it's most relevant. This is at the core of our case." Hutchinson folds his arms. "We contend that the nature of their relationship provided the central reason for my client's discharge."

"Go ahead and answer, Mrs. Kelbaugh," says Novack. "I reserve my objection."

"Oh, dear no." She frowns, yet does not seem to resent the question. "Nothing of that kind. It was pure business."

Bill Hutchinson sits staring at Diana Kelbaugh, fixing her brown eyes with his. He believes her to be a shrewd woman, a skillful actress and liar, and yet he can't be 100 percent certain. There's a possibility, however minute and remote, that Wendell and Diana did go to a motel in separate cars, engaged a room as a fictional married couple, and then sat around and discussed business. Instinct tells Bill to leave the Pompton Arms alone for a time while he tries to find another key to this woman's character. At the moment he's stymied.

Bill returns to other phases of Diana's work for Bluebird and the questions run on until the midafternoon break. After the recess the session continues for another hour and a half without noticeable enlightenment to Hutchinson and Oretta or damage to Martin Novack and his Bluebird clients.

Bill is just about to dismiss Diane from further testimony when he asks as though on a sudden whim: "Oh, by the way, Mrs. Kelbaugh, have you ever been to Borrego Springs?"

Diana hesitates, then says, "Yes."

"With Wendell Long?"

"Yes."

"And did you ever spend a weekend with Mr. Long at the arty town of Mendocino?"

She coughs. Her answer is indistinct.

"Could you please answer that in a voice loud enough for the court reporter to hear, Mrs. Kelbaugh."

"Yes, we stayed once in Mendocino."

"Mrs. Kelbaugh, did you ever spend three nights with Wendell Long at a hotel near Cabo San Lucas, Baja California, in Mexico?"

"That's right, Mr. Hutchinson." Her voice has shrunk, sounds like that of an embarrassed young girl.

"You flew from Los Angeles to La Paz in Baja and then drove south to Cabo San Lucas, did you not?"

"Yes."

"With Mr. Long?"

"Well, yes. The two of us."

"Mrs. Kelbaugh, tell me if you will, what was the purpose of these trips together?"

"We discussed marketing problems." Diana says it with a flourish as if challenging Hutchinson to prove otherwise.

"You flew all the way to the southern part of Baja California in Mexico to discuss marketing problems?"

"That's right." Diana Kelbaugh has a dogged air now.

"Did you occupy the same room at night?"

"Yes, we did. Mr. Long thought that a double room wouldn't cost the company as much money as two single rooms."

"Did the room have twin beds or a double bed?"

"Oh, twin beds." Her tone is that of an innocent woman falsely accused.

Hutchinson rummages among his papers, finally extracts a copy of a hotel bill. He hands the paper to Diana. "Doesn't this hotel bill indicate that you occupied a room with a double bed?"

"It does." She hands back the paper with a toss of her head. "But that has to be a mistake in the office. We had twin beds. I never slept with Mr. Long. It was a business trip."

"Did you occupy the same room on the trips to Mendocino and Borrego Springs?"

"Yes, but always with twin beds."

"Thank you, Mrs. Kelbaugh." Hutchinson begins gathering up papers, but then asks, seemingly as an afterthought: "Oh, by the way, one other thing, Mrs. Kelbaugh. What is your husband's first name?"

"Clarence."

"Did you ever tell your husband Clarence about your sessions with Mr. Long at the Pompton Arms?" This is the first mention of the motel in almost two hours.

"Yes, I did."

"When did you first tell him?"

Diana hesitates. "Oh, I'm not sure." For the first time, she seems uneasy. "I don't know just when it was."

"These meetings at the Pompton Arms began long ago. Did you tell him at the time of the first meeting?"

"No, I didn't." She colors slightly.

Bill bores in quickly. "When you did tell him, did you tell him about the fake registration as Mr. and Mrs. Hugo Angell, occupying the same room, coming in separate cars?"

"I'm not sure just what I told him when I told him." Diana's eyes flick toward her attorney. She needs help.

"Did you inform your husband last year about the Pompton Arms meetings with Mr. Long?"

"Last year?" She looks set upon. "No, I don't think so. No, not last year."

Bill sits for a long minute, tapping a pen on his stack of papers, gazing at the witness. "Actually, Mrs. Kelbaugh, isn't it true that you never mentioned the Pompton Arms meetings to your husband until after I first questioned Wendell Long about them in this room last month?" Bill thinks this intuitive shot has but minimal risk.

Diana Kelbaugh does not reply. She looks confused now, unprepared for this oblique attack. Oretta notes that she is twisting a hand-kerchief. Bill guesses that this was one line of questioning which Marty Novack neglected to review with his client. A half minute goes by in silence.

"Could we have your reply, please, Mrs. Kelbaugh?"

"No, I didn't." Diana does not look at Bill this time.

"You never told Clarence Kelbaugh about the Pompton Arms meetings with Wendell Long before January of this year then?"

"No."

"Mrs. Kelbaugh." Hutchinson drops his voice. "Have you told Clarence Kelbaugh about your trips to Mendocino, Borrego Springs, and Cabo San Lucas?"

"He knew I went on company trips, yes."

"But did you tell him that on these three trips, just you and Wendell Long went together?"

"No, I didn't." Her defenses are shattered.

Bill forbears to ask whether Clarence knows about his wife and her boss sharing the same hotel room. "Thank you, Mrs. Kelbaugh. I have no further questions."

When Oretta and Bill rehash Diana's deposition in Bill's office later, Oretta is once again riding a crest on her roller coaster ride. She compliments Bill on his tactics, lauds the way he held the crusher questions until the last. They agree that Diana is a skilled liar when properly prepared, but less than perfect when on her own. They also agree that on a one-to-ten scale of sexual attraction, Diana scores a two minus.

Oretta Long's own deposition is scheduled for the next week in the Century City law offices of Henderson, Shapiro, Novack and Kawagami, and on Friday she spends three hours with Susan Pennington, reviewing the interrogatories and other facets of the case. Early Monday morning she shows up at Bill's office for the drive to what all weekend she has been calling "the ordeal."

She is nervous, finds herself perspiring slightly in anticipation, and fusses a great deal with her hair although the new set needs no attention whatever.

"I can't understand it," she tells Bill. "There's not a single thing for me to worry about, but I'm jittery anyway."

"Like a runner before a race," says Bill. "You'll be fine after the first few questions. I'll brief you on the drive over there. But first, we have a decision. Marty Novack called me just before you arrived. Wendell and Arthur are making you an offer."

"Oh?" Oretta shakes out a cigarette from the pack and lights it. "I'm all ears. I figured our Pompton Arms surprise might bring some reaction."

"They're offering an even one hundred thousand to settle the case."

Oretta sniffs. "You want my short answer? . . . No."

Bill nods. "I told Marty I didn't think that kind of money would elicit much of a response. But since they're thinking settlement, this might be the time to make a counterproposal."

"All right." Oretta's case of nerves has been forgotten. She's concentrating on money now. "Tell Mr. Novack that your client will shut up and go home for an even million. No, give him a bargain. Make that nine hundred and ninety-five thousand dollars."

"No chance of that, Oretta."

"Could be, but I think the Pompton Arms bit, plus Borrego Springs and those other two weekends, are worth a lot of money."

"I'm inclined to agree." Bill studies his client. "Marty said he was making the offer in good faith before your deposition. He said if you didn't accept, you might regret the decision after being deposed. A not very veiled hint that he has something up his sleeve for today. You know anything they could surprise us with?"

Oretta shakes her head. "They'll find when they get through with me, that their case is as bad as it's always been."

"Okay, I'll call Novack now. Just make yourself comfortable."

When Bill reaches the other lawyer, he relays Oretta's rejection of the offer and listens a moment. "Do we have a counterproposal? Yes, we do. Mrs. Long says she'll settle for nine hundred and ninety-five thousand dollars. . . . That's right, it's bargain day. . . . You won't huh? . . . All right, we'll be at your place at ten as agreed."

Hanging up the phone, Bill shakes his head. "Novack said there's not a chance the Longs will consider our counteroffer. So he'll see us in a half hour for your deposition. . . . No problem. They'll come up with a higher offer before long."

Driving to the Century City building, Hutchinson schools his client on appropriate behavior when being questioned by Novack.

"You've seen how the taking of depositions works now, but there are some things I want to emphasize. Remember that your answers probably will be transcribed. Marty Novack will study them and undoubtedly bring them to court and quiz you about them on the witness stand."

Hutchinson says that he can recite almost verbatim the advice given by his law partner Andrew Tong to clients about to be deposed. Tong, says Bill, has a deep theatrical voice that makes an impression on clients and juries. A cassette tape of his advice can be found in several law school libraries now.

"Andy says there are three basic rules to observe when being deposed. First, listen carefully. Do not reply until you are sure you fully understand the question and its implications. Wendell, you may have noted, sometimes bolted ahead before he completely understood. If you are not sure, ask that the question be repeated. Take your time answering. If the question rattles you, remain silent until you have composed yourself."

Bill curses softly at the driver of a red sedan that swerves into his lane without warning. "Rule Two. In answering, use just the words that are necessary and not a single word more. Repeating, never add an unnecessary word. If the question can be answered by yes or no, use that one word and nothing more.

"Let me amplify. If Novack asks you, 'Mrs. Long, did you use any sales assistants in your work?' just say, 'Yes.' Don't say, 'Yes, I wanted to hire Dorothy Smith, but she wasn't available so I hired Marianne Kramer.' The longer response merely opens the door for Marty to come exploring. You'd be surprised how many witnesses, beguiled by the questioner, lose their case by revealing too much."

"Don't fret about me, Bill." Oretta pats his arm. "I'll be so close-mouthed, I'll wear out my lipstick."

"Good." Bill glances at her. "Rule Three. Tell the absolute truth. Diana Kelbaugh and Wendell Long didn't do that and they got themselves in deeper by the minute."

Bill talks some more, then concludes as they pull into the garage beneath the building that houses the opposing law firm. She should relax, answer only what she's asked, and leave everything else to him. "I'll be right at your elbow and if Novack asks anything irrelevant or barred by the rules, I'll jump right in with an objection. If Novack and I get into a hassle, just sit quietly until I tell you to answer. Trust me. After all, Oretta, that's why you hired me—to be your legal adviser and technician."

The Lawsuit

16

Los Angeles
February 26
Second Year

Part Seven: *Red Faces at the Blue Fox*

Discovery, Depositions

Unlike the scene when Hutchinson took the opposition's depositions and Oretta sat in as a silent observer, only Martin Novack and a legal stenographer await Bill and Oretta. They meet in the law firm's conference room, which might be a carbon copy of the one in Bill's law firm except for the magnificent view.

The firm of Henderson, Shapiro, Novack & Kawagami occupies a large suite on the seventeenth floor and one side of the conference room is the tinted glass exterior of the building. The four occupants look west toward the Pacific Ocean which today, thanks to less smog than usual over the city, actually can be seen.

Nothing is said about the rejected settlement offer and after the greetings, Novack gets right to work with his questions while the court stenographer taps away at his machine. Soon the lawyer focuses on the areas covered in his original letter to Hutchinson, Oretta's lack of diligence in servicing accounts, her use of "inexperienced and inept" sales assistants, her violation of orders in opening an East Coast market, and refusal to follow company "operating procedures."

All of this had been anticipated by Hutchinson and aside from a few minor points, none of it bothers Oretta. She answers as economically as possible, usually providing only yes and no responses. When Bill and Oretta go to lunch during the noon recess, they agree that Novack has advanced his clients' case not a bit. "He didn't lay a glove on you," says Bill with no apology for the cliché.

Soon after lunch, however, the first glove brushes Oretta. Martin Novack, swinging into the subject of expense accounts, fires his questions from behind a thick book entitled *Official Hotel & Resort Guide* and a stack of papers that turn out to be expense accounts filed with Bluebird Sportswear's accounting department by Oretta Long over a period of more than four years.

"Now Mrs. Long, was it your custom when traveling for Bluebird to stay in clean, respectable, medium-priced commercial hotels or the high-priced deluxe hotels?"

"I believed in going first class when on company business."

"Does that mean you always stayed at deluxe hotels?"

"No. Not always."

Novack takes a fistful of papers from a folder and puts on his glasses to inspect them. "All right. Here we have your expense accounts for Seattle. They show you visited the city eleven times in four years on sales trips for the company. Does that sound right to you?"

"Yes, give or take a time or two."

The attorney hands the sheaf of papers to Oretta. "Are those your expense accounts, Mrs. Long?"

Oretta takes several minutes to glance through the papers, then answers: "Yes."

"And are those your signatures?"

"Yes."

"Now, Mrs. Long, glance through those eleven expense accounts and tell me what other hotels you stayed at beside the Sorrento and the Olympic?"

"None. I always stayed at one or the other."

Novack picks up the book. "Now reading from the *Official Hotel*

& *Resort Guide*, published periodically by the Ziff-Davis people, the Sorrento is described as an intimate deluxe hotel with a turn-of-the-century European atmosphere. The book describes the Olympic as a deluxe classic resort that is on the register of historic places. Mrs. Long, would you agree with those descriptions?"

"In general, yes."

"Now would you please read into the record the single rates you paid and for which you billed Bluebird during those eleven stops."

Oretta reads out numbers that vary between $100 and $115 nightly at the Sorrento and between $130 and $170 nightly at the Olympic.

"Moving now to San Francisco," says Novack, "I find that you stopped at hotels in that city twelve times on company business during your employment." He holds up another sheaf of papers. "Does that agree with your memory?"

"About that, yes."

"Now where did you stay in San Francisco on company expense accounts?"

"Either the Huntington or the Clift."

"Any other hotel?"

"No."

"The *Guide* calls both hotels, discreet, superior, deluxe. Would you agree with that description?"

"Yes."

"I hand you these expense accounts and again ask you to read off the nightly single rates that you charged to Bluebird."

Oretta reads off numbers that average about $160 a night for both the Huntington and the Clift.

The attorney continues in the same pattern for half an hour, including such West Coast hotels as the Heathman in Portland, the Westgate in San Diego, La Valencia in La Jolla, and the Rancho Bernardo Inn some miles outside San Diego. Naming two-dozen hotels, he goes through the same routine from deluxe description to expensive nightly single rate.

"Look, Marty," says Bill at last, "we're willing to stipulate that Oretta invariably stopped at first-rate hotels as part of her philosophy of doing business. Must we waste time by naming all these hotels and their rates?"

"Bill, you had your time with my clients," Novack retorts, "with very little objection on my part. Now it's my turn. I'm heading right at the target, my friend."

Bill sighs and Marty continues thumbing through the expense accounts. He finds what he wants, holds up the paper, adjusts his eyeglasses, and reads for a few moments.

"All right. Mrs. Long, I hand you this expense account and ask you to identify the place and the hotel."

"It's the Hibbard Grove Hotel east of Oakland."

"Now, please, Mrs. Long, read the items listed under breakfast."

"Orange juice, toast, and coffee."

"And how much was the orange juice?"

"Seven dollars."

"Was that a small, medium, or large glass?"

"I can't remember a thing like that."

"Is it your custom to pay seven dollars for a glass of orange juice?"

"No. I never paid that much before."

"But you were quite willing to pay that much of the company's money, were you not?"

"Mr. Novack, I never saw how much the orange juice cost."

"Didn't you read the menu?"

"I suppose so. I can't remember."

"And didn't the menu include prices?"

"I don't recall."

Novack swings around to look at the view toward the Pacific as the afternoon sun begins to cast shadows through the city. "Did it ever occur to you to pay part of the cost of the seven-dollar orange juice?"

"No, I was traveling on business."

"Did it ever occur to you to pay part of those steep single rates at those exclusive hotels where you stayed?"

"No."

"Now, Mrs. Long, did there come a time when Mr. Wendell Long took you to task for flying first class and stopping only at deluxe hotels with their extravagant rates?"

"Yes."

"And wasn't the date of his reprimand May seventeenth three years ago?"

"About that, I guess. I don't recall exactly."

"So that you were on notice fairly early in your employment at

Bluebird, were you not, that Wendell Long disapproved of your lavish expense account spending?"

"Yes."

"And yet you continued to travel in the same royal style, spending top dollar. Is that not true?"

"Yes, but only after Wendell and I took it up with Arthur Long and Arthur sided with me. I said our type of customers wouldn't like a saleswoman who nickled-and-dimed her way, buying them cheap drinks in dingy bars and taking them to dinner in second-class restaurants. Arthur agreed with me and I never heard any more about it."

"No more about it?" Martin Novack's tone is one of cynical disbelief. He paws about among his papers, finds what he wants. "As a matter of fact, didn't Wendell Long order you last year to fly economy class and cease stopping at the deluxe hotels?"

"Oh yes, but that was just before I was fired—in violation of my written contract. I wasn't counting that final time."

"Did you agree to obey Mr. Long's orders?"

"No, we had a big argument. I told him going the el cheapo route was no way to get business, and he told me that I was being extravagant and that it wasn't paying off. Then Arthur showed up and the two half brothers said they'd talk it over and let me know their decision. Their decision was to fire me."

"Mrs. Long, you insist on calling Wendell and Arthur the half brothers. Are they not real brothers?"

"Well, yes. But they were half brothers to Frank, my husband, who founded the company."

"So in your final discussion with Wendell Long, you still refused to heed his demand that you cut your lavish expense account spending?"

"I put my views in vigorous terms, but obeying or not obeying became academic because I was fired before my next sales trip."

Novack spends another hour exploring various angles of Oretta's expense accounts, then recesses the deposition for the night with the understanding that his questioning will be resumed at ten the next morning.

Driving back to Hutchinson's Wilshire office building, where Oretta had left her car, they agree that Novack has not damaged her case to any significant extent.

"Of course, he lays a logical base for your dismissal," says Bill Hutchinson, "but I'm not persuaded that expense accounts are his best bet. The fact is that most jurors will think a profitable company's expense account is fair game. Some of them will have had expense accounts that they padded now and then. Others will wish they'd had the opportunity."

Oretta thinks she did quite well, goes out with a friend that night for a festive dinner, then retires early with a John McDonald paperback. Refreshed by a good night's sleep, she drives herself to the building garage in Century City and shows up, eager for the fray this time, a few minutes before ten.

If Martin Novack, gloved or bare-fisted, planned to punch out his adversary, there is no sign of his intentions throughout a dull morning and a dreary afternoon of questioning that roams through the normally placid relationships and uneventful business negotiations prevailing at Bluebird Sportswear.

A flurry occurs just before noon when Novack goes into the aptitude and experience of the two young women hired by Oretta Long to help her sell Bluebird's products in four western states. It soon turns out that one of the women, a Marianne Kramer, had no experience and few skills save for a troublesome talent for antagonizing customers. Ms. Kramer, it develops, regarded owners of retail sportswear shops as an inferior breed who failed to measure up to the standards expected by an English literature major fresh out of Sweet Briar. Hurt feelings and bruised egos littered Marianne's path through the sports shops of the West.

Novack matches wits with Oretta over the extent and significance of Ms. Kramer's admitted deficiencies as a saleswoman. Nearing the end of the encounter, Novack seeks to complete his portrait of Oretta Long as an inept executive.

"Now, Mrs. Long, you hired Marianne Kramer after a single interview, did you not?"

"Yes."

"Did you consider a graduate of Sweet Briar with no background save tennis, horseback riding, and English literature to be the kind of assistant you needed for Bluebird sales?"

"No."

"Your answer is no. So, why, Mrs. Long, did you hire her?" Late that night Marty Novack would confess ruefully to his wife that he was glad he asked this question during a deposition and not during the trial when the answer would surprise him and injure his case. Marty had transgressed a cardinal rule of witness examination: Never ask a question to which you don't know the answer.

Oretta's smile is one of her sweetest. "I hired her because Arlene Fields sent her to me."

Martin Novack looks as if he's been slapped in the mouth with a wet fish. "Arlene Fields . . ." He checks himself, leafs about among his papers as if searching for something. "You mean Arlene Fields, Bluebird's vice president for finance?"

"Yes."

"Are you speaking of Mrs. Arlene Fields, the same woman who gave her deposition in Mr. Hutchinson's office?"

"Yes."

"Mrs. Fields sent Ms. Kramer to you for a job?"

"Yes. She said the young woman was the daughter of a friend and maybe she'd fit in sales."

Novack snatches at the word "maybe" as a drowning man grasps at a life preserver. "*Maybe* she'd fit in. So Mrs. Fields did not recommend the hiring of Ms. Kramer?"

"I took it for a recommendation."

"Did Mrs. Fields make her request in writing?"

"No. She just called me on the phone, then sent the woman over to my office."

"The decision, however, was yours, was it not?"

"Yes."

"So that you hired this young lady from a fashionable college, this girl with no experience and a snobbish attitude toward people in business—excepting herself, of course. You hired her?"

"Yes, I did."

Marty Novack tries to manage a concluding look of triumph, but can't bring it off. The brief round has gone to Oretta, but Bill Hutchinson enjoys it only slightly more than Novack does.

"You should have told me about Mrs. Fields," Bill whispers to Oretta. "I can't defend us properly when I'm surprised."

"Sorry, Bill," she whispers back. "I thought I told Susan Pennington. Maybe I didn't."

But no glove more than grazes Oretta in this second day of her deposition and at three in the afternoon, seemingly as a sign of desperation, the enemy attorney returns to expense accounts. He goes through a number of dinner checks exceeding $100 that Oretta had turned into the accounting department after entertaining this or that store owner.

"Now here we have a dinner check for two hundred thirteen dollars and fifty-five cents from the Blue Fox in San Francisco. You entertained customers at the Blue Fox, did you not?"

"Yes."

"Frequently?"

"Fairly often when I was in town, yes."

"Mrs. Long, I hand you seven dinner checks and ask you to please strike an average for us." Novack hands her some papers along with a pocket calculator. "Just punch in the figures, will you, and then divide by seven."

Oretta looks inquiringly at Hutchinson. Her attorney shrugs, "Sure. Go ahead."

After several minutes of work, Oretta looks up.

"So," asks Novack, "the average cost of the seven dinners is what?"

"One hundred eighty-nine dollars and forty cents."

"In each case, that is a dinner for two, is it not?"

"Yes." Oretta suddenly suspects where this is leading.

"Presumably, at those prices, with a fine wine. Is that right?"

"Yes, we always had wine."

"Now, Mrs. Long, the Blue Fox is one of San Francisco's most distinguished, opulent, and expensive restaurants, is it not?"

"Yes, sir." The "sir" drops unexpectedly with a cold cube of fear.

"It is famous for its velvet-gilt-crystal appointments and its luxurious atmosphere, is it not?"

"That's right."

"Now each one of these seven times, you entertained on Bluebird expense account a person named Thelma Vallejo, did you not?"

"Yes." Oretta feels like shrinking.

Novack leaves his chair, strolls to the window-wall looking toward the Pacific and the lowering afternoon sun. He gazes out for a moment before he turns around. "What sportswear company does Thelma Vallejo work for?"

"She's not in sportswear."

"Oh?" Novack feigns surprise. This time he knows exactly where he's going. "What company does she represent?"

"None. She does some occasional part-time bookkeeping for a wine outfit in Napa Valley. That's all."

"What connection does Thelma Vallejo have then that justifies her entertainment on a Bluebird Sportswear expense account?"

"Well, you see . . ." Oretta falters.

Hutchinson, sensing trouble, cuts in. "Hold it, Oretta. . . . Marty, we'd like a five-minute recess."

"Be my guest." Novack beams.

Hutchinson takes his client down the law firm's carpeted hallway until he finds an unoccupied office along the same tinted window-wall.

"All right," he says when they're inside, "I can see we're in for something. Just what is it, Oretta?"

"Well, I guess I shouldn't have put Thelma down on expense accounts."

"Why not?" Bill tries not to be sharp. He detests surprises.

"She doesn't actually qualify, if you know what I mean. She's an old, old friend of Frank's and mine. Years ago she loaned Frank a couple of hundred dollars to go to college. He always took her to dinner when he came to San Francisco and I, well, I just continued the custom. She's really a dear old lady and she adores fancy restaurants."

"Is that all?"

"Yeah, that's about it." Oretta has a sheepish look.

"Did you tell this to Susan Pennington?"

"No, I didn't."

"Why not?" Bill's gentle tone masks his irritation.

"I really don't know. I guess because I didn't think Bluebird accounting knew about it. After all, they never questioned me. You see, I put Thelma down as representing North Beach Court Togs."

"Does that exist?"

"No, it doesn't. Bill, I'm sorry. I know I should have told you."

"Why didn't you take Thelma on your own money? You weren't broke by a long shot." Bill has to make an effort now to remain sympathetic. He ranks clients who withhold from him on next to the lowest rung of the ladder, just one step up from the liars.

"I could have afforded it easily." Oretta's distressed now. "I guess

I thought Bluebird kind of owed Thelma, since she had given Frank his start and everything."

"All right, let's control the damage as much as we can. In your answers, stress the sense of obligation to the woman who helped the founder of Bluebird."

"Okay." She's crestfallen.

"And when you're back in the room, you should say that you're sending a check to Bluebird covering the cost of those dinners with Thelma at the Blue Fox. If I remember the numbers, that would amount to something under fourteen hundred dollars."

"Okay, Bill. I'm sorry. I won't surprise you again."

"No, please don't." He smiles and gives her arm an encouraging grip. "But cheer up, the slip isn't fatal by any means. Before a jury, the fact that Thelma helped the founder of the company in time of need will play pretty well."

He talks some more, building her morale. He has seen stronger characters than Oretta crumble in similar circumstances and he wants to make sure that she regains her confidence and poise.

Back in the conference room, Oretta's attempts at damage control succeed only partially. Novack goes over and over the incident, forces an admission that Oretta falsified seven expense accounts by listing Thelma Vallejo as a buyer for a nonexistent sportswear store. His questions stress the gourmet meals, the atmosphere of luxury, and the easy spending of Bluebird funds. She says she regrets the error and will make restitution. Still she feels like a common criminal under Novack's pounding.

Oretta finds herself at low ebb when she walks away from her deposition that evening. She stops for a drink with Hutchinson on their way to the parking garage and he tries to cheer her up.

"It wasn't good for our side, true," he says. "But this won't be a major feature in the lawsuit, especially since you will have repaid Bluebird. Coming to the end of the discovery process now, our case is just as strong, if not stronger, as it was the day we filed our complaint. You were summarily fired without substantial cause in violation of a valid contract. That's the guts of the case and that hasn't changed."

"But I've booted the chance for a good settlement, haven't I?" The blues close in about her as she realizes that the first money to be exchanged in her lawsuit will go from herself to the half brothers.

"You're not in as good position as this morning, but don't forget that Wendell is in a far worse spot than you are. Diana's testimony on those trips with Wendell could get him in bad trouble with Internal Revenue. He charged them all off as business expenses. He doesn't want that kind of thing aired in public. Believe me, we haven't heard the last of their settlement offers."

When they part, Oretta has regained some of her usual spirit, but that night, alone in bed, she feels herself sinking again. She wonders whether she shouldn't drop this suit. It's dominating her life increasingly. Just last weekend Fred, the dentist from Santa Barbara, whom she likes more than a little, told her the case "was becoming an obsession" with her. Why not jettison the whole thing, take her loss, and go out and get another job? Fred's right. The suit's with her morning, noon, and night. Also it's starting to undermine her resolve and her career by focusing all her energy on legal maneuvers instead of on what she likes best: work, her love-life, and her daughter, Amy.

The Costs

With the depositions concluded, Oretta's bill after ten months of the lawsuit now stands:

Balance to Date (Paid)	$25,713.25
Motion to Compel	
Pennington, preparation (1 hr.)	75.00
Hutchinson, argument (2 hrs.)	300.00
Depositions, W. Long, D. Kelbaugh	
Hutchinson, attendance (8 hrs.)	$1,200.00
Court original transcript 231 pages ($2.50 page)	577.50
Working copy transcript ($1.25 page)	288.75
Settlement Phone Call, Hutchinson (15 mins.)	37.50
Oretta Long's Deposition	
Review with Pennington (3 hrs.)	225.00
Hutchinson, attendance (16 hrs.)	2,400.00
Hutchinson, briefing (15 mins.)	37.50
Working copy (472 pages) ($1.25 page)	590.00
Total	*$31,444.50*

Mediation

17

Part Eight: *Rosemary's Progress*

Rosemary Wofford, who together with her brother borrowed $1 million from Chase Manhattan to start her home furnishings store, makes her first repayment in person. She hands a check for $25,000 to the loan officer who handled the transfer somewhat more than a year ago.

Her store in Hopewell, New Jersey, ROSEMARY'S PLACE, has done well if not quite up to expectations. She and Stephen, her secret financial backer, decided in view of the store's modest profits to pay off their debt rather than to expand to a second store at this time.

Rosemary is in no way discouraged, however. The store has made money from the start, she has gained a favorable reputation in the area, and she's busy and happy.

She's a fan of mediation. She settled the dispute with her brother under the guidance of Mediator Seymour F. Weinstein seventeen months ago, enabling her to get ahead with her career. She knows that had she chosen litigation, she probably still would be mired in the court action.

The Lawsuit

18

Los Angeles
November 19
Second Year

Part Eight: *The Flexible Experts*

Expert Witnesses

Late one fall afternoon in Los Angeles, Bill Hutchinson calls Oretta
Long and tells her he has procured "the best expert in the women's
sportswear field." Earlier Oretta had given permission somewhat reluctantly to Bill to hire an expert witness. Hutchinson contends that
the favorable testimony of a recognized authority, added to other strong
elements of her case, is vitally necessary to carry the day for her in
court.

Oretta does not rush to assent. In truth, she feels burdened by her
suit. It has been nine months since the depositions and now she is
deep into other interests. Fred Yeager, the widower Santa Barbara
dentist, got her a job as director of social activities at the Five Oaks
Country Club near Santa Barbara, and with Amy away as a sopho-
more at the University of Chicago, Oretta has been spending almost
every night in Santa Barbara.

Susan Pennington has called a few times to keep her abreast of nondevelopments in the case, but there has been only one occurrence of any note. Back in September Bill Hutchinson reported that Martin Novack had relayed a new settlement offer from the Longs. If she'd drop the suit, they'd give her $150,000, a 50 percent boost over their original offer. Oretta countered, reducing her demand to $850,000. The Longs rejected that and there the matter rests.

She quizzed Hutchinson at some length on the value of an expert witness and assented only after Bill emphasized the necessity of corroborating her testimony that her marketing performance and expenditures stood well above industry standards. He said he was sure that Novack would hire his own experts, trying to show that Oretta performed poorly and spent unduly by industry standards. This was no time, Bill contended, to skimp on experts needed to bolster her position. It made no sense, he said, to let the other side, obviously hurting since the revelations of Wendell's affair with Diana Kelbaugh, get the better of them on other issues.

Now, calling Oretta to tell of engaging Judiah Piggott, Bill explains just who the man is. The longtime executive secretary of the International Women's Sports Apparel Association, he's recognized as the nation's top expert in the female sportswear field. Retired from the Washington, D.C., headquarters for three years now, he lives in Florida and makes a good living traveling about the country as an expert witness in cases involving women's recreational wear. He is noted for his precision of detail, his vast knowledge of the industry, and his impressive demeanor on the witness stand. He charges $130 an hour and $750 per diem when away from home.

"We're really lucky to get him," says Bill. "When Piggott tells the jury that your performance in marketing far exceeds the average, the jury will be all ears."

"But how do we know he'll say that?" Oretta is skeptical. "What if he says I did a lousy job?"

"He can't, Oretta, because you did a great job. He'll come out here and spend a few days, get himself well briefed by all of us." Though Bill doesn't say so, he knows the subtle play between the expert and the party that pays his fee. He knows of few experts who failed to render a favorable report to the side that hired them. "If he gives us a report adverse to our interests, we just won't use him. But there's not much chance of that. Not with our solid case."

Bill Hutchinson's prediction comes true. Judiah Piggott flies in from Florida and spends three days in Los Angeles in January, reads all the interrogatories and depositions, interviews Oretta, and goes exhaustively into the issues of the case. Early in February Hutchinson receives a fourteen-page report written by Piggott in his Sarasota home. The expert says that Oretta Long unquestionably did an outstanding job marketing Bluebird's products. She increased sales each year and placed the line in a great many new retail outlets. Key quote: "From my experience in the field, I would say that few individuals in the industry could have outperformed Mrs. Long during those four-plus years. Given the greater than average production and returns problems, she did a most creditable job."

Oretta likes the report upon reading, but is not thrilled by it. She didn't take to Piggott, found him pompous and overly concerned with his own importance, patronizing to women, and terribly expensive.

Hutchinson calls her the next month at Dr. Yeager's home in Santa Barbara and asks permission to hire a second expert, this one an accountant who'll verify the losses she suffered under her contract because of her firing by the Long brothers. Oretta assents, but urges Bill to try to obtain some one "less snotty and less expensive than that fat little guy from Florida."

Avery Easthammer, chief accountant in his own small but reputable Los Angeles firm, worked many years for Price Waterhouse and Peat Marwick Mitchell before branching out on his own. Unlike Piggott, he likes to joke with his clients and tell spicy stories. He roots through the books like a busy mole, but aside from his numbers he's not a serious man. Oretta takes a quick liking to him when she comes down to Los Angeles so that he can interview her on her expense accounts, commissions, and allied matters.

"Aren't we taking a big chance?" she asks when they finish business. "We pay you a lot of money and then after you nose around, what if you decide the other side's right after all?"

"You're the first client who ever asked that." Easthammer lights up a cigar. "I guess everybody just assumes that I'll work hard and find that their position is the correct one." He tells a long story about serving as a neutral expert to decide the value of an office building.

Oretta grins. "That's an interesting story, but you didn't answer my question. What if, after we pay you all this money you're getting, you come up with a report that favors the other side?"

"Well, I guess you're just stuck, aren't you?" He returns her grin. "Look, we bow to no one in our maintaining of ethical standards. But that doesn't mean we're not aware of who hires us. I wouldn't lose any sleep over it, if I were you."

As he prepares to leave the law firm, Easthammer adds that the West Germans do it differently. "I appeared once in a court in Munich. Over there, the judge, not the suers, calls in the expert. So there's no tendency over there to juggle the figures to favor the side that hired you."

Not surprisingly, Avery Easthammer's lengthy report concludes after a thorough analysis that the Long brothers owe Oretta $1,300,000 under the breached contract that still had more than five years to run. In twenty-one typed and well-reasoned pages, he projects the probable rate of inflation, sales prices, and continued growth of the Bluebird market developed by Oretta.

After reading the paper, Oretta talks to Hutchinson and is surprised to learn that, under an agreement with Martin Novack, he is sending both the Easthammer and Piggott reports to the opposition attorney.

"I just don't understand that, Bill," she objects. "Why do we show our hand like that, letting him see the reports we paid good money for?"

"Two reasons," Bill replies. "First, we get to see his reports, so we can go to work before trial and refute his conclusions. We might want to take depositions of their experts so we can pin down the basis of their findings and then have them analyzed and picked apart by Piggott and Easthammer. Second, if the Longs are impressed with our data, it'll be just one more factor influencing them to throw in the towel."

"Sure seems funny to me." Once again Oretta has the feeling of being a mere pawn in an elaborate legal chess game that has an infinity of moves, few of which she imagined when she brought suit.

"That's the system," says the lawyer, "and if you think about it awhile, you realize that it has a pretty good logical basis."

But the logic escapes Oretta. "Gee, Bill, if the experts side with the people who hire them, what's the value?" She tells him what Easthammer said about the West German system.

"Yes, I realize that other countries do it differently," Hutchinson replies. "But we're suing under the American rules of litigation where we get the opportunity to put your best foot forward."

"With both sides hiring their own experts, it sounds to me like you'd always wind up in a Mexican standoff."

"Not if you're careful about the caliber of your experts. Also, remember you'd be in sad shape if you failed to hire an expert and the other side paraded three or four weighty authorities before the jury."

Oretta forgets her feeling of powerlessness as the lawsuit again fades into the background and she becomes absorbed in her new busy and happy life in Santa Barbara. Then in early March the mail brings a package from Bill Hutchinson that evokes some of the same feelings in more intensive form.

The package contains copies of two reports to Attorney Martin Novack from prospective expert witnesses. One of them, Herman G. Aller, is identified as former executive vice president of the U.S. Marketing Society, a trade association of corporate sales departments, and a top authority on marketing. Aller also is retired and makes his living traveling about the country as an expert witness.

Aller's nine-page report, completely at odds with the view of Judiah Piggott, holds that Oretta Long performed far below the average as a marketing officer for Bluebird Sportswear. Her techniques were outdated, her training and supervision of subordinates were nonexistent, Aller reported, she failed to keep abreast of developments in the field, and she sold far less than an expanding company had a right to expect.

Aller made a special case of women's tennis socks of the type bearing a colored tassel at the back. At a time when national statistics showed a boom in women's tasseled tennis socklets, many companies showing annual increases of 50 percent and up, Bluebird managed to up its sales of the line less than 5 percent over four years.

"For God's sake!" Livid at the accusation, Oretta can't wait for Dr. Yeager to come back from the liquor store. She reads him the offending section while he's replenishing the bar cart. "The goddamn tassel line!" she explodes. "What that crooked so-called expert doesn't say is that the lousy tassels kept coming off. About half of all that returned merchandise was made up of socks that had lost their tassels."

Oretta strides about the library with the report in her hand. "Imagine, Fred. They were attaching those tassels with the flimsiest, skinniest yarn you ever saw. So naturally, women players would lose them first time out or the little balls would tear off during the first laundry. But would that crummy mercenary ever mention that in his so-called 'expert's' report? Not on your life. He's paid to make his big lies look like the truth."

Oretta calls Bill Hutchinson the next morning to channel her anger and Bill welcomes her ire as he might an old friend.

"I'm glad you caught that, Oretta," he says. "That one example of the tassels will destroy Aller's credibility. I'll have Susan go through those invoices of returned goods and pick out all the tassel complaints. I'm going to love taking that one before a jury.

"With that obvious error by Aller, I think I'll skip taking his deposition because if I did, Novack might catch the mistake too. It's funny the Long brothers didn't pick it up. Oh well, maybe they're paying attention to business, not the lawsuit."

Once again Oretta realizes that what troubles her invariably delights Hutchinson. His reaction mollifies her somewhat, but she can't shake the feeling that this whole case has gone far beyond her control.

The second report is from Dwayne Hill Utley, leading partner in the accounting firm of Utley Stampler Israel, which ranks just below the big eight giants in the world of accounting. In nineteen pages, Utley demonstrates by graphs and columns of statistics that Oretta Long's marketing performance at Bluebird fell "far below the national mean in the women's sportswear field." He classified her sales results as "mediocre to poor." He used many of the same indices as Avery Easthammer, Hutchinson's accountant expert, but drew contradictory conclusions. The bottom line: Due to her wretched performance, Oretta owes Bluebird $700,000.

Thus a $2 million gap has opened in the value of Oretta's services as seen by two reputable accountants, one hired by the plaintiff and one by the defendant.

The suit is now into its third year and still another month goes by with only two phone calls from Susan Pennington linking Oretta in Santa Barbara to what she now thinks of as That Thing in Los Angeles. Then one day in early April, after another phone call from Susan, Oretta receives an affidavit in the mail, which she is to sign in the presence of a notary public.

The statement sets out many of the facts of the case, including terms of her contract, and concludes: "Affiant believes Bluebird Sportswear, Arthur and Wendell Long acted intentionally, in concert, and together, to wrongfully dismiss Affiant from her position, and to deprive her of moneys rightfully due her."

Susan has told her that the affidavit will accompany a motion for "summary judgment" that Hutchinson will file in Superior Court, urging that the court throw out all the counterclaims made by the Long brothers against Oretta and hand down a decision upholding Oretta's contentions, including the breach of contract, the core of the case.

"This is the next step," says Susan. "We've gone through the discovery process and the experts. Now we're asking the court to see it our way, that the defendants just have no case at all whereas we have evidence to prove all our contentions."

"Why didn't we file something like this a year ago?" asks Oretta.

"We didn't have all facts in then." Susan speaks with a voice of experience now. "We're in a position now to show the judge just how thin Novack's case is."

Oretta gets a notary at the bank to witness her signature and she mails the paper back to the law firm. Hutchinson had intended to set the hearing date immediately after the required sixty-day notice period, but Martin Novack, upon receipt of his copy and needing time to prepare his countermotion for a summary judgment, calls Bill and asks for a delay.

"It's that case in Japan again, Bill," says Novack. "I have to go to Tokyo tomorrow and I just can't handle the motion for summary now. How about a ninety-day extension? I promise that'll be my last request in this Long brothers case."

Bill accedes and another season goes by before both attorneys file their responses to each other's motions for summary judgment. Argument is set for two weeks later when the same Judge Stewart Otterbein hears Hutchinson and Novack tell him why he should throw the other attorney's case out of court. Each man takes fifteen minutes to present his views in the same motions court where several whispering lawyers lounge on the back benches and the old lady with the voluminous handbag shuffles about on her own mysterious mission. Judge Otterbein listens respectfully, punctuating the declamations with several hand-shielded yawns, then tells the legal combatants that he will take their points under advisement and let them know his decision in due time.

A week later the judge's clerk calls Bill with word of the decision. Otterbein has granted Hutchinson's request that the counterclaims of libel and slander against Oretta be deleted from the proceedings, but he has denied the rest of the motion. Balancing this, he has denied Novack's plea for summary judgment in toto. Both attorneys are directed to write up the orders for Otterbein to sign.

Oretta is confused when Hutchinson calls to give her the news. "I don't understand. What does it mean?"

"A victory for us, Oretta. The judge says there's no evidence you libeled or slandered anybody. So now the case goes forward without those baseless charges. Otherwise, not much has changed."

"If nothing much is changed, why did we go to all that trouble on the motion then?" Oretta, increasingly in a cranky mood as far as her suit is concerned, challenges every move now.

"Because there was always a chance, Oretta, that the judge would see it your way and throw out all the claims against you." Bill goes through the particulars carefully and quietly. "It doesn't happen often, but often enough so that we didn't want to pass up the shot."

"So what's next?" she asks halfheartedly. Oretta is enjoying her job as social director at the country club and has about decided that she likes it far more than a career in sales. Also Fred has mentioned marriage and she's considering it. She does love the man and her only worry now is how Amy will take it.

"That's about it until we get a trial date and the court sets up the time for a mandatory settlement conference," Bill replies. "Not much chance though of getting to court for another two years yet."

"Bill, I'm getting sick of this thing." Oretta voices what she's been thinking lately. "If I could get five hundred thousand out of the half brothers, I'd drop it."

"I understand. Well, let's see. Let me try out that figure on Novack. He asked me when we were arguing the summary motions whether you'd had any new settlement ideas."

"Yes, please see what you can do."

Hutchinson calls back the next evening. "Sorry, Oretta. Novack said the Longs won't go anywhere near five hundred. In fact, he said they wouldn't budge above their last offer of one-fifty. He says Wendell especially has hardened his attitude recently."

Oretta, wondering what caused the vulnerable Wendell to reject compromise so handily, finds out the next week when gossiping on the phone with Tina Jordan, the young woman who had worked briefly for Oretta at Bluebird before transferring to the personnel office. Miss Jordan had quit Bluebird for a better job several days earlier.

"Did something come out in your lawsuit about Wendell Long and Diana Kelbaugh?" Tina asks.

"I'd like to tell you, Tina, but my lawyer has cautioned me about talking about that aspect of the case. Why, what's up?"

"Well, you know everybody knows they've been having an affair." Tina laughs. "Rich, no? The Lutheran deacon and that tubby Diana who looks like she just came out of a cake bake-off for grandmothers only. Anyway, the word around Bluebird is that in some kind of questioning in your lawsuit, it came out that they used to meet a lot at some motel somewhere on the shore. So Wendell went and confessed to Grace, his wife, and they had a big row. But Grace finally forgave him on condition he knock off seeing Diana, which I guess he has. I don't know whether it's true, but that's the way the story goes around the office."

Oretta relays the information to Susan Pennington who says she'll tell Hutchinson. Susan is full of brave words. "It really makes no difference, Oretta, what Wendell Long's attitude is. You've got a solid case. Your contract was broken in violation of the law and you're going to win a good award in court."

It is now June, two years and one month since Oretta walked into Bill Hutchinson's office with her complaint against the Long brothers. With her trial still some two years away, she has invested substantial money.

The Costs

(Fifteen Months Since Last Billing)

Balance to Date (Paid in full)	$31,444.50
Phone Calls to Client	
Pennington (5 hrs.)	375.00

Hutchinson (3 hrs., 15 mins.)	487.50
Phone Calls to Experts, Novack, Court	
Pennington (3 hrs.)	225.00
Hutchinson (2½ hrs.)	375.00
Judiah Piggott	
Inquiries, Los Angeles (23 hrs. at $130 hr.)	2,990.00
Per diem (4 days, $750 per day)	3,000.00
Preparing report (11 hrs.)	1,430.00
Avery Easthammer	
Inquiries (24 hrs. at $150 hr.)	3,600.00
Preparing report (9 hrs.)	1,350.00
Analyzing Opposition Aller, Utley Reports	
Pennington (3 hrs.)	225.00
Motion for Summary Judgment	
Preparation	
Pennington (13 hrs.)	975.00
Hutchinson (2 hrs.)	300.00
Argument	
Hutchinson (3 hrs.)	450.00
Court costs	
Filing motion	50.00
Total	**$47,277.00**

Mediation

19

Part Nine: *Rosemary in Hopewell*

Four years and a month have passed since Rosemary Wofford settled the dispute with her brother through mediation. ROSEMARY'S PLACE, her home furnishings store in Hopewell, New Jersey, is flourishing, she is about to be married, her two sons are working during college vacations, and she has paid down the million-dollar loan on the store to $425,000.

Rosemary is marrying a Princeton University professor of architecture next week and preparing to honeymoon the rest of the summer in the Greek islands. She's happy, in love with her man and her business, and is thinking of opening a second store in a Philadelphia suburb.

Only one dark cloud drifts across her sky. She's had another argument with her brother, Stephen Holloway. Despite his pledge not to meddle in the operation of the store of which he's the major owner, he nevertheless has tried to play an active role in recent months, second-guessing some of her purchases, faulting her for "a lack of taste," and pressuring her to take on one of his trusted employees from Holloway Interiors, Inc.

Finally she blew up and they had an angry falling-out climaxed by a mutual decision to end their joint business venture. This time, however, the split is taking place without resort to legal measures because their lawyers had the foresight to provide a mechanism should they come to a parting of the ways.

Rosemary is obtaining her own loan of $500,000 to pay off the balance owed Chase Manhattan on the note that her brother co-signed. She also is paying her brother $75,000, or $25,000 for each year of their commercial alliance as provided in their agreement signed shortly after the conclusion of mediation.

This time, as angry as brother and sister have been, they remain on speaking terms and manage to dissolve their corporation without another explosion. Actually, Rosemary feels that after they both cool down, they can become friends again. They're both just too strong and independent to work well together.

The Lawsuit

20

Part Nine: *The Trial Draws Near*

The Pre-Trial Conference

At long last the date for Oretta Long's suit against the Long brothers appears on the horizon. It is now July and the trial is scheduled to start in mid-October, four years and five months after she filed her complaint, charging rupture of a valid contract.

Just today, this second Monday in July, Lawyer Bill Hutchinson and his assistant, Susan Pennington, are meeting to refresh their memories on the Oretta Long matter and to set out their position for the paper that Judge Oscar Fowler Runn has requested. Runn, one of Los Angeles County's settlement judges, will preside at the pretrial negotiation conference scheduled for next week, three months in advance of the trial.

Aside from a few phone calls to Oretta, court functionaries, and the experts, Hutchinson and Pennington have done very little on the case in two years. In fact, fourteen cartons of documents piled against the wall of Pennington's office offer the chief evidence that the lawsuit still lives. Susan Pennington, a novice when the suit began, is now an experienced attorney with five years of practice to her credit, including several appearances before a jury. Her firm now bills her services at $100 an hour, although the price to Oretta has not been raised and still remains at $75.

This morning, Bill has difficulty fixing the main points of the Long case again in his mind. Susan, who spent most of the previous day reviewing, takes him through the highlights.

"All right," says Bill when the issues and names once more take on a familiar cast, "I want to call both Arthur and Wendell Long as adverse witnesses. That way we get the jump on Marty Novack and plant an unfavorable picture of his chief witnesses in the jury's mind."

Susan is to prepare the position paper that will go to Novack as well as to Judge Runn. She and Hutchinson decide on their key issues, the thrust of the case, the list of witnesses to be called, and what they'll be expected to prove. They plan the scenario for a trial they calculate will last about eight days.

The next day Bill and Susan meet with Oretta Long, down from Santa Barbara, to decide on their stance at the upcoming settlement conference. Oretta's in a breezy mood. She is now Mrs. Yeager, for the past year the wife of Dr. Fred Yeager, the Santa Barbara dentist. At the Five Oaks Country Club, she now manages all of the club's services save golf itself. She's content, laid back, and hasn't thought much about her suit in months.

"Let's see now," says Bill. "When I talked to Marty Novack yesterday, he wouldn't budge from their last offer of one-hundred and fifty thousand and I had no authority to go below the five hundred thousand that you gave me two years ago, Oretta. So that's where we are, three-fifty apart. Any new ideas?"

"Look, Bill," she says. "I lost interest in this thing a long time ago. On the other hand, we've come this far and you say our case is still strong, so I favor sticking at five hundred. If they won't come up, why should I be the one to give in?"

"All right, that's fine with me." Bill nods agreement. "We go in at five hundred."

The next day they gather outside the chambers of Judge Runn in the main Los Angeles Superior Court Building, a four-story beige structure next to the Music Center. Hutchinson and Novack go into the office of the settlement judge while Oretta sits outside. The other occupant of the anteroom is Wendell Long, apparently here to represent both brothers. He and Oretta exchange nods, but little else. Oretta, reading the *Los Angeles Times*, is relieved to note that she can look at him without touching off emotional flares. Wendell, Arthur, and Bluebird all belong to an old chapter in her life.

Inside, Hutchinson and Novack sit down at a walnut conference table on either side of Judge Runn, a large, broad-shouldered, friendly but decisive man whose only known weakness is for the Los Angeles Dodgers. A group photograph on the wall indicates that he once played second base for the University of Southern California. Other personal memorabilia share wall space with some bright watercolors above bookcases that are filled with tan-and-red law books. The judge is ready for business, his jacket off, his tie loosened.

Oscar Runn takes only several minutes to sketch the essence of the case as gleaned through the position papers. "As I see it," he concludes, "you both have wide vulnerability. Mr. Novack, there's no question your people broke a contract. On the other hand, Mr. Hutchinson, it seems a case can be made that your client breached some of her agreements. She spent expense account money like a Hollywood producer and she actually wined and dined the nonrepresentative of a nonexistent San Francisco sportswear store."

"She returned that money some years ago, Judge."

"Doesn't change the guts of the case one bit." Judge Runn dismisses the repayment with a wave of his arm. "So one party with a weak case wants five hundred thousand dollars and her opponent with an even weaker case will offer only one hundred and fifty thousand dollars. And there, gentlemen, we have perfect grounds for a swift settlement. So what numbers did you come in with this morning?"

"I am not authorized to go above one-fifty, Your Honor." Novack's tone is slightly apologetic. "My clients are in no mood to settle and I had to argue to keep the one-fifty offer open. You see, Wendell's affair with Mrs. Kelbaugh is long over and his wife forgave him some time ago. So they don't feel vulnerable on that score."

"What about all those shipments of shoddily made sports clothes?"

Judge Runn fires the question like a prosecutor. "You think the Long brothers want that spread on the record?"

"They think that's all in the past. They haven't had a single shipment returned this year for poor workmanship. Your honor, they'll go to trial before they'll go a penny above a hundred and fifty thousand."

"We'll see about that." The judge appears to take it as a personal affront. "How about your client, Mr. Hutchinson? She must be sick of this case by now."

"She is, Your Honor," Bill replies, "but she's determined to get five hundred thousand dollars. Yesterday she said that since she's gone this far, she might as well go the whole way if they won't pay what she wants."

"All right then." The judge gets up and walks toward the door. "You go out and talk to your clients. I want to see some substantial movement from both parties." The judge moves like a man determined to give the state of California a full day's work for a day's pay. "I want to see Mr. Novack and his client in here then. Let's say in ten minutes."

When the judge's efforts resume, he is seated with Wendell Long on one side of him and Martin Novack on the other.

"Mr. Long," he asks, "has your lawyer told you that you have certain weaknesses in your case?"

"He has." There's a dogged quality about Wendell Long today. "But he also tells me that the other side has some glaring weaknesses."

"Has he discussed with you the legal position of Mrs. Yeager?" Judge Runn turns to Novack. "Have you pointed out to your client some of the legal problems he has to overcome?"

"We've reviewed our situation," Novack replies, "and that's why we've made a fair offer."

"Mr. Long," says Judge Runn, turning back to Wendell, "I can tell you from experience that you've got a weak case. You can settle today or you can go into a courtroom and open yourself to hundreds of thousands of dollars of exposure. If you settle this right now, you save yourself endless headaches and possibly a lot of money."

"We'll take the risk." Wendell's tone is firm. He wants to show the judge that he won't bend under judicial pressure. "I don't intend to go higher than one hundred fifty thousand dollars, which is a very magnanimous offer. In fact, I regret ever offering a nickel. Why, Oretta is working now and could have gotten a job a long time ago."

"Would you be willing to put an offer of two hundred on the table?" Judge Runn acts as if Long owes the money.

Wendell shakes his head.

"All right then. What will you add to your offer?" Runn makes it sound as if Wendell Long, by coming into the judge's chambers, owes an entry fee of some kind.

"Nothing." Wendell thrusts out his jaw, but with his flaccid face, the gesture looks more odd than stubborn.

"You wouldn't even make it one-sixty as a sign of good faith?"

"One-sixty is as far as I'll go." Sweat breaks out on Wendell's forehead. He's not used to arm-twisting judges.

"Good. We've got movement. The offer is now one hundred sixty thousand dollars." Runn stands up before Wendell changes his mind. "Tell Hutchinson to come in here with his client."

Runn loses no time after Oretta and Bill are seated. He addresses Oretta. "I understand you've remarried since this suit began. It's now Mrs. Yeager, isn't it?"

"That's correct, Judge."

"Mrs. Yeager, you're in about the same position as your former brother-in-law. Your outlook before a jury is chancey." He turned to the attorney. "Mr. Hutchinson, can you tell me why, at this late date, you think your client is entitled to half a million dollars?"

"Because, Your Honor, She was fired in violation of a valid contract. She was humiliated and the firing jinxed her career. Actually, they owe her more than we're asking."

"Did she make efforts to find other employment in the sportswear field?"

"No, I didn't." Oretta cuts in with an edge of truculence.

"Are you working now?"

"Yes. I'm manager of a country club outside Santa Barbara."

"Good money, I suppose?"

"It's a decent salary. I have no complaints."

Judge Runn leans toward her, his forearms resting on the table. "Now, Mrs. Yeager, you must appreciate, I'm sure, how a jury would react to you. Has your lawyer told you about the law of mitigation, that you must try to reduce your damages by finding other work? Have you considered whether the jurors would wonder just what damages you've suffered? You've got a good job and a new husband with whom, I assume, you share an enjoyable marriage."

"True, but I don't see what that has to do with the fact that I was fired without cause, breaking a contract. So what are contracts for, Judge?"

The judge chuckles. "Good question. In my experience, they're now and then of some benefit, but not much, when people don't trust one another. I am, nevertheless, bound by the law which upholds the sanctity of contract."

"Exactly." Oretta is warming now to the challenges of the negotiating game. "The law says you can't break contracts, which is just what the half brothers did."

"The fact remains, Mrs. Yeager, that you're asking a half million dollars."

"I know you're trying to get a settlement, Judge." Oretta offers a smile that has more sugar than sincerity. "So I'm willing to match Wendell's offer. I'll go home right this minute if he'll put up four hundred and ninety thousand dollars."

Judge Runn spreads his arms like an evangelist welcoming sinners to Christ. "More movement! Four-ninety and one-sixty. That leaves a narrowed gap of just three hundred and thirty thousand between the parties." He gets up suddenly from the table, "All right, let's start doing some serious business. You wait outside, Mrs. Yeager. I want to talk to the attorneys."

Judge Runn closes the door, walks back to the table, and stands for a moment. "All right, gentlemen, let's get down to it. We all know that it would be an affront to the taxpayers of California to take this simple little dispute into a courtroom and spend a week or ten days on it. This is a clear-cut factual matter. You certainly can put a price on it and not set yourselves in concrete three hundred thirty thousand dollars apart. It's an imposition on the state, the trial judge, and the jury. This case had no business getting this far." The judge takes his seat again. "Now then, I want to see some major movement here."

Novack shakes his head. "I'm not authorized, Your Honor, to go any higher. In fact, I had specific instructions not to go beyond one-fifty. I was surprised when Mr. Long broke through his limit himself."

"I see good grounds for settling this somewhere between two and two-fifty." Judge Runn looks at Hutchinson. "I've thought that ever since I read your position papers."

"Too low, Judge," says Hutchinson. His mind clicks back to the day, more than four years ago, when Oretta Long came into his office. He recalls that after a half hour of listening to her he had estimated a probable settlement figure around $300,000. "And, at any rate, like Marty, I'm not authorized to drop lower than the four-ninety that Mrs. Yeager has agreed to settle for."

"Do you gentlemen realize that average time-to-trial is now running about five years in this county?" He addresses them like a teacher trying to prod slow students. "If we don't get some cooperation soon from the bar and its litigation-crazed clients, we may grind to a halt in this building."

Both lawyers murmur appropriate words of sympathy, but neither offers a new number. Judge Runn talks for five minutes about constipation in the nation's courts, then looks at his watch—he has three more settlement conferences scheduled for today—and decides to send the attorneys back to their principals with instructions to warn them of the heavier legal fees that a trial will trigger.

Ten minutes brings no new developments, so Judge Runn talks again with Marty and Wendell, then calls in Bill and Oretta again.

"Have you discussed the legal fee situation with your client?" he asks Bill.

"Yes, sir."

"How much have you spent on this case thus far, Mrs. Yeager?"

"Something over forty-five thousand dollars."

"I told her, Your Honor, that her costs would run about two thousand a day in court with a trial of perhaps eight days. Together with pretrial preparation costs, she'd be looking at about sixty-five thousand dollars by the time the jury came in with a verdict."

"And, of course, Mrs. Yeager, that expenditure does not guarantee you victory."

"I know that, Judge." Oretta makes a sour face. "And if I lost, I'd feel awful."

"But you're willing to risk sixty-five on the chance of winning two-fifty—which is about the outside I could see a jury giving you in a case of this sort?"

"Don't forget I've already spent forty-seven thousand or thereabouts."

This kind of dialogue goes on for ten minutes, but each push by the judge makes Oretta more determined not to give in to this man. He's picked the wrong person for these muscle tactics, she tells herself.

The judge talks again to the two attorneys to no avail. When the noon hour arrives and Judge Runn must end his participation in the negotiations, he admits failure. Oretta finally has come down to $475,000 and Wendell has edged up to $175,000, but both swear they will make no further concessions.

"That's it then," says the judge to the lawyers. "You're still three hundred thousand apart and you're headed for trial. I've got just one piece of advice for both clients. They should go home and sleep on this matter. The people of California do not deserve to have this case taking up valuable time in their courts. Your clients are not blazing new trails in the law. They're just staking out new claims in stubbornness."

Bill Hutchinson has an early afternoon appointment in an important case, but he takes time for a quick lunch with Oretta. He's somewhat surprised at her unwillingness to yield more than she has and he picks about for an explanation.

"How did you like the judge?"

"I didn't like him." Oretta taps a cigarette on her thumbnail. "It wasn't, well, dignified in there with this big bruiser of a guy sitting around in his shirtsleeves. I thought judges had to wear those robes."

"Only on the bench. I suppose Judge Runn is strong medicine when you don't know him. I'm used to him. He belongs to the Teamster school of negotiation. He does throw his weight around."

"He's a bully and I didn't like him." She lights the cigarette and inhales. "You'd think I was some kind of public menace just because I wouldn't give up my rights. Here I wait more than four years and spend forty-seven thousand dollars and he wants me to give up and go home. What gall!"

"What does your husband think you ought to do about the case?" Hutchinson still hasn't got a handle on Oretta's renewed resolve.

"Oh, he's thought for a long time that I ought to take their offer and run." She smiles fondly. "But Fred's not a fighter. He's a dear man, and I love him a bunch, but he always prefers the easy way. . . . I'll tell you how I feel, Bill. I've come this far, investing a lot of time and money, and now I'm going to see it through."

While Bill isn't satisfied that he has the complete answer to Oretta's fighting stance, he recognizes the signs. He's seen this happen before. The client wearies of the game, wants to withdraw and hear no more about the matter, then on the eve of trial suddenly stiffens, demands all rights, spurns talk of concessions, and prepares to wade into court and spill some blood. Well, some win and some lose, and it's certainly not for him to say they shouldn't try for victory in court.

The Lawsuit

21

Part Ten· *And So It Ends*

Trial and Settlement

Over the next ten weeks in Santa Barbara, Oretta Yeager goes through an emotional cycle over the case. At first, in telling husband Fred of the settlement conference, Oretta strides about like a boxer, showing how she stood up to a Superior Court judge and made him take a piece of her mind.

Then the next week, with summer business at the club especially heavy, she begins to wonder why she is putting up with this dreary, nagging lawsuit down in Los Angeles. Why not take the $150,000—no, it was up to $175,000 now—and treat Fred to that world cruise they've been talking about? After all, the prospect of taking revenge on Wendell and Arthur, once so appealing, just doesn't set her juices flowing anymore. Wouldn't it hurt them to lose their $175,000? Of course.

But another week, with club business slackening again, she finds herself beside the pool, refreshed after doing a few laps, actually looking forward to the excitement and challenge of a trial. She is sure they can bring off a winner. And she would love to see Diana Kelbaugh and Wendell struggling on the stand to explain away their bedroom marketing conferences at the Pompton Arms. Would they admit all, now that Grace had forgiven Wendell? But how about Mr. Kelbaugh? No, no, the unknowns in this drama render it so crammed with suspense that she couldn't bear to abandon it.

Later still, when Fred is helping her prepare her testimony by tossing unexpected questions at her, Oretta undergoes yet another emotional reaction. The thought of taking the witness stand and opening herself to God-knows-what kind of smart-aleck questions from Martin Novack at first bothers her, then frightens and finally fills her with dread. She hates to be made the fool in public and she surely would be, what with the seven-dollar orange juice, the deluxe hotel suites and expensive dinners, and cheating the company by lying about Thelma Vallejo's identity. That night she dreams of making a horrible gaffe on the witness stand and the next morning she awakens with the dry taste of defeat in her mouth. What if she goes through all that mess and still loses the case? She'd not only be out some $65,000 in legal fees, as Judge Runn pointed out, but she'd see a fool when she looked in the mirror.

After each emotional switch, she calls Susan Pennington, sometimes to suggest questions to be asked the Longs, sometimes to find out if any new offer has come in, and sometimes just hoping for reassurance. Finally, the week before the start of trial, she reconciles herself to going ahead. She isn't happy about it, but in the end curiosity triumphs over fear. The decision, however, saps her energy. In the nights before trial, she sleeps poorly, twisting and turning and awaking with a start in the small silent hours.

In this week just prior to the trial, Bill Hutchinson tears himself away from a complicated case involving a shopping mall and seven of its tenants. He spends two hours a day supervising the building of the case that he'll present in court for Oretta Yeager. Susan Pennington and a paralegal take most of the week going through the fourteen cartons of material, writing synopses of the testimony of witnesses, lining up the batting order, and listing and marking 221 documents with little green stickers that say, "Plaintiff's Exhibit No. _____." They make three sets of the exhibits—one for the court, one for Novack, and one for themselves. They contact the expert witnesses and write out a trial scenario under Hutchinson's orders that is as detailed and comprehensive as the outline of a history textbook.

Hutchinson moves in and out of the preparations, but on the Friday before trial he spends a good six hours reviewing all aspects of Long versus Long.

Then at 3:10 P.M. on Friday, disaster strikes. Mrs. Janet Easthammer, wife of Avery, the accountant expert witness, calls to say that her husband has just been taken to Cedars-Sinai Medical Center in an ambulance with a ruptured appendix. He'll be operated on within the hour. Chances of him appearing in a courtroom anytime next week are almost nil, she says. Could he be examined and cross-examined in his hospital bed with a video recorder? Bill wants to know. That depends on his speed of recovery, says the wife. She doubts it. Instead she gives Bill the name of Elroy Dempster, an accountant friend of Easthammer's who has done considerable work as an expert witness in the ready-to-wear clothing field.

Susan Pennington finally reaches Dempster, who agrees to serve as an expert provided he's paid double his $150 hourly rate for coming in to the office on Sunday to familiarize himself with the facts. Bill approves the higher rate and the deal is closed.

Near the end of office hours on that Friday, Martin Novack calls with a last offer before trial. The Long brothers are now willing to pay $200,000 to settle the matter.

Bill calls Oretta in Santa Barbara. Oretta refuses to accept $200,000 but says she's talked it over with husband Fred and is now willing to reduce her demands to $400,000. That too is a final figure, not to be lowered under any condition, she says.

Bill relays the information to Novack who contacts Wendell Long. The Bluebird executive refuses to pay $400,000 and declines to make a counteroffer. When he said $200,000 was his last offer, he meant it, he says.

"So we've still got a gap between us of two hundred thousand," says Bill.

"That's it, Bill," says Marty. He has come to like Hutchinson over the years of this case. "Too bad. If they left it up to us, we could settle this thing by dinnertime "

"Hell, yes. We'd split the two hundred down the middle and go off and have us a TGIF drink." Bill sighs. "Well, see you in court Monday, Marty."

At 9 A.M. October 14, Hutchinson and his little army—Susan Pennington, Oretta Yeager, a paralegal, a messenger, and the two expert witnesses—gather in a huge courtroom of the Superior Court building to hear the reading of the master calendar by the presiding judge of Los Angeles County.

The room, reputed to be the largest courtroom in California, overflows with attorneys, plaintiffs, defendants, and witnesses who are vying for one of the more than one-hundred courtrooms in the building so that they can begin at last to try their long-pending disputes.

Hutchinson's group spies Martin Novack with Wendell and Arthur Long and a cluster of other witnesses. Hutchinson confers with Novack, then tells Oretta and her fellow witnesses that they may wait outside if they wish or remain in the crowded room. Oretta decides to stay and see the action, but the others file into the corridor.

Oretta and Hutchinson sit in padded theater-type seats while the presiding judge, Ralph J. Isaacs, a thin graying man with a somewhat petulant voice, calls off cases and assigns them to courtrooms. He uses a microphone to make himself heard over a ceaseless murmur of voices.

"Good grief," Oretta whispers to Susan. "This is more like a cattle auction than a courtroom."

A fit of coughing runs like a string of small firecrackers around the ballroom-sized assignment center. The smog hits high on the index today.

"Oretta Long versus Arthur Long, Wendell Long, and Bluebird Sportswear, Inc." rasps the judge after a time. "Are the parties ready?"

"Ready, Your Honor," Hutchinson, rising, calls it out. Novack stands to announce that the defendants are ready as well.

"How many days?" The judge looks impatient.

"Eight," says Novack. Hutchinson nods his agreement.

The judge says nothing in response. Instead he continues calling his calendar. He runs through some eighty cases before taking a short break. The growl of several hundred conversations fills the room during the intermission, then the judge takes his place on the bench again and begins to assign specific courtrooms. Within a few minutes, he has exhausted his available spaces and Oretta realizes that Long versus Long won't start today after all.

Judge Isaacs soon returns to the Long case, thirty-first on the list. "Assignment or trail?" he asks the opposing attorneys. "Trail, Your Honor," says Hutchinson. "Trail, Your Honor," repeats Novack.

"All right," says the judge, "Long versus Long is trailing."

Hutchinson explains as he escorts Oretta into the hall. "That means we're on the waiting list for a courtroom. It might be a couple of hours. It might be a week. We have to keep in touch. If we took 'assignment,' we'd have to wait another three months." Outside Hutchinson tells his group that everyone must remain on the alert, reachable within minutes. Once notified of an open courtroom, they must assemble within two hours.

Oretta, who has driven down from Santa Barbara and who's staying at the old Beverly Hills Hotel, decides that she'll return to the hotel and do her waiting beside the swimming pool. She's annoyed, feels she's been tricked. Having wound herself up for battle, she finds herself away from home and job with nothing on which to expend her energy.

Hutchinson goes back into the courtroom, makes his way to the "Rent-A-Beeper" desk and obtains one of the radio-wave devices for a week at a cost of $25. Court congestion in Los Angeles is so thick and time so valuable that rental of the beepers has been moved inside the big Department 1 courtroom to save hard-pressed attorneys a few minutes. Some lawyers awaiting trial space take their beepers to the golf course or yacht harbor, but Bill wants his for protection when he visits the shopping mall tenants who are suing the owners for $4 million. He'll swing in a few minutes from Long versus Long to Cruise Travel et al. versus Pollenode Corp.

Four days pass in tense waiting. Oretta feels like a prisoner. She doesn't want to leave the hotel and despite the atmosphere of breezy action about the place, she soon tires of tanning by the pool, drinks in the Polo Lounge, working crossword puzzles, breakfast on her little terrace, and dining alone. Susan Pennington comes out one night for dinner and Oretta confesses that she now wishes she'd never started the lawsuit in the first place. Susan assures her the discomfort and anxiety are almost over. Oretta crosses her fingers. She hopes so.

The call comes at last at 11:25 A.M. on Friday while Oretta is

fretting over 6 Down, Milk in Acapulco, five letters, third letter probably a c. She is told by the operator at the law firm to get herself at
once to the Superior Court building where Long versus Long will
begin promptly at 1:30 P.M. in the courtroom of Department 28.

Oretta arrives with minutes to spare to find that Hutchinson and
Novack already are closeted with the trial judge, Clovis R. Gabrielson. Hutchinson soon enters from a door near the judge's bench and
beckons to Oretta.

"Another effort to settle, this time by Judge Gabrielson," says Bill.
"Novack has come up to two hundred and fifty thousand dollars. Are
you interested at that figure? We're getting into reasonable territory
now, Oretta."

She shakes her head. "No. I'll come down to three hundred and
fifty thousand, you can tell them, but that's the lowest I'll go." The
instant she says this, Oretta realizes that subconsciously she has changed
her mind since last night when, sick and tired of the whole thing,
she told Fred that she'd take anything over $200,000 that Wendell
would come up with. But it's a game again and she's not about to be
outplayed in the final period.

"Okay, it's three hundred and fifty thousand as our last word." Bill
turns to leave.

"Bill . . ." She's about to give ground again, but when Hutchinson faces her, she changes once more. "Nothing. Go ahead. I'll talk
to you when you finish in there."

Hutchinson returns in a few minutes. No dice. They're still $100,000
apart. They seat themselves at a table for counsel and Novack and
the Long brothers take chairs at the other table a few yards away.
They all rise when Judge Gabrielson takes his place on the bench.

A bailiff calls thirteen jurors into the jury box and the judge questions them as a group as to acquaintance with the principals, famil-
iarity with Bluebird Sportswear, and prejudices. Two jurors are excused
as a result of this exercise, and two replacements are called.

Hutchinson and Novack then question individual jurors under the
ancient voir dire procedure. At the end of an hour and fifteen minutes, two more jurors have been excused.

Judge Gabrielson, a small precise man who wears glasses with thick
black rims, tilts his head to listen to the whispered message of a court
functionary, then declares the court in recess for ten minutes.

Martin Novack follows Hutchinson into the hall, takes his arm, and leads him a few steps away from the crowd around the courtroom entrance. "I've got a new offer from the Longs," he says.

"It figures," says Bill. "If this case doesn't settle today, we've all got rocks in our head."

"They'll go to two hundred and seventy-five thousand. That's cash."

"What kind of cash?"

"A check drawn on Bluebird. Mrs. Yeager can cash it tomorrow."

"Fair enough," says Bill. "Let me talk to Oretta and I'll get back to you soonest."

Hutchinson goes back to the plaintiff's table where Oretta is chatting with Susan Pennington. He relays the new offer. Oretta cocks her head, reflects, appears uncertain.

"What do you think, Bill?" She questions with her eyes as well.

"I just told Marty that if we can't settle this case today, we've all got rocks in our head. I would suggest this, Oretta. Tell them you'll settle for three hundred thousand, then give me authority to negotiate. That means I'll bring you back something better than two seventy-five."

"I was thinking of going down only to three twenty-five." Oretta is once again into gameswomanship. "After all, they only went up twenty-five."

"That's all right, if you want to do it." Bill nods. "But my hunch is they'll have a psychological barrier somewhere below three hundred. Don't forget, if you settle today, you're going to save yourself about fifteen grand in fees." He smiles. "My clock's running, you know."

"Okay, let's go your route. Tell Novack I'll pack up and go home for three hundred thousand cash. You and I understand that we'll agree to something between two seventy-five and three."

Hutchinson says, "Fine," and as he turns away on his mission, Oretta sighs heavily. Four long years and five longer months, for God's sake.

Hutchinson finds Novack waiting for him in the hall. "Oretta wants three hundred, cash. Put the check in her hot little hand and she'll climb off your clients' backs."

Novack shrugs. "Bill, I have no authority to go above two seventy-five."

"Come on, Marty. We're down to only twenty-five between us.

Let's make a joint recommendation to our clients."

"For how much?"

"We split it clean down the middle. That makes it two hundred eighty seven thousand five hundred. A deal?"

"You're on." He shakes Bill's hand. "Two eighty-seven five it is."

Bill does not loosen his grip. "Cash, right?"

"Sure, if they accept, by immediate corporate check."

The two lawyers stride back into the courtroom. The judge has not yet returned.

"I got you two hundred eighty-seven thousand five hundred dollars," he says to Oretta. "That's a joint recommendation from Marty and me to our clients. Is it okay?"

"I'll take it."

"Good." Hutchinson looks toward the defendants' table and catches Novack's eye. Bill holds up a circled thumb and forefinger.

Novack nods and calls, "Give us a few minutes." The attorney is seen in conversation with the Long brothers. Wendell and Arthur seem to be disagreeing, but then they both make assenting gestures and Novack gets up and comes over to the plaintiffs' table.

"We have a settlement. Two hundred eighty-seven thousand five hundred dollars cash."

Novack and Hutchinson shake hands and Hutchinson nods toward the Longs.

"I don't have to shake hands with them, do I?" asks Oretta.

"I think they'd just as soon leave things as they are," says Novack.

Judge Gabrielson comes in a few moments later, raps his gavel, and looks inquiringly toward the two lawyers.

"Your Honor." Hutchinson stands up. "We have just reached a settlement."

"Counsel come up to the bench, please." Judge Gabrielson beckons to the attorneys.

Ten minutes later the judge has entered the stipulated judgment on his record, dismissed the jury, adjourned court, and notified officials in Department 1 that this courtroom is cleared for the next case in line.

Arthur Long writes out the check at his table, Novack hands it to Hutchinson who in turn delivers it to Oretta Yeager. She kisses him on the cheek, puts the check in her purse.

"Come on," she says to Bill and Susan, "I'm buying for the celebration drink. You know, TGIO, thank God it's over."

They go to Otto Rothschilds, a bar located downstairs in the nearby Music Center, much frequented by lawyers and litigants from the Superior Court building. They sit at the bar and when the drinks are served, they clink glasses.

"Good job, Bill," says Oretta.

"I had an understanding client and a fine associate," Bill replies. "Too bad we couldn't have gotten you more money, but you know the final figure was within a few thousand of what I'd kind of thought all along. After a time in this business, you get a nose for settlement numbers."

"What was your estimate?"

"Three hundred thousand."

"Close enough," says Susan. "I wish I could call them that neatly."

"Did you think we'd actually go to trial?" asks Oretta.

"The first of the week, yes. Neither you nor the Longs seemed to want to make serious concessions. But then, this morning, when the Longs came up to two hundred and fifty thousand dollars, I knew we'd never get to the first witness. Two-fifty meant they were earnest and that they didn't want a trial. My hunch is that the Kelbaugh matter still bothered Wendell more than we thought. Especially the IRS angle."

"Bill, if you had a fix on the probable settlement figure a long time ago, why didn't you try hard for a settlement back a couple of years?" Oretta lights a cigarette as she talks.

Bill shakes his head. "Nope. The case wasn't ripe. Not until we got under the gun of trial did both you and the Longs get serious about negotiation." He leans back and stretches. "That's the great thing about our system. It seems complicated and unwieldy at times, but it has a curious way of imposing justice at the right time."

"You mean you think this settlement was just?"

"Perhaps not from our viewpoint, Oretta. But if I were a judge, looking closely at both sides, I think I'd say that if justice wasn't served, it came pretty damn close."

Oretta shrugs. "Maybe, but it took a long hard haul to get there."

"But until a lot of time passed," says Susan, "you wouldn't have been willing to settle, Oretta. Remember how you used to cuss the half brothers?"

"You got something there." Oretta isn't sure. She needs time to evaluate what has happened today. She beckons to the bartender. "Another round, please."

"Not for me." Bill glances at his watch. "I've got to get back to the office. I have a shopping mall case that's proving an awful tough one. Trouble is, the other side's got most of the law going for them."

So Oretta has a final drink with Susan, then the two women kiss good-bye and wish each other luck.

Oretta Long Yeager's case ends four years, five months, eight days, and four hours, twenty-five minutes after she walked into Bill Hutchinson's law office with fire in her heart, vowing to sue Arthur and Wendell Long out of their socks.

Final Costs

Balance to Date (Paid in Full)	$47,277.00
Phone Calls Since Last Billing	
Hutchinson (1½ hrs.)	225.00
Pennington (3 hrs.)	225.00
Preparation for Pretrial Settlement Conf.	
Hutchinson (3 hrs.)	450.00
Pennington (8 hrs.)	600.00
Phone, Settlement Talk, Novack	
Hutchinson (45 mins.)	112.50
Settlement Conference, Judge Runn	
Hutchinson (4 hrs.)	600.00
Phone Talks with Client	
Hutchinson (½ hr.)	75.00
Pennington (2 hrs.)	150.00
Preparation for Trial	
Hutchinson (10 hrs.)	1,500.00
Pennington (24 hrs.)	1,800.00
Paralegal (24 hrs.)	960.00
Oct. 14 Expected Trial Date	
Hutchinson (2 hrs.)	300.00
Pennington (2 hrs.)	150.00
Rent-A-Beeper	25.00
Experts on Standby	
Elroy Dempster (emergency Sunday prep. at overtime rate) (8 hrs.)	2,400.00

Four days (per diem $200)	800.00
Judiah Piggott 4 days ($750 per diem)	3,000.00
Trial Day	
Hutchinson (3 hrs.)	450.00
Pennington (3 hrs.)	225.00
Total	$61,324.50

The Practice of Mediation and Litigation:
The Longs and the Holloways 22

The Bill Hutchinson–Oretta Long Yeager story is fiction, but it is based squarely on the experience of one of us in working with clients, courts, and opposing attorneys within the prevailing litigation system. We believe the steps taken fairly represent the typical procedure in a case of this size and kind. However, lawyers who read this book will take issue with and argue about Hutchinson's strategy and tactics. Some may contend that certain aspects of the case have been exaggerated, whereas other traditional procedures have been slighted or underdeveloped by us. Some attorneys would not use interrogatories, for example. Others may argue that further motions could have been filed to advance Oretta Long's cause or a different approach taken toward her damages.

All the critics may be right or partially right, for the practice of law is an art in which hunch, luck, psychology, timing, and a bent for drama all play a part. It is not a science in which the use of certain established procedures will yield a definite predictable result. A hundred lawyers attacking a common problem might take twenty, fifty, or even a hundred different paths to persuade a judge or jury.

The point of the Long versus Long lawsuit story lies not in the value of the specific steps taken by Bill Hutchinson and his friendly foe, Marty Novack, but in the fact that when they finished their painstaking labors, their motions, and their depositions, they settled the case on approximately the same terms that they could have embraced some years earlier.

Never forget that some 95 percent of all lawsuits filed in America are settled or withdrawn prior to a decision in court. We keep coming back to that figure because it is basic to the kind of legal approach we advocate in this book. Bill Hutchinson and Marty Novack, like thousands of American lawyers, are aware that only about one in twenty lawsuits reach the trial and decision stage and yet they act as if almost every case they handle were headed for a courtroom, judge, and jury. Mark Bianchi, on the other hand, not only knows the percentage but conducts himself accordingly.

Some lawyers and laypersons alike may contend that our Rosemary Wofford–Stephen Holloway case was easy for Bianchi to take to mediation, whereas the dispute between the widow Long and her late husband's half brothers was much less amenable to the mediation process. We think not. We hold that the great majority of disputes are ready for mediation at an early stage. We believe that had Hutchinson and Novack been mediation-minded, they could have persuaded their clients to take their dispute to mediation with a distinct probability of success.

Most lawyers who've spent their careers at litigation argue something like this: Oh, but the average case has to "ripen." Clients aren't ready for mediation at the outset. They aren't ready emotionally. They want to fight, to sue the bastards. Not until the facts are fully developed through the litigation process does the client realize that settlement may be preferable to the risk of an expensive and perhaps painful trial.

We hold that many lawyers, schooled in the wear-'em-down tradition, adopt a negative attitude toward early settlement that quickly permeates the thinking of their clients.

Why shouldn't attorneys explore all avenues to settlement as early as possible? Do they not have an obligation to their clients to set out the merits of swifter, less-expensive mediation or arbitration as well as the advantages of conventional litigation? We believe that they do.

Federal Judge H. Dale Cook of Oklahoma believes that lawyers who fail to inform their clients of alternative methods to litigation should be held accountable. "Without a question," he says, "a lawyer representing a client stands in a fiduciary relationship. There exists a *duty* to resolve a client's legal disputes in the most reasonable, inexpensive, and expeditious manner. A failure to so inform a client as to all means and methods to resolve such dispute would constitute a breach violation of the attorney's fiduciary duty."

U.S. Senator Mitch McConnell of Kentucky has introduced federal legislation that would require lawyers to inform their clients of the alternatives to litigation. With other voices joining those of Judge Cook and Senator McConnell, we may be nearing the day when attorneys will be subject to malpractice charges if they limit their advice to litigation without mentioning the alternatives.

In the Long versus Long dispute, a skilled mediator might have gone beyond the mere transfer of dollars to help fashion a resolution more satisfactory to the contending parties. Oretta Long, it may be recalled, at first wanted her job back. A good mediator, working with that fact, might have brought Arthur and Wendell Long to concede that Oretta had been an effective marketing officer in the face of production and return problems. She had a base of broad customer goodwill, dating from the early days with her husband, which Bluebird Sportswear might have used to its advantage while expanding under the brothers.

The mediator would understand that Arthur and Wendell had legitimate quarrels with Oretta's performance. She had become independent of their lines of authority, had used less than proficient assistants, and had indulged her taste for travel luxuries at the company's expense.

The three Longs obviously once had envisioned a long-term business relationship when they signed a ten-year contract without giving it much thought. Starting from that intention, a good mediator would have stressed the ways in which Oretta still needed the company and those in which the company still needed her. Instead, Bill Hutchinson at the outset assumed that Oretta's anger at the brothers automatically cast her into an adversarial role. That role quickly hardened into the studied animosity of the plaintiff at law. On the other side, Marty Novack, treating Arthur and Wendell as enemies of Oretta, paved the way for them to adopt conventional roles as the outraged defendants in a lawsuit.

In essence, Hutchinson and Novack stressed all the negative aspects of the Longs' dispute, whereas Mark Bianchi, in a somewhat similar conflict between Rosemary Wofford and her brother, emphasized the positive factors. We do not disparage Hutchinson and Novack as lawyers. They did what comes naturally to men trained to litigate through the complexities of our legal system. We do, however, find fault with a system that encourages those playing the game to accentuate the negative and slight the positive.

In litigation, judges, often persons of great talent and insight, sit passively as neutral umpires. They are neither negative nor positive. Mediators, on the other hand, have a personal stake in working out an agreement. They therefore use their influence, skills, and knowledge of human nature to stress the upbeat possibilities and to dampen the negative fires that frequently consume the disputants.

The mediation process, although it might have vented feelings about Wendell's affair and Oretta's high style of expense account traveling, would have cast these negatives aside as it focused on positive ways in which Oretta, Arthur, and Wendell Long might have framed a new business relationship. If exploration proved that to be infeasible, mediation would have come up with a simple exchange of money, seeking a solution that harmed and alienated the parties as little as possible.

Instead litigation magnified Wendell's liaison with Diana Kelbaugh out of all proportion to its significance among the factors leading to the firing of Oretta Long. By exposing similar inviting vulnerabilities to opposing lawyers, the lawsuit way essentially distorts the total picture and thus makes an equitable solution more difficult.

Lawyers who review their conduct of a trial often talk about winners and losers and what tactics they might have used to crush the opposition. Mediators who reminisce tend to talk about the healthy new relationship they helped create and in special memorable cases of the burst of mutual goodwill that engulfed the contending parties at the finish.

New Roads to Justice

23

"*Discourage litigation. Persuade your neighbors to compromise whenever you can. Point out to them how the nominal winner is often a real
loser—in fees, expenses and waste of time.*"

ABRAHAM LINCOLN, 1850

It has taken almost a century and a half for Lincoln's advice to sink
in, but now, at long last, Americans have set about transforming
their system of civil justice. They are seeking swifter, cheaper, simpler, less combative, and less rule-hobbled ways of settling their disputes or gaining redress of the wrongs suffered at the hands of others.

The old county courthouse, with its leisurely trials, its memorial
Civil War cannon on the lawn, and its odor of disinfectant and stale
tobacco smoke coasting along its worn marble floors, no longer holds
a monopoly on the delivery of justice. The courthouse does remain,
as it should, the hub of our civil legal system. Its judges and juries
still function, not only as the symbols of our equality before the law,
but as the chief umpires of our quarrels and our brawls. Now, however, a movement to resolve most disputes outside the courthouses
and away from judges and juries gathers momentum and more ad-
herents every year.

America has had previous waves of legal reform—the rise of family and juvenile courts earlier in the century, the coming of mandatory collective bargaining between management and labor in the New Deal years, the birth and growth of small claims courts—but none of them had the scope, power, financing, and quality of leadership of the current surge.

This contemporary movement, under way in strength since the mid-seventies, seeks to establish for the aggrieved citizen a whole range of options in gaining satisfaction, recompense, or restitution for his or her injuries. It gains its name, "alternative dispute resolution" or ADR, from the variety of methods now open to the person who once had but three choices: (1) try to work out a personal settlement, (2) hire a lawyer and threaten to sue, or (3) forget the whole thing.

While still retaining those options, an injured person or group now may pursue any one of a number of other paths to justice. In general these alternative methods are cheaper, faster, simpler, and less stressful. They provide satisfactory resolution of the great majority of disputes, but for certain cases, particularly those involving public policy, fundamental rights, or a wide imbalance of power, conventional lawsuits remain the preferred and most suitable vehicle. A brief description of the alternative methods follows.

Mediation.   As we saw in the Wofford–Holloway chapters, two or more parties seek to work out their own solution under the guidance of a neutral third person. Sometimes two or more mediators participate. Mediation, the most promising of the alternative methods, almost always takes place outside the formal legal structure although many court jurisidictions now mandate the procedure for certain categories of disputes such as child custody.

In most mediations only the good faith and self-interest of the principals insure that the agreement will be carried out. However, any mediation agreement can be turned into a binding instrument if the parties so wish. The mediator merely turns him or herself into an arbitrator at the end of the sessions and signs the agreement as the arbitrator. If the document is then filed in court, the agreement can be enforced legally.

Arbitration.   Disputants argue their cases before a mutually selected umpire who then hands down a decision much like a judge. Arbitration can be voluntary or mandatory. Hundreds of thousands of contracts provide for mandatory arbitration of disputes, especially in the construction industry. Most arbitration rulings have the force of law. A growing number of jurisdictions now require arbitration of court cases where less than a stipulated amount, such as $50,000, is involved. In Pittsburgh and Philadelphia court-mandated arbitration of this type of case has been in successful operation for more than three decades. Much of the nation's private arbitration takes place through the American Arbitration Association, a nonprofit organization that has been functioning since 1926.

MED–ARB. Disputing parties agree to submit their fight to mediation with the proviso that they will go on to binding arbitration if the mediation fails. This is frequently used now in commercial disputes where the contract stipulates arbitration. The parties try mediation first in the hopes of saving time and money because arbitration usually entails more formal legal presentations.

Mini-Trial. Invented by lawyers in 1977 to resolve a knotty patent infringement dispute, the mini-trial has been used largely by corporations that are headed toward an expensive lawsuit. In the mini-trial, company lawyers present the core of their opposing cases to a panel composed of top executives of the contending corporations. Instead of a lengthy trial, the mini-trial takes two or three days. After hearing the presentations of fact and law, the executives seek to settle the case on the basis of what they've learned. The process sometimes fails, but it has produced many striking successes.

Ombudsman. This development, imported from Scandinavia, calls for the appointment of an official within an institution who entertains complaints from customers, clients, employees, and other individuals, investigates the charges, and tries to give satisfaction to the complainant. Many newspapers, business corporations, government agencies, and universities now have ombudsmen. The concept is spreading.

Rent-A-Judge. The contending parties gain court approval to hire a neutral person, often a former judge, who hears abbreviated versions of the cases opposing lawyers would present in court. He or she then renders a decision. Unlike binding arbitration, the private judge's ruling may be appealed through the regular court system.

Quickie Jury Trial. Opposing lawyers present brief versions of their case to a jury selected from the regular jury pool. The jury, deliberating only a short time, renders a nonbinding verdict. Lawyers may then question jurors as to their reactions. Often settlement follows this telescoped trial because both sides get a clear picture of what a real jury might do. The process, formally known as the summary jury trial, was developed by Federal Judge Thomas Lambros of Ohio's north district, one of many state and federal judges who are seeking to shorten and simplify the procedures of civil justice.

Variations of these new methods spring up around the country as more people learn to innovate in resolving their differences.

The new roads to justice, with but few exceptions, lead to resolution within weeks or months as opposed to the years consumed by lawsuits. And most disputes, whether commercial or personal, can be mediated or arbitrated to a conclusion at a tenth to a fifth of the costs they would incur in the legal process leading to trial.

The new methods also encourage a psychology of compromise in those who use them, holding the potential for a profound transformation in the way Americans tackle disputes, confrontations, and settlements. The conventional civil lawsuit pits plaintiff against defendant as adversaries, one of whom will win and one of whom will lose at the conclusion of an often bruising struggle. "As a litigant," the scholarly Judge Learned Hand told the New York Bar more than a half century ago, "I should dread a lawsuit beyond almost anything else short of sickness and death."

Today's alternatives to lawsuits would please the famous jurist. Instead of setting the disputants in the concrete stance of courtroom enemies, the new methods seek common ground and often yield a mutually crafted agreement in which neither party wins nor loses. This is especially true in mediation where each side gives some to get some and seldom winds up with the sour feelings of a courthouse loser.

The alternative methods owe much of their recent growth to the intolerable congestion in the nation's courts. In Los Angeles, the country's largest trial court system, it now takes fifty-nine months, just one month shy of five years, for an average case to get to trial. There has been a great deal of talk about Americans becoming more litigious, that more of us are rushing into lawsuits now than our fathers and grandfathers did. However, an Institute for Civil Justice (Rand Corp.) study indicates that may not be the case. In Los Angeles, at least, the civil lawsuit filings have remained fairly even with population growth in recent decades, about one filing a year per 200 people.

What has happened is that many of the cases have become far more complex. Simple suits, like debt collection, used to comprise about half the docket. Now heavy court traffic occurs in personal injury suits—product liability, malpractice, sex and race discrimination in employment, civil rights. These take more time and cost more money. Americans may not have become more litigious in the number of lawsuits we file, but we have become more deeply enmeshed in the intricacies of the law and the legal system.

Support for an Idea

Alternative dispute resolution has taken on the trappings of a major movement, prodded along by such influential critics of the legal system as former President Jimmy Carter, former Chief Justice Warren Burger, and President Derek C. Bok of Harvard.

Chief Justice Burger rattled the cages in his 1984 State of the Judiciary address: "The entire legal profession—lawyers, judges, law teachers—has become so mesmerized with the stimulation of the courtroom contest that we tend to forget that we ought to be healers of conflict. For many claims, trials by adversarial contest must in time go the way of the ancient trial by battle and blood. Our system is too costly, too painful, too destructive, too inefficient for a truly civilized society."

Burger placed the prestige of his office in the forefront of the ADR movement and used tough language in speech after speech. "We may well be on our way," he warned, "to a society overrun by hordes of lawyers, hungry as locusts, and brigades of judges in numbers never before contemplated."

Harvard's Bok in his annual report to the Board of Overseers criticized the American legal system in 1983 as expensive, cumbersome, and wasteful. "There is far too much law for those who can afford it," he said, "and far too little for those who cannot."

He said the law siphoned off "exceptionally gifted" young people from business, teaching, engineering, and public service, producing a "giant bar" to run a complex system "that is the most expensive in the world, yet cannot manage to protect the rights of most of its citizens."

"Everyone must agree," he said, "that law schools train their students more for conflict than for the gentler arts of reconciliation and accommodation. This emphasis is likely to serve the profession poorly. Over the next generation, I predict, society's greatest opportunities will lie in tapping human inclinations toward collaboration and compromise rather than stirring our proclivities for competition and rivalry."

Former President Carter, viewing us as "overlawyered and underrepresented," said that by "resorting to litigation at the drop of a hat, by regarding the adversary system as an end in itself, we have made justice more cumbersome, more expensive and less equal than it ought to be."

Supreme Court Justice Sandra Day O'Connor, citing a great need for such alternative methods as mediation and arbitration, said that "the courts of this country should not be the places where the resolution of disputes begins. They should be the places where disputes end—after alternative methods of resolving disputes have been considered and tried."

Former Chief Judge Lawrence H. Cooke of New York, who pushed installation of the nation's first state-supervised dispute resolution service, noted that "mediation offers a radical departure from the judicial process. Most notable is its dedication to the parties' self-resolution of their disagreement. The mediator differs from the judge in that he or she is not present to hear evidence and then to inform the disputants as to the resolution of their problem.

"Instead, the mediator encourages communication, assists in the identification of areas of disagreement, as well as agreement, and then works to bring the parties to a resolution, but a resolution reached and defined by the parties themselves."

U.S. Senator Mitch McConnell of Kentucky, author of several bills to stitch alternate dispute methods into the legal fabric of the nation, says the American "mad romance" with civil lawsuits must end lest the system snarl itself beyond hope.

The major drive for alternative methods dates from 1976 at a meeting with the head-spinning title of "National Conference on the Causes of Popular Dissatisfaction with the Administration of Justice." Leaders dedicated the conference to the late Roscoe Pound, a brilliant dean of the Harvard Law School, who had been a tenacious critic of the nation's judicial and legal system since 1916.

The movement is becoming organized as professional groups spring up and multiply. The American Bar Association has an active committee on dispute resolution. We now have the Society of Professionals in Dispute Resolution (SPIDR), the Academy of Family Mediators, the National Academy of Arbitrators, the Family Mediation Association, National Association for Mediation in Education, and the National Association of Community Justice among others. State and regional societies have been formed to advance mediation and other forms of alternative dispute resolution.

Backing an Idea with Money

Foundations and corporations are funneling substantial sums of money into the drive to widen and modernize our system of civil justice. Some are motivated by a simple desire to save time, money, and energy on legal matters. Others with a broader philosophical approach seek a system that fosters cooperation, compromise, and mutual benefits rather than one that tends to lock disputants into hard adversarial roles producing winners and losers in a climate of ill will.

The National Institute for Dispute Resolution in Washington, D.C., holds seminars, publishes papers, and gives research grants in the field. Originally funded by the Ford, Hewlett, MacArthur, and Prudential Foundations and the American Telephone & Telegraph Corporation, NIDR now attracts contributions from other foundations and corporations.

Another organization, the Institute for Civil Justice, established within the Rand Corp. in 1979, has spent more than $14 million publishing a series of excellent research studies on facets of the nation's civil justice system. In general, the reports supply ammunition to critics of the system and to those experimenting with alternative ways to resolve disputes. The list of those financing the Institute's work reads like an honor roll of American corporations, most of which obviously want to cut their legal costs.

Still another heavyweight in the movement is the Center for Public Resources, launched in New York City by James F. Henry, a foundation veteran. Financed by corporate treasuries, CPR tries to persuade large corporations to settle their differences by means other than full-blown litigation. More than 200 corporations have signed CPR's pledge to explore alternative methods of resolving disputes that arise with any of the corporate cosigners, thus obviating some of those long courtroom battles between economic giants that sometimes cost tens of millions of dollars. CPR also sponsors symposiums and publishes one of the best of the many newsletters now flourishing in the ADR field. The Center's slick-page monthly is entitled "ALTERNATIVES to the High Cost of Litigation," a succinct expression of the reason many corporations help finance the Center.

Foundations have pumped substantial funds into the ADR movement, supporting research, backing conferences, and financing publications and experiments. One of the most active has been the William and Flora Hewlett Foundation (computer money), which has distributed more than $14 million in the field under the direction of Robert C. Barrett, the officer for programs in conflict resolution. Hewlett provided initial funding for twelve university projects, the Program on Negotiation at Harvard, and centers for dispute resolution studies at Colorado, George Mason, Hawaii, Michigan, Minnesota, Northwestern, Penn State, Rutgers, Stanford, Syracuse, and Wisconsin universities. Hewlett has also backed a number of neighborhood justice centers including those in Atlanta, Honolulu, and Minneapolis.

Law Schools Get in the Act

An indication of the growing strength of the ADR movement is its impact on the nation's law schools. A decade ago not a single law school offered a course in dispute resolution, according to Ronald L. Olson, former chairman of the American Bar Association's special committee on dispute resolution. Now more than half the nation's law schools offer one or more courses on mediation and other alternatives to courtroom litigation.

Located at Harvard Law School, the Program on Negotiation, a consortium of Boston schools devoted to the theory and practice of dispute resolution, has taken a leading role as an innovator in the field. Emory University now has its Carter Center for conflict resolution. The University of Missouri School of Law publishes the annual *Missouri Journal of Dispute Resolution* and Ohio State's College of Law has begun publishing its semiannual *Ohio State Journal on Dispute Resolution*. Willamette University College of Law has established a Center for Dispute Resolution and the *Willamette Law Review*, like some others in the country, has devoted an entire issue to the alternative methods.

A decade ago law school library shelves held only meager materials for classroom use on the alternatives to litigation, but now scholarly papers, articles, and books pour from the word processors of academia. A weighty text, *Dispute Resolution*, bound in the familiar tan-and-red covers of law books, was published by Little, Brown & Co. The authors, Law Professors Stephen B. Goldberg, Eric D. Green, and Frank E. A. Sander, play prominent, innovative roles in the ADR movement. Business schools also have caught the ADR fever. More than twenty business schools, including those at Dartmouth, Columbia, and Michigan, offer courses in the negotiation field. Professors report that student interest has ballooned in the last decade.

The Liability Insurance Mess

While no single remedy exists for the crisis in liability insurance— multimillion-dollar jury awards to injured persons, soaring insurance rates, and the closing down of vital facilities and services because of the inability to obtain insurance coverage at any price—mediation already has made modest headway toward reducing costs and restoring a measure of sanity to the chaotic area of the law of personal injury.

Despite the attention paid to the occasional spectacular failure of a widely used product or the huge damages awarded the cruelly maimed victim of medical malpractice, the vast run of personal injury suits involve people who have undergone only moderate "pain and suffering" and who have scant chance of winning a fortune from even the most liberal jury.

Sizable numbers of those with claims against manufacturers, physicians, and business concerns are now accepting the offer of insurance companies to mediate, arbitrate, or otherwise negotiate the matter without going to court.

In 1983 the Travelers Insurance Companies, in conjunction with the American Arbitration Association, embarked on a pilot mediation venture, forerunner of a large mediation program launched by Henry J. Naruk, general counsel of Travelers. In 1985 Travelers offered claimants alternate dispute resolution channels in more than 3,000 cases nationwide. Somewhat less than 500 accepted. In 1986 acceptances jumped to 1,400 out of 3,745 offers. Naruk says he estimates that Travelers is saving about $1,000 per case in legal costs by avoiding litigation. While there are no statistics on finances of claimants, presumably they are saving as much or more than the company. Both sides, of course, reach settlement much faster.

"No question that these alternative forms are here to stay in the liability claims field," says Naruk. "They're bound to grow as people become more familiar with them."

Another project initiated and pursued by Travelers involves twenty-one insurance companies, including some of the largest, funneling claims into five dispute resolution firms operating outside the court system. The program, started in late 1986 and centered in Hartford, found that 65 percent of the early mediations resulted in agreement. The remaining claimants went on to litigation. At the outset all claimants had the option of mediating or going at once into a lawsuit.

Much more than the introduction of mediation and arbitration needs to be done to bring about reason and justice in the area of liability claims, but whatever finally happens, alternative methods will be a major part of the package.

Abundant research indicates the high tolls of litigation. A major insurance industry study shows that 36 percent of the amounts paid out for general liability claims goes for legal and defense costs. A 1984 Honolulu study estimated that only about 30 percent of the sums spent on liability claims in the construction industry reached the aggrieved party. Philip J. Hermann, chairman of Jury Verdict Research of Cleveland, offers some persuasive figures: If a plaintiff with a $100,000 product liability claim settles before litigation, he will average $64,990 net. But if he goes through a lawsuit, the eventual jury award will return him a net average of only $24,282.

Since mediation costs both sides much less than litigation, we firmly believe that wide use of mediation would not only increase amounts received by claimants, but would allow substantial cuts in insurance premiums, especially in those that have reached absurd heights.

Feuding Spouses

Mediation works best where the feuding parties share a relationship that will continue no matter how angry the contenders get with one another. Customers and companies, contractors and subcontractors, wholesalers and retailers of a product, citizens and City Hall, neighbors, relatives, all must look forward to some kind of continuing connection. You can't eat your own trash just because you had a run-in with the city sanitation department. You can't deport your nephew because he fails to pay the $250 he owes you.

Perhaps no segment of quarreling America is better suited to the process of mediation than married couples who have decided to split. No matter how much they may loathe each other, all but a small fraction of them are fated to have some kind of a relationship in the future. Those with children will have to talk to each other for years to come. In recognition of this fact, many jurisdictions, including the state of California, now require mandatory mediation in child custody cases. Eighteen states are using mediation in some manner to resolve custody and visitation arguments.

But money, property, mutual friends, relatives, all the bric-a-brac of married life will compel communication of some sort between even childless marital warriors. Having elected to dissolve THE relationship, they nevertheless find themselves snared by remnants of the same intimate connection.

Recognizing that litigation tends to intensify the bitterness of splitting couples, many toilers on the rocky turf of domestic relations— social workers, judges, court personnel, and even lawyers—are urging mediation for those about to end their marriages. Divorce mediation clinics are springing up around the country and a number of court jurisdictions now stipulate mediation as a first step for those heading into divorce. Maine has made mediation mandatory prior to any contested divorce action. In Hawaii divorcing couples must attempt mediation within seventy-five days of filing the case. Although statistics are fragmentary, mediation for divorce and child custody disputes appears to be growing faster than in any other field.

Gail Rappaport of Santa Barbara, California, provides a flesh-and-blood sample of the trend. A successful divorce lawyer, she became distressed at the bitterness attending the legal splitting of wife and husband. She recalls strolling on the beach one day and "wondering whether this is the way I want to spend my life," serving as an instrument for increased hostility between people who once loved each other. The answer was no. She switched from litigation to mediation and in 1982 opened the Mediation Center for Family Law in Santa Barbara.

Barking Dogs and Wayward Kids

Within a decade several hundred centers for resolving personal and neighborhood disputes have sprung up around the country. The most successful perhaps are those located in Atlanta, Honolulu, and San Francisco, but most large cities now have one or more places outside the courts where people can go with their complaints against neighbors, friends, relatives, and trespassing children. New York State has a dispute resolution center in more than fifty counties now and plans to have one soon in every one of its sixty-two counties.

Commonly called Neighborhood Justice Centers or Community Justice Centers, the facilities normally operate with a small professional staff and a large number of volunteers who go through training courses to become mediators. The most successful ones work in conjunction with the local court system. Judges refer a variety of cases to the centers for mediation: arguments over property lines, the relative cleanliness and appearance of adjoining properties, fallen trees, roaming children, barking dogs, loud parties, and blaring stereo sets. Complaints about noise predominate in one form or another. To savor the range of these day-by-day quarrels over the frictions of modern living, just think of the last five controversies on your own street. Whatever they were, the neighborhood justice centers have handled them many times over.

Until they become institutionalized in the life of the community, these centers appear to depend for their success on the energy, commitment, and executive ability of the director. Typical of the high-energy movers and shakers is Edith B. Primm of Georgia's Justice Center of Atlanta, Inc., who not only sells local court officials on the value of mediation, but raises funds, rallies her troop of volunteers, runs her center, and spreads the word at local and national seminars and conferences.

In Hawaii the success of the Honolulu Neighborhood Justice Center (about 1,000 mediations a year with over 700 agreements) has inspired a number of spin-offs, the most promising of which brings mediation to the many military bases on the island of Oahu. Closely packed housing, the strictures and discipline of military life, racial strains, and the sporadic absence of husbands on maneuvers intensify emotions in the normal run of neighborhood quarrels. Traditionally commanders have had to take time from their military duties to settle hassles over turf, noise, kids, parties, and intake of booze. Now, under the sponsorship of the Armed Services Y.M.C.A., trained volunteers are mediating many of these cases and some commanders automatically turn over housing-born disputes to the Mediation Service. The potential for the nation's huge military establishment is impressive.

At the back of this book readers will find a state-by-state directory of mediation services. These include neighborhood justice centers, offices of the American Arbitration Association, law firms offering substantial alternative methods of dispute settlement, family and divorce mediators, and a variety of offices specializing in solving conflicts outside the court system.

First Corinthians 6: 1, 7

"Dare any of you, having a matter against another, go to law before the unjust, and not before the saints? . . . Now therefore there is utterly a fault among you, because ye go to law one with another. . . ."

The Apostle Paul's admonition to the early Christians to steer clear of the Roman system of civil justice found its way not only into the pages of the ancient New Testament but also into a modern Los Angeles home where a group of lawyers had gathered to study and discuss the Bible. Members of the Christian Legal Society, the attorneys found Paul's words troubling and challenging. Long discussions followed in 1979 and 1980 as to whether a sincere believer could simultaneously serve both Christian principles and American legal institutions that transformed disputing citizens into adversaries primed for courtroom combat.

Result: Foundation of the Christian Conciliation Service, which offered counseling, mediation, and arbitration as ways to resolve differences outside the civil justice system. The new facility quickly expanded and now, only a few years later, includes branches in more than thirty cities nationwide with every indication of continued growth. CCS offices, listed in the directory in this book's appendix, provide private methods of settling a broad range of disputes from commercial to marital. People of varied occupations serve as conciliators, but lawyers remain the nucleus of professional help.

This kind of creative reaction to our sluggish legal system has resulted in such groups as the Mennonite Conciliation Service, Society of Professionals in Dispute Resolution, Academy of Family Mediators, and statewide dispute settlement programs in Massachusetts, New York, and North Carolina.

The VORPS

The process of mediating disputes has spread into almost all phases of American life including the area of minor crimes when victims and offenders are brought together with a mediator to work out penalties and restitutions together with reconciliation if possible.

More than sixty of these VORP (Victim–Offender Reconciliation Program) centers are operating in the United States, Canada, England, and New Zealand. The daddy of them all, the most successful and the best-known, is the Night Prosecutor Program in Columbus, Ohio. The Columbus program has been going since 1971, has resulted in the mediation of almost 300,000 misdemeanors, currently handles about 30,000 cases a year, and has spawned imitative programs in other cities. NPP has a professional staff, but employs an active squad of mediators, mostly law students.

The most common problems brought to mediation are threats and various forms of assault, usually between members of a family, neighbors, or friends. Officials running the program claim a settlement rate of 93 percent when both parties appear for a hearing.

The Graybeards of Mediation

Although the modern surge of mediation and arbitration has come in the last decade, both forms have historic roots in America. Many of the original colonies settled almost all disputes outside the English courts. In 1635 Boston's town meeting decided that no residents could "sue one another at lawe" until the dispute had been heard by an arbitration panel. Merchants generally preferred to settle their money differences by arbitration. Almost all the early Utopian communities handled their conflicts outside the courts. Dedham, founded outside Boston early in the seventeenth century, referred disputes to mediation by several "judicious" or "understanding" men.

In the successive waves of immigration to the United States, the newcomers, fearful of strange justice, tended to steer clear of the courts. The Dutch, Scandinavians, Greeks, Italians all had their own forums for resolving disputes within their ethnic group. The Jews in East Coast cities, particularly in New York and Baltimore, began settling their personal, commercial, and religious differences by arbitration and mediation and by this century had established many local arbitration boards. The Chinese, at first denied citizenship and the target of onerous discrimination, settled all their disputes among themselves, usually by mediation within the family, benevolent or business associations flourishing in the big city Chinatowns, or through the offices of a "go-between" who specialized in mediating fights.

The federal government itself got into mediation before World War I when the newly created post of Secretary of Labor was given mediation powers and a U.S. Conciliation Service was established. In 1926 Congress created the National Mediation Board to handle disputes involving railroad unions. Then in 1947, with passage of the Taft–Hartley labor–management relations act, there came into being the Federal Mediation and Conciliation Service, a remarkable federal agency which mediates tens of thousands of disputes between labor unions and their employers.

This lean agency with 216 mediators stationed about the country has few rules, little red tape, and not many surplus employees. Some mediators operate out of a single-room office with a tape machine on the telephone and no secretary. Very little paper accumulates because the parties to a dispute are notified that no records will be kept and all notes torn up at the end of mediation. Since each mediator works alone, using his or her own style, there is but minimal contact with Washington headquarters, thus escaping the usual evils bred of bureaucracy and hierarchy.

More recently the establishment of the Community Relations Service within the U.S. Department of Justice has brought federal officials with mediation talents into towns and cities torn by racial strife. Many states have created mediation agencies to help solve labor–management disputes.

Into the Classrooms and Corridors

Nowhere has the spread of mediation been more promising than that into schools of the nation. In some inner-city schools, where brawls and knifings were common occurrences, mediation has cut the crime rate significantly. Once they get the hang of the process, elementary and high school students take pride in forging agreements and keeping their pledged word.

Some of the school programs have attracted special attention. Cleveland's Law and Public Service Magnet School began training students in mediation in 1982 and since then the program has expanded into a number of elementary schools. Student mediators not only settle disputes among their peers but train other students in the process. In New York City a program of student mediation that began at William Cullen Bryant High School in Queens has spread to other schools. In New York's Suffolk County a program under way for six years trains students, parents, teachers, and administrators to mediate disputes in the school communities of three districts. In San Francisco elementary pupils and teachers have been trained by the city's Community Boards, the equivalent of neighborhood justice centers. In North Carolina's rural Chatham County, elementary and high school teachers and students are trained to mediate disputes in the schools.

Some states, particularly California and Massachusetts, now provide by law for the mediation of disputes between parents and school officials over the special services to be extended slow, limited, or otherwise handicapped children. Both Massachusetts and California have a corps of professional mediators for cases of the children with special needs. Formerly such disputes were decided after formal hearings with sworn testimony, witnesses, and other courtlike features. While such "due process" hearings are always an option of the parent, most differences are now resolved in the relaxed informal atmosphere of mediation that, according to evaluators, satisfies most parents and school officials.

Mediation within the schools holds great potential, not only as a means of curbing teenage violence but for its impact on adult society as school-trained mediators grow into positions of responsibility. Most kids like the process. It gives them self-esteem, pride in helping peaceful change, and a tool to deal with tough group situations.

Back to Business

The business of America is business, as Calvin Coolidge once observed, and it is mediation in the area of commercial disputes that holds great promise of swifter, cheaper justice for the nation's economic enterprises, freeing executives from time-consuming involvement in litigation. In business the dollar reigns and money, for settlement purposes, is infinitely divisible.

Commercial disputes, as knotty and as emotion-strewn as some may be, quickly come down to money. And money dictates the route a company will follow to collect what it believes a customer or supplier owes it. If mediation can fetch approximately the same amount cheaper and faster (and time translates into dollars) as a lawsuit, then a wise executive will choose mediation. That simple exercise in arithmetic and logic is propelling more and more businesses into mediation and other alternatives to litigation. Catering to the trend are such new enterprises as EnDispute in Chicago, American Intermediation Services in San Francisco, Judicate, Inc. in Philadelphia, Dispute Resolution, Inc. in Hartford, U.S. Arbitration Service in Seattle and other cities, and ADR, Inc. in Boston. In addition, the American Arbitration Association, with thirty-three offices around the country, recently has expanded and stressed its mediation services as an auxiliary to its historic role in arbitration.

If the growth in alternative forms continues at its current rate, by the turn of the new century a majority of the disputes now litigated through the courts may be settled outside the conventional legal system. The hopes of such men as Abraham Lincoln, Roscoe Pound, Learned Hand, and Warren Burger for a dual system that yields justice within a reasonable time at a reasonable cost will be realized

Personal Reflections:

What Mediation Does for the Mediator

24

Gerald S. Clay's Account of His Experiences with Mediation

Mediation often rewards the mediator as much as it does the parties who decide to settle their dispute by talking it out with a third person.

Perhaps that opinion of mine stems from a matter of temperament. I know there are some lawyers who are happiest when they're battling it out toe-to-toe with another legal slugger who also enjoys crushing the opposition. Actually, I don't know many of that type. Most lawyers I know are negotiators, peaceable men and women who like their work best when they can achieve an equitable solution. The only reason they don't take their cases to mediation, in my view, is that they're unfamiliar and ill at ease with the process. They are trained to sue, not talk, even though talking is what they spend most of their career doing.

I've chatted with many mediators who feel much as I do. When I ask them what they like about mediating a dispute, they use such phrases as getting "a big charge out of it," "personal fulfillment," "a sense of usefulness," "helping people," "doing it the commonsense way," or "solving the problem quickly."

Bringing off an agreement cossets the mediator's ego in a special way. Usually both parties have a positive feeling toward me and that warms me in a manner that no courtroom victory could. A well-crafted, solid agreement buoys my confidence. After all, I've gone into the pit with two angry combatants and witnessed their transformation, under my guidance, into reasonable human beings who, through self-interest, arrive at a solution that yields mutual benefits. This kind of ego satisfaction is at once more subtle and more deeply enduring than the kind that comes from winning an important case in court. The glow of defeating someone soon fades. The pride that comes from shaping a solution where everyone wins almost never loses its luster.

Then come the mediation bonuses, those rare, special times when the contenders start off in a rage, slowly calm down, and then reach an agreement in a burst of euphoric fellowship. Several times I've seen the once clashing foes embrace one another and then go out with me for a drink to celebrate our newfound wisdom. Most mediators have experienced similar climactic outpourings of goodwill.

Although mediation has had a major impact on my life, I had only passing contact with the art for most of my career. Then one fine Honolulu day in April 1984, my whole view of our legal system changed sharply.

On that day, after seventeen years of practice as a conventional attorney, largely on commercial matters, I took a course in mediation sponsored by the American Arbitration Association. The session featured Robert Castrey, formerly the Honolulu chief of the Federal Mediation and Conciliation Services, as a principal trainer.

We viewed a mediation training film and did several simulated mediations. I found I slipped naturally into the role of the neutral third party who guides, prods, and nudges the disputants toward an agreement. The process felt good to me. In a sense I had nothing to learn, but instead instinctively seemed to make the proper moves. Unlike litigation, it was not ponderous, detailed, and highly structured. I left the training in an exuberant mood. A door had opened and I had glimpsed new vistas in the practice of law.

Federal Judge Cook of Tulsa, Oklahoma, one of the many jurists trying to speed traffic within America's congested legal system, says that when he first heard of mini-trials several years ago, "a light bulb" went on in his head. A light flashed in my head too and, like Judge Cook, ever since then I've seen the law through new eyes.

Actually I had watched mediation at work as far back as 1977 in some truck driver–building supplier contract negotiations. Though I was impressed with the procedure, it never occurred to me that mediation could be used elsewhere than in the labor–management context. Obviously I had my blinders on. I was trained as an adversary attorney and I saw myself as a gladiator for my clients, doing combat in the courts.

I had done a lot of arbitration, however, taking some of my own cases to arbitration and deciding perhaps 150 cases as an arbitrator. Arbitration saves time and money, but it much resembles the court system in that contending parties fight with one another and then turn their fate over to a third person who decides the issue.

Mediation, after my brief training, appealed to me in part because it allowed the disputants to forge their own settlement with the help of a neutral third party. I realized I always had been vaguely dissatisfied with the adversarial lawsuit. Somehow court decisions offended my sense of fairness and balance. Very few people are 100 percent right or 100 percent wrong—except in a courtroom when a judge or jury announces its decision.

Eager to conduct a real negotiation, I got my chance a few weeks later when Keith Hunter, head of the Honolulu office of the American Arbitration Association, named me as mediator in a dispute between a lecturer and a film company. Although both contenders started off in a fever pitch of emotion, throwing barbs back and forth, they soon settled down and five hours later we had an agreement. Total cost: $750. The parties split the tab.

A number of things about this initial mediation impressed me. First, the speedy resolution. It took only ten days between the decision to mediate and the implementing of the agreement. This would have been impossible had they taken the matter to court. At the end of ten days the average lawsuit still lies in embryo.

Second, the cost. Had this gone to a lawsuit, each side would have spent several thousand dollars even if the issue never reached trial stage. A trial, of course, would have increased expenses substantially.

Third, the relationship and attitudes of the contenders. After blowing off steam at the outset, they wound up in a friendly mood, ready to do business again. A lawsuit, by contrast, would have exacerbated their original hostility and probably have prohibited any further business dealings.

Fourth, my own mood, I left the mediation on a high. This, I realized, was the kind of lawyering I wholeheartedly enjoyed. I had helped people reach a workable solution to their altercation and had been paid for doing it. I felt like a healer who had cooled angry foes and guided them to a fair result that pleased both sides. Don't misunderstand me. If the game is a win-or-lose lawsuit, I like to win as well as the next person. But this process felt so much better. I had helped carve out a solution, rather than outplayed, outwitted, or outschemed a losing party who went away empty-handed and bitter.

The Mediator's Style

Although I anticipate the continued growth of alternative forms of dispute resolution, at the moment mediation remains a minor percentage of my practice. At this writing, about three years have passed since I took the mediation training. I have acted as a paid mediator in eighteen commercial cases, all but two of which resulted in an agreement, and one husband–wife hassle that I helped settle. I've also been a volunteer mediator at Honolulu's Neighborhood Justice Center in four family disputes. In addition I've taken seven of my own commercial cases to mediation and helped write the agreements that disposed of six of them. The seventh is pending.

Every mediator has his or her own style. Mine is the bulldog approach, not in the sense that I growl at or antagonize the contending parties, but in the sense that I sink my teeth into the case and determine that I won't let go until an agreement is signed, whether it takes all day and night or all week. I have a set procedure, first talking with both parties together and then shuttling between them with offers and suggestions, but my tactics vary with the personalities and circumstances. I'll wheedle, cajole, promise, threaten, praise, challenge, confront, blast, manipulate, anything within the bounds of ethics and propriety to get those signatures on a durable agreement. That word "durable" is pivotal. There is no sense forcing an agreement that one party dislikes or submits to under duress. The agreement must serve the interests of all (sometimes a number of people are involved) contending parties or it will be broken, probably sooner than later.

I am an intervening mediator rather than one who goes by the book. I take the line followed by Frank Schoeppel, the current federal mediator in Hawaii. A veteran of hundreds of labor–management fights, Frank believes that mediators should use any tool at their disposal to gain an agreement. The point of the game is to settle the dispute. Later they can mull over their methods.

Here in Honolulu, our Neighborhood Justice Center believes in sticking close to procedural regulations. The mediators work in pairs and they are schooled to guide the disputants gently toward an agreement. The mediators are not to push, prod, or manipulate, but are urged to create an atmosphere in which the contending parties will come to their signed compact.

This difference in style led to a revealing incident. Frank Schoeppel, assuming that his long years of federal service would be of value, volunteered to mediate at the NJC during his spare time. After a few months, he told friends that he had been "fired" because the center officers did not like his aggressive methods. Leland Chang, director of the center, denying that Schoeppel had been ousted, said that he had quit rather than conform to certain NJC procedures. Whether fired or not, Schoeppel had not gone back to mediate at the justice center at the time of this writing.

The differences illustrate the spread in methods used in mediation. Federal mediators operate in disputes where unions and employers have continuing relationships, usually governed by contracts and complex rules. Much gamesmanship is involved and the skilled players accord great latitude to the mediator whose role is a familiar one to them. Honolulu's Neighborhood Justice Center, on the other hand, uses 150 volunteer mediators who work with people who have grown angry at one another outside any formal dispute-settling structure. In these circumstances the mediators move cautiously, often having to overcome suspicions, fears, and misreadings of their roles by the disputants.

I understand why the NJC operates as it does. I have mediated there, following the center's rules, and I can appreciate the need for prudence. The structure helps assure consistency by volunteers, who generally mediate once a month.

Steady workaday experience, on the other hand, builds the kind of confidence that breeds innovation and a personal willingness to take chances. Schoeppel, a talented professional mediator with hundreds of successes behind him, has a quiet but solid confidence in his own abilities, a belief that allows him wide maneuvering room. "I'll mediate anything, anywhere, anytime" is his motto. Talent often writes its own rules.

On this question of talent, I agree with both Schoeppel and Keith Hunter of the Honolulu AAA office. Schoeppel believes that one either has the mediator's touch or one hasn't and if a person has the talent, only a minimum of training is necessary. Hunter believes that he can tell within a few minutes of watching prospects in training whether a person will or will not make a good mediator.

I know that I felt comfortable and confident in the mediator's role from the outset. I'm not sure I could compile a definitive list of the preferred qualities, but among them I'd put flexibility, lack of prejudice, a sense of fairness, a desire to solve problems, an insight into human motivation, imagination, tenacity, boldness, and a flair for innovation. I don't want to imply that I possess all these qualities, but I've mediated long enough to know what to look for in a top-drawer mediator.

An ability to innovate is important because sometimes the ideal solution, a brainstorming flash out of left field, is one that neither side has thought of. An understanding of psychology is no less important. What a contending tiger wants is not always what he says he wants. If the mediator can suggest an approach derived from the disputant's hidden agenda, he or she often strikes the responsive chord that produces the solution. It therefore follows that a mediator must be a good listener, paying close attention to pick up the subsurface clues to a person's real wants.

I suppose the most valuable quality for a mediator is a liking for people and a desire to help them mold a mutually beneficial agreement. Without that basic feeling and desire, the most talented of people will fail as mediators.

In my own field of business disputes, I also think that a knowledge of the law helps immensely. Not every lawyer has the skills of a mediator, but a good mediator who is also a lawyer has a distinct advantage. It should be said, however, that some fine mediators don't agree with me. On the contrary, they actively oppose lawyers taking part in the mediation process. As a sample, one volunteer mediator, Karen Leichtnam, Washington, D.C., legislative representative for HALT, a pro-consumer organization seeking reform of the legal system, says that "bringing a lawyer into a mediation session is like wheeling a tank into a peace conference." I agree that most lawyers don't fit the mediation mold. But then neither do most people of whatever profession or trade. Only a minority of people make good mediators and when that good mediator happens to be a lawyer, he or she brings superior knowledge to the table. That special knowledge and experience in working with the traditional legal system can make the difference between success and failure.

Mediation Succeeds Where Adversary Methods Fail

My longest and most gratifying mediation illuminates much of what I've been saying. I will alter some of the facts and numbers in order to preserve the privacy of those involved. Not the least of the superior features of mediation as against litigation is the fact that mediation is conducted in private, whereas almost all aspects of a lawsuit are open to public scrutiny.

The case involved an architectural firm with six partners who split their sizable profits annually into six equal shares. They worked and socialized harmoniously together for many years until one of them— we'll call him Jeff—became seriously ill. When he returned to the office at last, disabled and lacking the old fire, Jeff was perceived by the others as able to work at only a fraction of the pace of his five partners, three men and two women.

Jeff felt differently. He believed he was carrying his share of the load. After a few months the five healthy partners decided they had to persuade Jeff to quit or sell out. He refused their terms, so they hired attorneys and negotiated for a year, but wound up with frayed emotions and hardened positions. They were farther away from a solution than when they started.

Jeff at last shifted from his business attorney to a lawyer in the litigation department of a large Honolulu law firm. After hearing all the details, the lawyer said he'd take the case, but warned that litigation expenses would run as high as $100,000. He asked a retainer of $25,000. The architect said he'd think it over. At this point his original business attorney suggested that Jeff might go to the AAA office and try their new mediation approach.

Jeff did so and I was called in as the mediator. My initial meeting with the six architects got nowhere despite the long hours we spent together. They were all polite, bland, and agreeable on the surface, but it became obvious that they were suppressing many resentments and ill feelings. I had the impression that a slight tilt of the lid would release a gush of emotion like steam from a boiling pot. I left with only a few insights, none of them bearing on a possible solution. I feared that I faced not just one hidden agenda, but perhaps as many as six.

I told them that I would be available to any of them at any time of day or night. In the ensuing weeks, I had long individual sessions with each architect, including four hours with the near invalid. Now I saw that the firm held two quarreling factions arrayed against Jeff, one with three architects, including one of the two women, and the other composed of the two remaining partners.

It was agreed finally at one session that the firm would be dissolved and the assets divided equally. Thereupon Jeff would set up his own establishment, the trio would open its shop, and the other two members would form a third entity. But now the cruddy work began. In addition to its assets, which included such matters as work in progress and accounts receivable, the firm had considerable liabilities, chiefly heavy mortgage payments on real estate that had been purchased for investment but which had tumbled in value. We spent more than twenty hours trying to divide this conglomeration equally, but ran into multiple frustrations over this or that indivisible fragment.

We finally jettisoned that approach when the senior partner crumpled a lengthy fact sheet and tossed it in a wastebasket. It was clear to all of us that we'd attempted an impossible task. After a few more false starts, the five nonailing partners agreed to absorb all the liabilities and to offer Jeff $150,000 for his share of the firm. Jeff agreed to sell on those conditions, but insisted on more money. I got the five to raise their offer to $180,000 and Jeff accepted what amounted to about a year and a half of his normal income from the six-person partnership.

What fascinated me about the whole procedure was how much

time the partners spent unloading their emotions and frustrations on me. They called me at all hours, usually to persuade me of the validity of the position they'd taken or to shake off guilt over some move they'd made. I've come to realize how important it is to people to express their emotions during an ostensible legal proceeding.

I also came to cherish the friendship, even affection I'd formed for all six partners as well as for one of the spouses who had become involved in the mediation. I liked them all. I could understand and empathize with everyone's position. As a consequence, as a mediator, I became effective in helping to fashion a road map for settlement.

Mediation permits necessary psychological eruptions. Litigation and a court of law do not. A witness who exposes feelings about matters or people connected with the case will be warned by the judge and counsel just to answer the question, please. In the case of the architects, their ability to sound off emotionally had as much to do with the eventual fair settlement as their interest over the money at stake.

After they all signed the agreement, I gave a dinner party for the partners and their spouses. The gathering generated enough warm reconciliation that the final dissolution was made with a minimum of carping. The two new firms even referred some business to their old partner, Jeff.

I spent fifty-five hours on the case, which cost the architects $5,500. They also asked me to draft the working documents and close the matter legally. That took another thirty-eight hours. They paid $1,000 to the AAA for setting up the mediation. In short, they were able to dissolve their firm to the satisfaction of all for a total of approximately $10,000. Had they gone to litigation, surely with three law firms to represent the three factions, the total cost might have run easily to over $200,000. Our mediation spread over several months. Litigation culminating in a trial would have taken a minimum of two years. As for energy depletion, although mediation took its toll, litigation would have made deep inroads into the psychic reserves of the partners and might have killed Jeff. For remember, litigation would have hardened the adversary positions that mediation tended to soften.

Sue but Rarely

In my own cases that I take to mediation, I assume that my client will eventually cool down and come to reason. And I always accompany my client to mediation. I'm there to advise, give legal counsel and perspective, help get the best settlement and to prevent the client from accepting a blatently unfair deal. I think that all the agreements thus far were fair and although several brought less money than a court victory could have, we must remember that we might have lost in court and that the mediated agreement saved the client money, time, and energy, all of which would have been lavished on litigation.

Courts, rather than mediation or arbitration, do have their place. The courtroom is the forum for simple uncontested legal procedures such as debt collection, mechanics' liens, or evictions. However, if the debtor, liened party, or tenant puts up a valid defense, then the matter becomes a dispute where voluntary mediation may better serve all parties.

I agree further with critics that mediation does not serve the person whose fundamental rights have been violated or whose case involves an emerging area of law or culpability, such as a claim of tobacco company liability in event cancer strikes a smoker.

Also, when corporations attempt to conceal known injurious effects of products, only pioneering lawsuits, with their depositions, subpoenas, and other tools of discovery, can bring the offenders to justice. This happened in the asbestos and birth control fields when manufacturers tried to picture lethal products as harmless. Once the culpability of a manufacturer has been established in court, however, mediation of subsequent liability claims, whether in the dozens or in the thousands, becomes a sensible method of saving time, money, and energy.

Pioneering cases, as newsworthy and as critical for society as they are, occupy only a small part of the nation's court calendars. In the ordinary practice of business law, it's the rare case that fits that kind of framework. In fact, I can't remember more than a handful of my cases in twenty years of practice that could not have been mediated to the advantage of the client. In business disputes almost never is one party 100 percent right and the other all wrong. Rather the cases are steeped in ambiguity, for no contract or venture can foresee and make provision for every eventuality.

Since my day of awakening several years ago, I've come to believe that our legal system needs drastic revision. The vast majority of cases now clogging the channels of civil justice could and should be settled by mediation, arbitration, or some other process outside formal court litigation. I believe that lawyers have a special responsibility to take the lead in reforming our system of civil justice, but every adult American involved in a dispute should realize what the options are when he or she takes the grievance to an attorney. Just what a new client should expect and demand of a lawyer is the subject of our next chapter.

Legal Consumerism:
You and Your Grievance

25

First Off, Cool It

When you get a raw deal that puts you in a vengeful "sue the bastards" mood, the first thing to do is nothing.

After you do that for a while, go take a long walk with no loose change in your pockets. At this stage you want to stay away from people and telephones. Your priority goal is to cool off sufficiently to permit you to consider your situation calmly and thoroughly.

Focusing on the dispute, you confront the first of a series of decisions. Can you settle this yourself through negotiation?

We assume for the purposes of this chapter that your answer is no. Perhaps you've already tried and failed. We mention this basic decision mainly to remind you that before you rush off to a lawyer, you should give serious consideration to negotiating yourself out of trouble. After all, most disputes are settled outside the legal framework without specialized assistance.

If you decide to seek professional help, your selection of an attorney becomes critical. You want a skilled lawyer, of course, but you also want one who will outline all the options for you clearly and simply, who'll answer all your questions, and who'll give you frank estimates of costs, time, and your chances of gaining satisfaction. While these qualifications seem modest enough, you'd be surprised how many attorneys fail to fill the bill.

If you've been through a lawsuit before, this is the time to reflect again on what happened. Did you recognize the roller coaster emotional ride that Oretta Long experienced in earlier chapters? Was your case settled? If so, at what stage? Was the settlement within the range that you considered probable at the outset of your action? Did you ever go to trial and lose? If not, can you imagine how you'd feel if a judge or jury shot down your case, shattering your belief that your blameless behavior must be evident to everyone? How much did your legal action cost you in dollars, time, and emotional wear and tear? Did your experience in the civil legal system leave you feeling satisfied or dismayed?

If you have never been through a legal action, we urge you to use this time to recall what happened in Oretta Long's case, a representative sketch of what goes on in the average lawsuit. Are you prepared to weather the course or would you prefer to investigate alternative methods of redressing the wrong visited on you?

You should, in short, have a rough idea of how you want to proceed before you consult a lawyer.

Choosing the Right Lawyer

How to select an attorney? Unfortunately there are few benchmarks by which to judge the qualifications and skills of a lawyer and fewer guides on how to become a sophisticated consumer of legal services. Unlike certification of specialties in medicine, there are no certifying boards for specialties in law except for the practice in patents. Therefore you, the consumer, cannot look to an independent body for assurance that the lawyer you're considering has passed an exam in a certain area of expertise. Instead you must rely on what the lawyer tells you and on his or her reputation among people you trust.

Yet the ability and quality of the lawyer can be the prime factor in determining the outcome of your case. The famous criminal lawyer who argued his blundering client out of a murder rap may have brought tears to the eyes of the jury, but he could prove a dud in your civil case against your do-nothing landlord. Achieving a good attorney–client match is often a matter of luck. To diminish the luck factor, proceed cautiously in your selection.

If you already have an able lawyer whom you trust, fine. But if you don't know a good lawyer, we suggest that you locate one through the recommendations of friends or business associates in whom you have confidence or by soliciting help from faculty members at the regional law school. Not recommended: Letting your fingers do the walking through the yellow pages. The yellow-page ad is written by the lawyer to tell you what he thinks of himself, not what others think of him.

Interviewing the Lawyer

After you make a tentative selection, you will talk with the lawyer on the telephone to arrange an appointment. At this point on the phone, ask if he or she works with litigation only or whether mediation, arbitration, and other alternative forms of resolution are part of the available tool kit.

If the attorney disparages alternative methods or says that he or she handles only conventional civil lawsuits, offer your thanks and say you'll look elsewhere. We urge that you do not hire a lawyer who dislikes or is unfamiliar with alternative routes. Once you commit yourself to an attorney who limits himself to litigation, you foreclose your options and bind yourself to the most expensive, lengthy, and troublesome method of resolving your grievance. Perhaps in the end it may turn out that litigation best serves your cause and you may return to the specialist who litigates only. But don't make that assumption *before* checking out the speedier and less costly alternatives.

If the phone contact with the attorney proves promising, make a date to call at the firm's office for an interview. And be sure to prepare for this session. Remember that it's *your* interview, not the lawyer's. You're the person who should be in charge, the one who should conduct the interview and do the hiring. We stress this point because many professional people, particularly physicians and lawyers, have a way of assuming the role of authority.

Be prepared to pay the attorney's regular hourly fee (except for lawyers on contingency fees) for the first interview. In return for your money, *you* guide the questioning. Be courteous and low-key, but keep command. Don't be maneuvered into a position where the lawyer is running the show. Here's a suggested plan for this first talk:

1. Sketch your problem. Be concise. Give all necessary particulars, but don't ramble.
2. Bring all pertinent documents with pages tabbed at key points for handy reference.
3. Obtain any additional information the lawyer may request.
4. Ask the attorney the following:
   a. What's his or her estimate of the probable outcome under the best and worst scenarios?
   b. How long will it take under the best and worst conditions?
   c. How much will it cost under best and worst circumstances (including anticipated use and costs of investigators, experts, etc.)

If you find this attorney compatible and are considering hiring him, ask for his written opinion on these questions. If he declines, ask him why. It's your money. There's no reason why a reputable lawyer shouldn't put these opinions in writing. If the explanation fails to satisfy you, best you consult another lawyer.

Since the attorney being interviewed already has indicated that he includes alternatives to litigation in his practice, question him about mediation as a possible vehicle for your case. Can your dispute be mediated? If he thinks not, why not? How about arbitration as a second choice? If he thinks the case is unsuited to arbitration, what about other alternative time-saving procedures such as mini-trial, rent-a-judge, or the quickie jury trial? Can he recommend any other course that will cut down on the time, money, and effort involved in a lawsuit? If he or she insists that litigation is the only way to go, demand the explanation in some detail.

Second Opinion

If not entirely satisfied with the interview, obtain a second or third opinion from other lawyers. In an art like the practice of law, second opinions can be revealing and helpful. And don't hesitate to discuss another lawyer's opinion. Remember, you've paid for that opinion and it belongs to you.

You'll pay additional hourly fees for these consultations, but the costs are insignificant when compared with the sums you would expend on a lengthy lawsuit. If the second opinion varies widely from the first, find out why. Suppose the first lawyer estimates that you might collect from $50,000 to $75,000 upon resolution of your case, but the second puts the range at a more modest $10,000 to $20,000. Find out the reasoning behind such varying numbers. Suppose the first lawyer called your grievance unsuited for mediation, but the second one sees mediation as a good route to go if the other side agrees. What accounts for these opposing views and which lawyer impresses you as the most forthright, logical, knowledgeable?

Remember that just as you, not your doctor or clergyman, are responsible for your own well-being, so it is you, not the lawyer, who is responsible for legal maneuvers and decisions in your case, including the ultimate decision on how to resolve your problem. Just as surgeons obtain a patient's consent for an operation, so your lawyer should get your permission before taking any significant step. The lawyer may recommend an appropriate course of action, and you should pay close attention to his or her professional advice, but the final decision will always rest with you.

How to Select a Mediator

If you elect to take your case to mediation with the assistance of your lawyer—and if your opponent agrees—you'll want an able, experienced mediator. Since mediators, unlike lawyers, are not licensed by the state, you must cast about for a person on whom both sides can agree. Your lawyer is your primary source of advice and he or she undoubtedly will have recommendations. Other sources of help: the nearest Neighborhood Justice Center, the regional office of the American Arbitration Association, the area's law school, the Society of Professionals In Dispute Resolution, or one of the mediation firms now located in large metropolitan centers. You will find a mediation directory at the back of this book.

If your case calls for specialized knowledge, you may want a mediator with a working grasp of the subject. As a sample, if yours is a malpractice complaint against a physician, you will want a mediator with a background in medicine and law as well as mediation. If you think a builder has done sloppy work on your new house, you should seek out a mediator who knows about construction and contracts in your area.

Although some experts disagree with us, we favor lawyers as mediators in most business disputes, and it is the fights in the commercial world that account for a majority of civil litigation in the United States and which chiefly concern us in this book. Most business wrangles involve a falling out over money or contract terms. No one yet has written a dispute-proof contract. Business lawyers spend a great deal of time drafting, interpreting, and revising contracts. We believe that a lawyer–mediator gets to the nub of a contract issue faster than a layperson and is able to advise either side when the law supports or fails to support that side's contention.

We hasten to add, however, that whatever a mediator's field of expertise—the law, medicine, manufacturing, engineering, domestic relations—that credential takes a distant second place to the prime qualities one seeks in a mediator. And what are they? Above all, wisdom. America brims with experts and specialists in every field, however narrow, but wise men and women do not abound. After wisdom as desirable traits of a good mediator, we'd list a sense of fairness and those other qualities we mentioned in the preceding chapter. Fortunately most cities and towns now have a number of experienced mediators who rate well in most or all of the desired characteristics.

Make sure the mediator suits you as well as your opponents for this is not a win/lose proposition, but rather a last opportunity to surmount the problem before a lengthy, costly battle. Obtain a prospective mediator's biographical reference sheet, which should list credentials and experience. If possible, you'll want to question those who have used the mediator. People who have been through mediation seem to enjoy talking about it. The process satisfied most of them and they realize that they've experienced an event that only a minority of Americans has shared.

If you do go to mediation, the chances of a favorable outcome are good. Various studies of the process indicate a high rate of satisfaction among opposite parties. Only a minority of participants come away feeling that the signed agreement yielded less than a fair settlement. The odds are high that you'll see your grievance disappear on terms as good as or better than you'd obtain in a court of law—and at an enormous saving of your time, money, and emotional reserves.

And remember: If the mediation fails and you leave the conference table without an agreement, you can always press your cause through a lawsuit. Mediation forecloses no options, barricades no routes. What's more, your brief experience with mediation will prepare you to look more realistically at your case and will equip you to make your own forecast of the probable outcome.

Guesstimating the Future

26

. . . Will make a far journey, encountering many obstacles. May find romance in the halls of justice. Good bet to wind up in the establishment. Career will bring satisfaction to many. Even money to remake the American justice system. . . .

If we were to cast the horoscope of mediation, it would read something like the preceding. Most signs point to a healthy expanding future for what is essentially another art form of the dispute resolution field.

In litigation, the traditional art form, lawyers play leading roles as agents of the decision-making process. In mediation the clients become the principal agents and the mediator becomes the guide in reaching a decision. In mediation the attorneys are relegated to supporting roles, a change that will prove healthy for society.

While still in its infancy in the modern American civil justice system, mediation is growing steadily. Each year more cases go to mediation, more mediators are trained, more mediation centers open, more law schools teach the process, more elementary and high school students learn how to settle their quarrels through mediation, more corporations learn the economic advantages of the process, more divorcing husbands and wives seek the path that skirts the acrimony of lawsuits, more people become aware of the method as one of their options when seeking to redress a wrong, and more workers and stars of the media publicize the values of mediation.

A number of factors insure that alternative forms of dispute resolution, mediation in particular, will have a secure place in our civil justice system. These include the quality of leadership, both within and without the legal establishment, the continuing flow of foundation money, the new teachers from elementary grades through university graduate schools, the growth of the new professional organizations, and public dissatisfaction with a sluggish, congested, often unresponsive system of justice.

There is a difference of opinion within the ADR community on just how large a role the alternative methods will play. A few people think that mediation may prove to be a passing fad. Some others have doubts about its staying power, but the majority of practitioners and experts in the field think that mediation will have a continuing steady growth until it becomes nationally recognized as a favored option to litigation.

We share the majority view. We believe that by the turn of the century, only a few years away at this writing, many alternative forms will be championed by the courts and widely used by the legal profession. We predict that mediation will become the preferred option by those undertaking to resolve a grievance, however severe, except in those minority of cases where filing a lawsuit is necessary to protect fundamental rights, clear up an uncertainty in the law itself, or chart new areas of public policy.

We also believe that this shift from legal combat to mutual accommodation eventually will bring profound changes in American society. The gradual shriveling of the long, expensive lawsuits as the norm means that business executives will be able to turn their backs on time-consuming litigation and devote themselves to commerce.

Lawsuits take a tremendous toll of this nation's supply of productive energy. Estimates on the total cost of the civil justice system vary widely between $40 billion and $80 billion annually. Our research inclines us to the view that the sum is closer to $80 billion than to $40 billion. Whatever the figure, an increase in mediation and a diminution of litigation will save the nation billions of dollars. Translated into action, that means a major shift from legal maneuvering into productive enterprise.

The resolution of disputes is essential to the smooth operation of any society, but a resolution system that absorbs an inordinate amount of the nation's first-class brainpower acts as a drag on the nation's economy. A shift from litigation to mediation, in reducing that drag, also eventually will reduce the number of lawyers, now at a burdensome level, and turn many of our best and brightest young minds to more beneficial endeavors.

We thus envision mediation contributing to the leaner, trimmer stature that America will need to regain some of its old industrial and commercial clout on world markets. America has grown fat and slovenly on now souring successes and excessive litigation is one manifestation of the national torpor.

We do not pretend that mediation is a cure-all by any means, but we do contend that it, along with such matters as tax reform, increased productivity, and improved education, will help the country back to economic health. Costly, tedious, and energy-draining lawsuits are a luxury a debt-ridden nation can no longer afford. We must settle our differences faster and cheaper with much less commitment of human resources.

This calls for a revolution in the way that Americans think about themselves in relation to the law and justice. Instead of rushing into a lawsuit to sue the bastards, no matter how long it takes in money, time, and effort, the goal must be to "settle this thing" and get on with life. The seeds of revolution are in the ground, are taking root, and soon will grow and bear fruit.

Appendix:
Directory of Dispute Resolution Services

This list is by no means definitive. New mediation and arbitration offices are opened every week in this rapidly developing field. The directory is helpful, however, to those looking for a way to remedy a grievance without going to court. If you cannot find what you want in the list below, the chances are good that someone at the office you contact will be able to refer you to the proper service or person in your area.

The list does not contain the many offices of the Federal Mediation and Conciliation Service located in cities throughout the country. The service mediates labor-management disputes. People with individual grievances must look elsewhere.

Although this directory includes the names of a number of law firms, it cannot cover every law firm handling alternatives to litigation. As yet, there is no reliable source for this information. This directory names the law firms that have been in the forefront of the ADR movement.

In the area of automobile complaints, we suggest that you contact the Better Business Bureau in your vicinity. Most BBB offices have an arbitration program for automobile disputes in which the major car manufacturers participate.

The directory is provided for information only. No recommendation of any listed organization or person is given or implied. As phone numbers change frequently, it is a good idea to check local listings before making your call.

C - Commercial	AFM - Includes a senior member of Academy of Family Mediators
E - Education, Schools, Research	L - Law firms doing sizable mediation, arbitration, etc.

Alabama

Fairhope
Christian Conciliation Service
PO Box 471, Fairhope 36532
(205) 928-0282

Mobile
Divorce Mediation Center
829 University Blvd. S., Mobile 36609
(205) 343-2597

Alaska

Anchorage
Divorce Mediation Center (AFM)
3941 Steller Dr., Anchorage 99504
(907) 279-9824

College
Interior Alaska Dispute Resolution Service
PO Box 81596, College 99708

Arizona

Florence
Conciliation Court Pinal County (AFM)
383 N. Main St., Florence 85232
(602) 868-5801 (Ext. 680)

Mesa
Conciliation Court (AFM)
1837 S. Mesa Dr., Mesa 85202
(602) 926-9011

Peoria
Tobin-Singer Mediation (AFM)
9444 W. McRae Way, Peoria 85345
(602) 997-9544

Phoenix
American Arbitration Assn. (C)
3033 N. Central Ave. (608), Phoenix 85012-2803
(602) 234-0950

Society Professionals in Dispute Resolution
1035 W. Mission Lane, Phoenix 85021
(602) 997-1213

United States Arbitration & Mediation of Arizona, Inc. (C)
7226 N. 16th St. (200), Phoenix 85020
(602) 870-4400

Conciliation Services (AFM)
Superior Court, 201 W. Jefferson St., Phoenix 85003
(602) 262-3296

Conciliation Services (AFM)
3910 Goldfinch Gate, Phoenix 85044
(602) 262-3298

Divorce Services Center (AFM)
5315 La Plaza Circle, Phoenix 85012
(602) 265-7077

Dashiell Mediation (AFM)
5040 N. 15th Ave. (402), Phoenix 85014
(602) 870-0053

LaVelle Mediation (AFM)
4524 N. 13th Ave., Phoenix 85013
(602) 264-7601

Scottsdale
Scottsdale Mediation Services, LTD
6040 E. Thomas Rd., Scottsdale 85254
(602) 994-5947

Conciliation Services (AFM)
3500 N. Hayden (1504), Scottsdale 85251
(602) 262-3296

Family Mediation Center (AFM)
7520 E. Second St. (3), Scottsdale 85251
(602) 955-6187

Tucson
Community Mediation Program
423 N. Tucson Blvd., Tucson 85716
(602) 323-1706

Divorce Mediation Service (AFM)
1910 E. 5th St., Tucson 85719
(602) 622-6075

Neighborhoods Mediation Project
101 W. Irvington St. C-1, Tucson 85714
(602) 746-0914

Conciliation Court (AFM)
177 N. Church St. (400), Tucson 85701
(602) 792-6344

Musty Mediation (AFM)
2902 E. Croyden, Tucson 85716
(602) 881-7791

Christian Conciliation Service
6842 E. Tanque Verde (E), Tucson 85715
(602) 886-2529

Arkansas

Little Rock
Small Claims Program
Municipal Court, Markham & Spring Sts.,
   Little Rock 72201
(501) 372-8501

BeyonDispute, Inc.
First Federal Savings Plaza, Little Rock
   72203
(501) 376-8800

John S. Miller, Associate Dean (E)
University of Arkansas–Little Rock
33rd St. & University, Little Rock 72204
(501) 569-3000

Consumer Protection
Attorney General's Office, Heritage West
   Bldg.
201 E. Markham St., Little Rock 72201
(501) 371-2341

Arkansas Dispute Resolutions (C)
2 Financial Centre (400), 10825 Financial
   Pkwy., Little Rock 72211
(501) 225-6942

Family Mediation Service
2024 Arkansas Valley Dr. (305), Little Rock
   72212
(501) 224-0099

California

Anaheim
Christian Conciliation Service
3855 E. LaPalma (112), Anaheim 92807
(714) 630-2622

Arcata
Humboldt Mediation Service
3260 West End Rd., Arcata 95521

Berkeley
Society Professionals in Dispute Resolution
   (Walter Merlino)
1580 Milvia St., Berkeley 94709
(408) 293-7993

Family Law Counseling Services
1854 Thousand Oaks Blvd., Berkeley 94709
(415) 548-5551

Berkeley Dispute Resolution Service
1771 Alcatraz Ave., Berkeley 94703

Beverly Hills
Elkin Mediation (AFM)
1217 Shadybrook Dr., Beverly Hills 90210
(213) 271-6929

Concord
Housing Alliance of Contra Costa County
1583 Galindo St., Concord 94520
(415) 825-4663

Corte Madera
Northern California Mediation Center
   (AFM)
100 Tamal Plaza (175), Corte Madera 94925
(415) 927-1422

Encino
American Assn. for Mediated Divorce
5435 Balboa Blvd. (208), Encino 91318
(213) 986-6953

Fullerton
Petrossi Mediation (AFM)
2555 E. Chapman Ave. (612), Fullerton
   92631
(714) 999-7057

Hollywood
Christian Conciliation Service
1800 N. Highland Ave. (502), Hollywood
   90028
(213) 467-3331

Huntington Beach
Society Professionals in Dispute Resolution
PO Box 5007, Huntington Beach 92615
(714) 963-7114

La Mesa
Divorce Alternatives (AFM)
5555 Jackson Dr. (206), La Mesa 92042
(619) 589-9333

Los Angeles
American Arbitration Assn. (C)
443 Shatto Place, Los Angeles 90020-0994
(213) 383-6516

Hearing Office Program
District Attorney's Office
310 W. Temple (780-23), Los Angeles
    90012
(213) 974-7401

L.A. City Attorney Program
808 N. Spring St. (4th Floor), Los Angeles
    90042
200 N. Main St., Los Angeles 90012
(213) 485-5433

JUDICATE
3435 Wilshire Blvd., Plaza Level (152), Los
    Angeles 90010
(213) 383-2100/1-800-631-9900

United States Arbitration & Mediation of
    Los Angeles (C)
Wilshire Palisades Bldg., 1299 Ocean Ave.,
    Santa Monica 90401
(213) 458-2923

Judicial Arbitration & Mediation Services,
    Inc. (C)
World Trade Center (296), 350 S. Figueroa,
    Los Angeles 90071
(213) 620-1133

Parker, Milliken, Clark, O'Hara & Samue-
    lian (L)
333 S. Hope St. (27th Floor), Los Angeles
    90071
(213) 683-6500

Petillon & Davidoff (L)
9841 Airport Blvd. (1500), Los Angeles
    90045
(213) 776-1684

Los Angeles Family Court Services (AFM)
111 N. Hill St. (241), Los Angeles 90012
(213) 974-5524

Society Professionals in Dispute Resolution
200 N. Main (1490), Los Angeles 90012
(213) 485-2066

Constitutional Rights Foundation (E)
1015 Cotner Ave., Los Angeles 90025
(213) 473-5091

Greenwald Mediation (AFM)
1100 Glendon Ave. (1510), Los Angeles
    90024
(213) 208-7406

Newman Mediation (AFM)
3309 Club Dr., Los Angeles 90064
(213) 838-8192

Mammoth Lakes
Dispute Resolution Center
PO Box 2535, Mammoth Lakes 93546
(619) 934-9688

Martinez
Family Court Services Superior Court
928 Main St., Martinez 94553
(415) 372-2681

Monterey Park
Cohen Mediation (AFM)
500 N. Garfield Ave. (312), Monterey Park
    91754
(818) 571-1717

Mountain View
Mountain View Tenant/Landlord Service
415 E. Middlefield Rd., Mountain View
    94043
(415) 856-4062

Newport Beach
Family Mediation Associates (AFM)
4000 MacArthur Blvd. (5500), Newport
    Beach 92660
(714) 752-2727

Novato
Christian Conciliation Service
PO Box 617, Novato 94948
(415) 382-9162

Oakland
Pastoral Mediation Services
Holy Names College, 3500 Mountain Blvd.,
    Oakland 94619
(415) 436-0111

Lemmon Mediation Institute (AFM)
5248 Boyd Ave., Oakland 94618
(415) 654-3650

Conciliation Forums of Oakland
5549 Claremont Ave., Oakland 94618
(415) 547-2290

Pacific Palisades
Kardener Mediation (AFM)
15515 Sunset Blvd. (220), Pacific Palisades
 90272
(213) 281-8600

Palo Alto
Task Forces, Human Relations Commission
PO Box 10250, City of Palo Alto 94303
(415) 329–2375

Family Mediation Service
285 Hamilton Ave., Palo Alto 94301
(415) 328-7000

New Family Center
PO Box 60872, Palo Alto 94306
(415) 328-3218

Geoff Ball & Associates
991 Commercial St. (4), Palo Alto 94303
(415) 424-8808

Alternative Dispute Resolution Associates
399 Sherman (5), Palo Alto 94030

Pasadena
Community Dispute Resolution Center
330 S. Oak Knoll Ave. (11), Pasadena 91101
(818) 793-7174

Rancho Palos Verdes
Baker-Jackson Mediation (AFM)
7405 Via Lorado, Rancho Palos Verdes
 90274
(213) 377-5311

Sacramento
Society Professionals in Dispute Resolution
Cal. State Mediation Service
3501 Cutter Way, Sacramento 95818
(916) 739-8898

Sacramento Neighborhood Mediation Center
PO Box 5275, Scramento 95817
(916) 739-7069

Complaint Assistance Unit
1020 N St. (501), Sacramento 95814
(916) 323-5999

Merksamer Mediation (AFM)
248-3 Selby Ranch Road, Sacramento 95864
(916) 487-6949

San Bernardino
Judicial Arbitration & Mediation Services
290 North D St. (7th floor), San Bernardino
 92403
(714) 885-7473

San Diego
American Arbitration Assn. (C)
525 C St. (400), San Diego 92101-5278
(619) 239-3051

Community Mediation Programs
San Diego Law Center, Alcala Park, San
 Diego 92110
(619) 260-4815

Judicial Arbitration & Mediation Services,
 Inc. (C)
401 B St. (296), San Diego 92101-4223
(619) 236-1848

Community Mediation Center
315 Laurel, San Diego 92107
(619) 238-1022

Christian Conciliation Service
3430 Camino del Rio N. (300), San Diego
 92108-1796
(619) 563-9965

Angel-Levy Mediation (AFM)
5431 Barkla St., San Diego 92122
(619) 569-7320

Roth Mediation (AFM)
3235 Fourth Ave., San Diego 92103
(619) 297-7181

San Francisco
American Arbitration Assn. (C)
445 Bush St., San Francisco 94108-3792
(415) 981-3901

American Intermediation Service (C)
One Montgomery St., West Tower 2100,
 San Francisco 94104
(415) 788-6253/800-262-6253

Community Boards of San Francisco
(Also Nat. Assn. for Community Justice)
149 Ninth St., San Francisco 94103
(415) 522-1250

Thelen, Marrin, Johnson & Bridges (L)
2 Embarcadero Center (2100), San Francisco 94111
(415) 392-6320

Bronson, Bronson & McKinnon (L)
555 California St., San Francisco 90017
(415) 986-4200

Judicial Arbitration & Mediation Services
111 Pine St. (710), San Francisco 94111
(415) 982-5267

California Community Dispute Services
445 Bush St., San Francisco 94108
(415) 434-2200

Arts Arbitration & Mediation Services
Bldg. B, Fort Mason Center, San Francisco 94123
(415) 775-7715/7200

Consumer Fraud Unit
District Attorney, 732 Brannan St., San Francisco 94103
(415) 552-6400

Family Law Mediation (AFM)
465 California St. (200), San Francisco 94104
(415) 989-8999

Connections (E)
40 Delano Ave., San Francisco 94112
(415) 585-1647

Cal. Mediation Service (AFM)
530 Bush St. (600), San Francisco 94108
(415) 981-7272

Family Mediation Center (AFM)
2739 Laguna St., San Francisco 94123
(415) 923-9252

National Center for State Courts
720 Sacramento St., San Francisco 94108
(415) 392-7151

Interaction Associates, Inc.
185 Berry St. (105), San Francisco 94107
(415) 777-0590

Sanger
Mennonite Conciliation Services
3075 N. Bethel St., Sanger 93657
(209) 441-1017/252-4800

San Jose
American Arbitration Assn. (C)
50 Airport Parkway (64), San Jose 95110-1009
(408) 293-7993

Consumer Affairs
1553 Berger Dr., San Jose 95112
(408) 299-4211

Neighborhood Mediation & Conciliation Service
70 W. Hedding St. (East Wing), San Jose 95110
(408) 299-2206

Neighborhood Small Claims Night Court
200 W. Hedding St., San Jose 95110
(408) 299-2272

San Jose Housing Service
425 Stockton Ave., San Jose 95126
(408) 287-2464

San Luis Obispo
Human Relations Mediation Services
PO Box 8100, San Luis Obispo 93403-8100

San Mateo
Peninsula Conflict Resolution Center
177 Bovet Road (230), San Mateo 94402
(415) 571-0367

San Rafael
Mediation Services
Administration Bldg., Civic Center, San Rafael 94903
(415) 499-6191

Santa Ana
Judicial Arbitration & Mediation Services, Inc. (C)
Centre Pl. (205), 1900 E. 4th St., Santa Ana 92705-3919
(714) 972-1616

Santa Barbara
Mediation Center for Family Law
1231 State St. (206), Santa Barbara 93101
(805) 965-4525

Rental Housing Mediation
1136 E. Monticello St., Santa Barbara 93101
(805) 963-4373

Santa Cruz
Program for Consumer Affairs
701 Ocean St. (204), Santa Cruz 95060

Santa Maria
Mediation Center Family Law
906 S. Broadway (E), Santa Maria 93454
(805) 928-3661

Santa Monica
Neighborhood Justice Center
1320-C Santa Monica Mall (3), Santa Monica 90401
(213) 451-8192

Dispute Resolution Services, Inc.
2830 Pico Blvd., Santa Monica 90405
(213) 450-5252

Institute for Civil Justice (Rand Corp.)
1700 Main St., Santa Monica 90406
(213) 393-0411

American Intermediation Service, Inc. (C)
2401 Colorado Ave. (280), Santa Monica 90404-3500
(213) 453-0089/800-262-6253

Center for Dispute Resolution (AFM)
1337 Ocean Ave. (Garden Suite), Santa Monica 90401
(213) 451-1615

Wildwood School (E)
3111 Olympic Blvd., Santa Monica 90404
(213) 828-4431

Santa Rosa
Sonoma County Mediation Services
324 Santa Rosa Ave., Santa Rosa 95405
(707) 575-8787

Seaside
Community Boards Program, Monterey Peninsula
PO Box 1538, Seaside 93955
(408) 394-1992

Sherman Oaks
Nancy Lydick Mediation
14937 Ventura Blvd. (317), Sherman Oaks 91403
(818) 906-2291

Richard H. Millen & Associates (C)
15235 Valley Vista Blvd., Sherman Oaks 91403
(818) 501-2787

Stanford
Stanford Research Center for Conflict Resolution (E)
Stanford Law School, Crown Quadrangle, Stanford 94305
(415) 723-1931

Operation Sentinel
860 Escondido Rd., Stanford 94305
(415) 497-0354

Stockton
Family Court Services
30 S. San Joaquin St., Stockton 95202
(209) 944-2601

Ukiah
Ukiah Counseling Services (AFM)
813 S. Dora St., Ukiah 95482
(707) 463-1305

Ventura
Mediation Center Family Law
Bard Memorial Bldg. (B), 121 N. Fir St., Ventura 93001
(805) 643-3543

Walnut Creek
United States Arbitration & Mediation of Northern California
590 Ygnacio Valley Rd. (200), Walnut Creek 94596
(415) 946-9696

Housing Alliance
1963 Tree Valley Bldg. (82), Walnut Creek 94596
(415) 943-1997

Woodland Hills
Mediation Institute
2231 Mulholland Hwy. (207-A), Woodland Hills 91364
(818) 702-9526

Colorado

Aurora
Landlord/Tenant Mediation Project
2302 Emporia St., Aurora 80010
(303) 366-9571

Boulder
Landlord/Tenant Mediation Project
City of Boulder, PO Box 791, Boulder 80306
(303) 441-3140

CDR Associates/Center for Dispute Resolution (AFM)
100 Arapahoe Ave. (12), Boulder 80302
(303) 442-7367/800-MEDIATE

Boulder Community Mediation Service
2480 Balsam Dr., Boulder 80302
(303) 447-2187

Judicial Arbiter Group (C)
2919 Valmont Rd., Boulder 80301-1350
(303) 449-1945

Boulder Bar Assn. Mediation Project
Boulder District Court, PO Box 471, Boulder 80306

Family Mediation Center
PO Box 1978, Boulder 80306
(303) 440-4318

Colorado Springs
Neighborhood Justice Center Assn.
326 S. Tejon St., Colorado Springs 80903
(303) 520-6016

Sutton Mediation (AFM)
801 N. Weber St., Colorado Springs 80903
(303) 632-0465

Christian Conciliation Service
PO Box 25658, Colorado Springs 80936
(719) 635-1190/596-7880

Denver
American Arbitration Assn. (C)
1775 Sherman St., Denver 80203-4318
(303) 831-0823

Center for Dispute Resolution
1900 Wazee St. (311), Denver 80202
(303) 295-2244

Dispute Settlement, Inc. (C)
2105 E. Virginia Ave., Denver 80209
(303) 733-9403

United States Arbitration & Mediation of Colorado, Inc. (C)
ı050 17th St. (1710), Denver 80265
(303) 534-8722

Bear Valley Baptist Peacemakers
2600 S. Sheridan Blvd., Denver 80227
(303) 861-1444

Christian Conciliation Service
1980 S. Wolff, Denver 80219
(303) 936-8919

Consumer Protection
1525 Sherman St. (215), Denver 80203
(303) 866-3611

Divorce Mediation Research Project
1720 Emerson St., Denver 80218
(303) 837-1555

Child Protection Mediation Project (E)
430 W. 9th Ave., Denver 80204
(303) 295-2244

Swartz Mediation (AFM)
443 S. Corona, Denver 80209
(303) 442-7367

Dillon
Keystone Center
PO Box 606, Dillon 80498-0606
(303) 468-5822

Hotchkiss
North Fork Counseling Services
PO Box 636, 207 W. Bridge St., Hotchkiss 81419
(303) 872-2550

Lakewood
Frontrange Mediation Associates
720 Kipling St. (200), Lakewood 80215
(303) 237-4322

Wheat Ridge
Serendipity Center for Mediation, Inc. (AFM)
4120 Independence Court, Wheat Ridge 80033
(303) 431-4528

Connecticut

Danbury
Danbury Counseling & Mediation (AFM)
35 Padanaram Road, Danbury 06811
(203) 748-3241

Darien
American Intermediation Service (C)
14 Old Parish Road, Darien 06820
(203) 655-9722/800-826-5605

Greenwich
Thode Mediation (AFM)
80 Perkins Road, Greenwich 06830
(203) 629-1131

Von Schmidt Mediation (AFM)
37 Arch St., Greenwich 06830
(203) 622-5900

Hartford
American Arbitration Assn. (C)
2 Hartford Square West, Hartford 06106-
    1943
(203) 278-5000

Dispute Resolution, Inc. (C)
179 Allyn St. (508), Hartford 06103-1421
(203) 724-0861

Superior Court Mediation Program
28 Grand St., Hartford 06106
(203) 566-8187

Cummings & Lockwood (L)
Cityplace, Hartford 06103
(203) 275-6700

Day, Berry & Howard (L)
Cityplace, Hartford 06103-3499
(203) 275-0100

Tyler Cooper & Alcorn (L)
Cityplace, Hartford 06103-3488
(203) 522-1216

Mediation Write/Right Decisions (E)
Noah Webster School
5 Cone St., Hartford 06105
(203) 521-6952

New Britain
Family Services Unit
177 Columbus Blvd., New Britain 06051
(203) 827-7130

New Haven
Fair Haven Community Mediation
126 Grand Ave., New Haven 06513-3908
(203) 787-9586

North Stonington
Bishop Mediation (AFM)
RFD 1, Box 318A, North Stonington 06359
(203) 442-4416

Riverside
Divorce Mediation Center (AFM)
25 Tower Road, Riverside 06878
(203) 646-9160

Delaware

Wilmington
Dispute Resolution
Family Court, PO Box 2359, Wilmington
    19899
(302) 571-2237/571-2615

Fee Dispute Mediation Committee
Delaware State Bar Assn.,
820 N. French St., Wilmington 19801
(302) 658-5278/1-800-292-7869

Wilmington Citizen's Dispute Settlement
    Center
800 N. French St., Wilmington 19801
(302) 571-4200

District of Columbia

American Arbitration Assn. (C)
1730 Rhode Island Ave. NW (509), Wash-
    ington, DC 20036–3169
(202) 296-8510

ENDISPUTE of Washington, DC (C)
1820 Jefferson Place NW, Washington, DC
    20036-2587
(202) 429-8782

Multi-Door Courthouse
DC Superior Court, 515 Fifth St. NW,
    Washington, DC 20001
(202) 879-2828

Civil Arbitration Program
DC Superior Court, 500 Indiana Ave. NW,
    Washington, DC 20001
(202) 879-1133

National Institute for Dispute Resolution
1901 L St. NW, Washington, DC 20036
(202) 331-2258

Arent, Fox, Kitner, Plotkin & Kahn (L)
1050 Connecticut Ave. NW, Washington,
    DC 20036-5339
(202) 857-6000

Hogan & Hartson (L)
555 13th St. NW, Washington, DC 20004-
5600
(202) 637-5600

Howrey & Simon (L)
1730 Pennsylvania Ave. NW, Washington,
DC 20006
(202) 783-0800

Kaye Scholer Fierman Hays & Handler (L)
1575 Eye St. NW, Washington, DC 20005
(202) 783-1200

Lane & Edson (L)
2300 M St. NW, Washington, DC 20037
(202) 955-9600

McGuire, Woods, Battle & Boothe (L)
1627 Eye St. NW (1000), Washington, DC
20006
(202) 857-1700

Steptoe & Johnson (L)
1330 Connecticut Ave. NW, Washington,
DC 20036
(202) 429-3000

Wilmer, Cutler & Pickering (L)
2445 M St. NW, Washington, DC 20037-
1420
(202) 663-6000

Christian Conciliation Service
PO Box 396, Fairfax, Va., 22030
(703) 591-1142

Fund for Research on Dispute Resolution
1901 L St. NW (600), Washington, DC
20036
(202) 466-4764

Center for Dispute Settlement
918 16th St. NW, Washington, DC 20006-
2902
(202) 296-2565

Committee on Dispute Resolution, American Bar Assn.
1800 M St. NW, Washington, DC 20036
(202) 331-2258

DC Mediation Service
Superior Court Bldg. A, Washington, DC
20001
(202) 724-8215

Community Relations Service, U.S. Dept.
of Justice
5550 Friendship Blvd. (370), Chevy Chase,
Md. 20815
(301) 492-5970

Multinational Legal Services, P.C.
11 Dupont Circle NW (505), Washington,
DC 20036-1207
(202) 955-1064

14th Street Community Services Center
3031 14th St. NW, Washington, DC 20010
(202) 673-6989

Family Mediation Service
918 16th St. NW (503), Washington, DC
20006
(202) 722-0194

PMK Associates, Inc.
1418 Jonquil St. NW, Washington, DC
20012
(202) 722-0194

Conservation Foundation
1250 24th St. NW, Washington, DC 20037-
1175
(202) 293-4800

Federal Mediation & Conciliation Service
2100 K St., Washington, DC 20427

International Council for Dispute Resolution
1150 17th St. (600), Washington, DC 20006
(202) 775-9172

InterAmerican Commercial Arbitration
Commission
1189 F St. NW (449-c), Washington, DC
20006
(202) 293-1455

Federal Trade Commission (Marketing Practices)
6th & Pennsylvania Ave., Washington, DC
20004
(202) 523-5809

Pretrial Services Resource Center
918 F St. NW (500), Washington, DC
  20040
(202) 653-5290

Society Professionals in Dispute Resolution
1730 Rhode Island Ave. NW (909), Washington, DC 20036
(202) 833-2188

Gridner Mediation (AFM)
3100 Connecitcut Ave. NW (145), Washington, DC 20008
(202) 483-4376

U.S. Office of Consumer Affairs
1009 Premier Bldg., 1725 I St. NW, Washington, DC 20201
(202) 634-4329

Environmental Mediation International
1775 Pennsylvania Ave. NW (475), Washington, DC 20036-4605
(202) 457-0457

Harter & DeLong Resources
2301 M St. NW (404), Washington, DC
  20037
(202) 887-1033

Maida Mediation (AFM)
6242 29th St. NW, Washington, DC 20015
(301) 454-6634

ICF, Inc.
1850 K St. NW, Washington, DC 20006
(202) 828-3449

Nat. Institute Citizen Education in the Law
  (E)
Georgetown University Law Center, 605 G
  St. NW (4th Floor)
Washington, DC 20002
(202) 624-8217/244-1357

Florida

Bartow
Citizen Dispute Settlement
State Attorney's Office, PO Box 9000, Bar-
  tow 33830
(813) 533-0731

Cocoa
Juvenile Alternative Service
Brevard Community College, 1519 Clearlake
  Rd., Cocoa 32922
(305) 632-1111 (Ext. 4560)

Shepard Mediation (AFM)
2420 Elsie Circle, Cocoa 32922
(907) 688-3667

Coral Gables
Counseling Center
University of Miami, PO Box 248186, Coral
  Gables 33124
(305) 284-5511

Crestview
Small Claims Mediation
Okaloosa County Courthouse, Crestview
  32536
(904) 862-7478

Daytona Beach
Volusia County Citizen Dispute
440 S. Beach St., Daytona Beach 32014
(904) 258-1490

East Naples
Mediation & Arbitration
Collier County Courthouse, Bldg. A, East
  Naples 33962

Fort Lauderdale
Family Mediation & Conciliation Program
507 SE 6th St. (2nd Floor), Fort Lauderdale
  33301
(305) 765-4012

United States Arbitration & Mediation, Inc.
  (C)
1600 SE 17th St. Causeway (304), Fort Lauderdale 33302
(305) 523-8400

Mediation, Inc.
4331 N. Federal Highway, Fort Lauderdale
  33308
(305) 764-1000

Irving Mediation (AFM)
1501 E. Oak Knoll Circle, Fort Lauderdale
  33324
(305) 370-1356

Mediation, Arbitration, Negotiation (E)
814 SW 30th St. (2), Fort Lauderdale 33315

Citizens Dispute Settlement
Court Administrator's Office
516 SE Fifth Court, Fort Lauderdale
  33301
(305) 765-4488

Fort Myers
Citizens Dispute Settlement
Lee County Justice Complex
1700 Monroe St., Fort Myers 33901
(813) 335-2884

Gainesville
Citizens Dispute Settlement
State Attorney's Office, PO Box 1437,
  Gainesville 32602
(904) 374-3675

Community Behavorial Services (AFM)
1212 NW 12th Ave., Gainesville 32601
(904) 372-6645

Family Mediation
Alachua County Ct. Services, 26 E. University, Gainesville 32601
(904) 377-0974

Jacksonville
Citizens Dispute Settlement
State Attorney's Office, Duval County
  Courthouse (501)
330 East Bay St., Jacksonville 32202
(904) 633-6643

Family Mediation
1283 E. 8th St., Jacksonville 32206
(904) 680-2028

Lakeland
Divorce Mediation
Peace River Center, 1835 N. Gilmore Ave.,
  Lakeland 33805
(813) 683-5701

Melbourne
Citizens Dispute Settlement/Small Claims
  Mediation
Brevard County Courthouse, 50 S. Neiman
  St., Melbourne 32935
(305) 727-9712

Christian Conciliation Service
427 Timberlake Drive, Melbourne 32940
(305) 242-1421

Miami
American Arbitration Assn. (C)
2250 SW Third Ave., Miami 33129-2092
(305) 854-1616/1617

Citizens Dispute Settlement
Court Administrator's Office
Metro Justice Bldg., 1351 NW 12th St.,
  Miami 33125
(305) 547-7885

Community Conflict Resolution
5400 NW 2nd Ave.(204), Miami 33142
(305) 638-6735

Small Claims Mediation
Dade County Courthouse (700)
73 W. Flagler St., Miami 33135
(305) 375-3864

Family Mediation
Dade County Courthouse (2201)
73 W. Flagler St., Miami 33135
(305) 375-1650

Miami Beach
G.C.A. Peace Education Foundation (E)
PO Box 1153, Miami Beach 33119
(305) 377-8161 (Ext. 49)

New Port Richey
Family Mediation
Pasco County Center, 7530 Little Rd., New
  Port Richey 33553
(813) 847-8174/847-8172

Orlando
Citizen Dispute Settlement/Family Mediation
Orange County Bar Assn.
880 N. Orange Ave. (101), Orlando 32801
(305) 423-5732/659-7009

Christian Conciliation Service
PO Box 1649, Orlando 32802
(407) 658-3005

Palatka
Community Arbitration
State Attorney's Office, PO Box 1346, Pal-
  atka 32078-1346
(904) 328-4944

Pensacola
Community Juvenile Arbitration
1800 St. Mary's Ave. (Box 10), Pensacola
  32501
(904) 434-3431 (Ext. 208)

Bingham-Turner & Associates (AFM)
4400 Bayou Blvd. (8-D), Pensacola 32504
(940) 474-9882

Plantation
Waxman Mediation (AFM)
9780 NW 16th St., Plantation 33322
(305) 472-7458

St. Petersburg
Citizens Dispute Settlement, Family Mediation
Court Administrator's Office
150 Fifth St. N., St. Petersburg 33701
(813) 825-1796/825-1797

Sanford
County Juvenile Program/Family Mediation
County Courthouse, 100 E. First St., Sanford 32771
(305) 322-7534/830-8919/323-4330 (Ext. 397)

Sarasota
Citizens Dispute Settlement/Family Mediation
Sarasota County Courthouse
2000 Main St., Sarasota 33577
(813) 365-1000 (Ext. 2225)/951-5700

Stuart
Family Mediation
100 E. Ocean Blvd., Stuart 33494
(305) 286-4613/334-2919

Tallahassee
Citizens Dispute Settlement
Leon County Courthouse (200), Tallahassee 32301
(904) 488-1357

Dispute Resolution Alternative Committee
Supreme Court Bldg., Tallahassee 32301
(904) 488-8621

Tampa
Mediation Diversion Services/Family Mediation
Hillsborough County Courthouse Annex (200)
800 E. Kennedy St., Tampa 33602
(813) 272-5642/272-5885

Tavares
Citizen Dispute Settlement
Lake County Courthouse
315 W. Main St., Tavares 32778
(305) 343-9718/347-1718

Titusville
Family Mediation
Brevard County Courthouse (3rd Floor W.)
400 S. St., Titusville 32780
(305) 269-8943

Vero Beach
Family Mediation
699 17th St. Causeway (D), Vero Beach 32960
(305) 778-2525

West Palm Beach
Court Mediation Services
PO Box 1989, West Palm Beach 33402-1989
(305) 820-2739

Northwood Medical Center (AFM)
2617 N. Flagler Drive (204), West Palm Beach 33407
(305) 832-7668

Georgia

Atlanta
American Arbitration Assn. (C)
1197 Peachtree St. NE, Atlanta 30361-3598
(404) 872-3022

Justice Center of Atlanta, Inc.
976 Edgewood Ave. NE, Atlanta 30307-2580
(404) 523-8236

King & Spalding (L)
2500 Trust Company Tower, Atlanta 30303
(404) 572-4600

Society Professionals in Dispute Resolution
6400 Blackwater Trail NW, Atlanta 30328-2723
(404) 658-2792

United States Arbitration & Mediation of Georgia, Inc. (C)
1670 Bank South Bldg., 55 Marietta St. NW, Atlanta 30303
(404) 688-0088

Interaction Associates, Inc.
5285 Amhurst Dr., Norcross 30092
(404) 446-9165

Pershing Point Center Counseling (AFM)
1375 Peachtree St. NE (780), Atlanta 30309
(404) 876-3025

Christian Conciliation Service
120 Allen Rd. (B), Atlanta 30328
(404) 851-9466

Fee Arbitration Program
State Bar, 84 Peachtree St. (11th Floor)
Atlanta 30303
(404) 522-6255

Governor's Office Consumer Affairs
2 Martin Luther King Drive (356 East
Tower), Atlanta 30334
(404) 656-1760

Divorce Mediation Associates
1780 Century Blvd. NE (B), Atlanta 30345
(404) 231-1414

Decatur
Manley Mediation (AFM)
321 Drexel Ave., Decatur 30030
(404) 378-3238

Douglasville
Kitchens Mediation (AFM)
8995 Laurel Drive, Douglasville 30135
(404) 378-3238

Savannah
Neighbor to Neighbor Justice Center, Inc.
1810 Bull St., Savannah 31401
(912) 236-0918

Hawaii

Aiea
Aiea Intermediate School Mediation (E)
99-600 Kulawea St., Aiea 96701
(808) 488-8421

Hilo
Conflict Mediation Program (E)
Waikea High School
155 W. Kawaili St., Hilo 96720
(808) 935-3721

Ku'ikahi YMCA Mediation Center
300 W. Lanikaula St., Hilo 96720
(808) 935-7844

Hilo H.S. Conflict Mediation (E)
556 Waianuenue St., Hilo 96720
(808) 935-4881

Honolulu
American Arbitration Assn. (C)
810 Richards St. (641), Honolulu 96813-
4728
(808) 531-0541

Neighborhood Justice Center
200 N. Vineyard St. (501), Honolulu 96817
(808) 521-6767

JUDICATE (C)
220 St. King St. (1250), Honolulu 96813
(808) 545-7242

American Intermediation Service (C)
900 Fort St. Mall (1777), Honolulu 96813
(808) 538-7754/800-826-5605

Program on Alternative Dispute Resolution
PO Box 2560, Honolulu 96804
(808) 548-3080

Kuniyuki & Chang (L)
900 Fort St. Mall (310), Honolulu 96813-
3771
(808) 524-4111

Stanton, Clay, Tom & Chapman (L)
567 S. King St. (101), Honolulu 96813
(808) 531-6894

Rush, Moore, Craven, Kim & Stricklin (L)
745 Fort St. Mall (20th Floor), Honolulu
96813
(808) 521-0400

Court-Annexed Arbitration Program (C)
The Judiciary, State of Hawaii
4th Floor, Kaahumanu Hale
777 Punchbowl St., Honolulu 96813
(808) 548-4380

Mediation Specialists of Hawaii (C)
233 Merchant St. (2nd Floor), Honolulu
96813
(808) 526-3899

U. of Hawaii Student Mediation Service (E)
2425 Campus Road (208), Honolulu 96822
(808) 948-8178

Armed Services YMCA Mediation Services
1148 B Vitex Pl., Aliamanu, Honolulu
96818
(808) 833-1386

Wheeler Air Force Base, Wahiawa 96854
(808) 624-5997

Marine Corps Air Station
Bldg. 455, Kaneohe 96863
(808) 254-4719

Barbers Point Naval Air Station
Bldg. 1890, Barbers Point NAS 96862
(808) 684-2263

Divorce Clinic
Kapiolani Women's & Children's Medical
    Center (638)
1319 Punahou St., Honolulu 96826
(808) 947-8368

Dispute Management in the Schools (E)
Kaimuki Intermediate School
631 18th Ave., Honolulu 96816
(808) 737-5837

Honolulu Board of Realtors Mediation
505 Ward Ave., Honolulu 96814
(808) 538-3641

Hawaii School Mediation Alliance (E)
College of Education, U. of Hawaii, Hono-
    lulu 96822
(808) 948-7817

Medical Claims Conciliation
1010 Richards St., Honolulu 96813
(808) 548-6245

Program on Conflict Resolution (E)
Porteus Hall, U. of Hawaii, Honolulu 96822
(808) 948-6433

Pacific Arbitration & Mediation Services,
    Inc. (C)
Pioneer Plaza (1400), 900 Fort St. Mall,
    Honolulu 96813
(808) 524-4854

Mediation Hawaii (C)
2085 Ala Wai Blvd. (17-4), Honolulu 96815
(808) 922-2955

Kahuku
Kahuku H.S. Mediation (E)
PO Box 308, Kahuku 96731
(808) 293-9245

Kahului
Lihikai School Mediation (E)
335 S. Papa Ave., Kahului 96732
(808) 877-5474

Project T.O.P.S. (E)
Maui High School
660 S. Lono Ave., Kahului 96732
(808) 871-5868

Kailua
Mediation Clinic
415 A Uluniu St., Kailua 96734
(808) 262-0730

Kalaheo H.S. Mediation (E)
730 Iliaina St., Kailua 96792
(808) 254-3551

Kamuela
West Hawaii Mediation Services
Opelo Cottage, Opelo Road, PO Box 1890,
    Kamuela 96743
(808) 885-5525/326-2666

Kaunakakai
Mediation Services of Molokai
PO Box 1275, Kaunakakai 96748
(808) 553-3844/567-9052

Lihue
Kauai Economic Opportunity Mediation
2786 Wehe Rd., PO Box 1027, Lihue
    96766
(808) 245-4077

Pahoa
Pahoa H.S. Mediation Club (E)
PO Box 3, Pahoa 96778
(808) 965-8411

Waianae
Waianae Intermediate School Mediation (E)
85-626 Farrington Highway, Waianae 96792
(808) 696-2922

Wailuku
Mediation Associates (C)
2233 Vineyard St. (A), Wailuku 96793
(808) 242-6623

Mediation Services of Maui, Inc.
95 Mahalani St., Wailuku 96793
(808) 244-5744

Idaho

Boise
Hawley Mediation (AFM)
750 Warm Springs Ave. (B), Boise 83712
(208) 343-4164

Idaho Human Rights Commission
450 W. State St., Boise 83270
(208) 334-2873

Lewiston
Idaho Arbitration & Mediation Services, Inc.
  (C)
PO Box 321, 504 Main St. (432), Lewiston
  83501
(208) 746-0344

Illinois

Bloomington
Hammer Mediation (AFM)
202 N. Center St., Bloomington 61701
(309) 828-7331

Chicago
Neighborhood Justice Center
53 W. Jackson St. (1511), Chicago 60604
(312) 939-7383

American Arbitration Assn. (C)
205 W. Wacker Drive (1100), Chicago
  60606-1212
(312) 346-2282

ENDISPUTE of Chicago (C)
222 S. Riverside Plaza (800), Chicago
  60606-5901
(312) 648-4343

American Intermediation Service, Inc. (C)
3 First National Plaza (1400), Chicago
  60602
(312) 606-0936/800-826-5605

Baker & McKenzie (L)
Prudential Plaza (2800), Chicago 60601
(312) 861-8000

Jenner & Block (L)
One IBM Plaza, Chicago 60611
(312) 222-9350

Kirkland & Ellis (L)
200 E. Randolph Drive, Chicago 60601
(312) 861-2000

Phelan Pope & John, Ltd. (L)
180 N. Wacker Drive, Chicago 60606
(312) 621-0700

Sidley & Austin (L)
1 First National Plaza, Chicago 60603
(312) 853-7000

Society Professionals in Dispute Resolution
  1853 N. Cleveland Ave., Chicago 60614
(312) 787-4145

  29 S. LaSalle St., Chicago 60603
(312) 332-7760

United States Arbitration of Northern Illinois
  (C)
5301 W. Dempster, Skokie 60077
(312) 965-8206

RESOLVE Dispute Management, Inc. (C)
7 East Huron, Chicago 60611-2705
(312) 943-7477

Center for Families in Conflict
1725 W. Harrison St. (9344), Chicago
  60612
(312) 829-1463

Breslin Mediation (AFM)
151 N. Michigan Ave. (805), Chicago 60601
(312) 565-1888

Zoub Mediation (AFM)
155 N. Michigan Ave. (600), Chicago 60601
(312) 938-0011

Des Plaines
Clean Sites, Inc.
1400 E. Touhy Ave., Des Plaines 60018-
  3305
(312) 635-7580

Evanston
Society Professionals in Dispute Resolution
1225 Oak St., Evanston 60202
(312) 869-2244

Mediation Research & Education Project
  (C)/(E)
Leverone Hall 3-191, Northwestern Law
  School, Evanston 60201-2940
(312) 866-8576

Dept. of Organizational Behavior (E)
Kellogg School of Management, 2001 Sheridan, Evanston 60201
(312) 491-3470

Family & Legal Social Services (AFM)
2234 Asbury Ave., Evanston 60201
(312) 866-6231

Lombard
Mennonite Peace Center
528 E. Madison St., Lombard 60148
(312) 627-5310

Park Ridge
Divorce Mediation Center
1580 N. Northwest Highway (111), Park Ridge 60068
(312) 696-6023

Pastoral Psychotherapy Institute (AFM)
Parkside Center (365), 1875 Dempster St., Park Ridge 60068
(312) 696-6023

Springfield
Consumer Protection
Office Att. Gen., 500 S. 2nd, Springfield 62706
(217) 782-9011/1-800-252-8666

Indiana

Anderson
Community Justice Center
PO Box 149, Anderson 46015
(317) 649-7341

Bloomington
Smith Mediation (AFM)
PO Box 1965, Bloomington 47402
(812) 332-2558

Elkhart
MCC Office of Criminal Justice (VORP Program)
220 W. High St., Elkhart 46516
(219) 293-3090

Evansville
Community Mediation
609 SE Second St., Evansville 47713
(812) 423-3681

Goshen
Mennonite Conciliation Services
1021 S. 7th St., Goshen 46526
(219) 533-9739

Greencastle
Cummins Mental Health Center (AFM)
600 N. Arlington St., Greencastle 46135
(317) 653-2669

Indianapolis
Consumer Protection
Att. Gen. Office, 219 State House, Indianapolis 46204
(317) 232-6330

United States Arbitration & Mediation of Indiana, Inc. (C)
2345 S. Lynhurst Dr. (213), Indianapolis 46241
(317) 243-2174

Williams Mediation (AFM)
8801 N. Meridian (314), Indianapolis 46260
(317) 846-4937

Mishawaka
Mediation Center
Family & Children's Center, 1411 Lincolnway W., Mishawaka 46544
(219) 259-5666

Richmond
Dunn Mental Health Center (AFM)
831 Dillon Dr., Richmond 47374
(317) 983-8010

South Bend
Night Prosecutor's Program
Prosecutor's Office, County-City Bldg., South Bend 46601
(219) 284-9544

Valparaiso
PACT Institute of Justice
254 S. Morgan Boulevard, Valparaiso 46383
(219) 462-1127

Iowa

Ames
Committee on Criminal Justice Mediation
304 Lynn Ave., Ames 50010
(515) 292-3820

Cedar Rapids
Community Dispute Settlement Center
445 First St. SW, Cedar Rapids 52404
(319) 398-3693

Des Mones
Citizens Aide/Ombudsman
515 E. 12th St., Des Moines 50319
(515) 281-3592

Att. Gen.'s Program
Asst. Att. Gen., 1300 E. Walnut St., Des
    Moines 50314
(515) 281-5926

Neighborhood Mediation Center
12th & University Sts., Des Moines 50314
(515) 286-3057

United States Arbitration & Mediation of
    Iowa, Inc. (C)
930 Grand Ave., PO Box 65204, West Des
    Moines 50265
(515) 226-0100

Divorce Mediation Center
435 E. Grand Ave., Des Moines 50309
(515) 284-1434

Fort Dodge
Webster County Mediation Center
Courthouse, 701 Central St., Fort Dodge
    50501
(515) 955-2773

Iowa City
Divorce Mediation Clinic
308 North Hall, University of Iowa, Iowa
    City 52242
(319) 353-4852

Mason City
North Iowa Dispute Settlement Center
County Courthouse, 220 N. Washington
    St., Mason City 50401
(515) 421-3119

Ottumwa
Sieda Mediation Service
PO Box 658, Ottumwa 52501
(515) 682-8741 (Ext. 19)

Kansas

Eldorado
Mental Health Center
2365 W. Central St., Eldorado 67042
(316) 321-6036

Kansas City
Victim-Offender Restitution
229 S. 8th St., Kansas City 66105
(913) 621-1504

Lawrence
Psychological Clinic
University of Kansas, Lawrence 66045
(913) 864-4121

McPherson
Prairie View, Inc.
1102 Hospital Drive, McPherson 67460
(316) 241-4556

Mission
Fox Counseling & Mediation Group
5509 Foxridge Dr., Mission 66202
(913) 384-2727

Newton
Mennonite Conciliation Services
Rt. 2, Box 32A, Newton 67114
(316) 283-6826

Olathe
Project Early Dispute Settlement
465 S. Parker St. (103), Olathe 66061
(913) 764-8585

Family & Youth Services (AFM)
905 W. Spruce, Olathe 66061
(913) 782-7252

Salina
Conflict Resolution (AFM)
227 N. Santa Fe St. (302), Salina 67401
(913) 823-5091

Shawneee Mission
Jewish Family & Children Services
4550 W. 90th Terrace, Shawnee Mission
    66207
(913) 649-1056

Topeka
Dispute Alternative Resolution center
3600 SW Burlingame Rd. (1A), Topeka
    66611
(913) 267-5622

Menninger Foundation
234 Kansas Ave., Topeka 66603
(913) 232-7214

Law School Clinic
Washburn University, 17th & MacVicar
Sts., Topeka 66621
(913) 295-6691

Wichita
Psychological & Counseling Services
310 W. Central St. (212), Wichita 67202
(316) 268-9079

Mediators of Domestic Disputes
2525 E. Central St., PO Box 3351, Wichita
67214
(316) 682-6498

Bethel Presbyterian Church
1200 Sullivan Circle, Wichita 67204
(316) 838-1954

Kentucky

Covington
Kenton-Campbell Pretrial
Municipal Bldg. (308), 3rd & Court Sts.,
Covington 41011
(606) 292-6517

Crestview Hills
Criminal Justice Program
Thomas Moore College, Crestview Hills
41017
(606) 344-3385

Frankfort
Pretrial Service Agency
403 Wrapping St., Frankfort 40601
(502) 564-7486

Lexington
Fayette Mediation Program
136 Walnut St. (201), Lexington 40507
(606) 233-4085

Louisville
Pretrial Services
514 W. Liberty St. (105), Louisville 40202
(502) 588-4142

United States Arbitration & Mediation of
Kentucky, Inc. (C)
1 Riverfront Plaza (2014), Louisville 40202
(502) 585-5090

Family Mediation Service (AFM)
3711 Hillsdale Rd., Louisville 40222
(502) 426-8161

Murray
School Mediation Consultant (E)
Office Academic V.P., Murray State University, Murray 24071
(502) 762-6466

Louisiana

Baton Rouge
State Consumer Protection
PO Box 94455 Capitol Station, Baton Rouge
70804
(504) 925-4401

Lafayette
David S. Foster III (L)
PO Drawer 52389, Lafayette 70505
(318) 232-9313

Family Mediation Center (AFM)
PO Box 31422, Lafayette 70503
(318) 981-8304

New Orleans
American Arbitration Assn. (C)
605 Poydras Center (2035), New Orleans
70130-6101
(504) 522-8781

Custody Mediation
Family Service Center, 2515 Canal St.
(201), New Orleans 70119
(504) 822-0800

United States Arbitration & Mediation of
Louisiana (C)
Equitable Plaza Bldg. (210), 3626 N. Causeway Blvd.
Metairie 70002
(504) 831-2141

Divorce Mediation Center
4400 General Meyer St. (311), New Orleans
70114
(504) 363-7020

Community Mediation Service
1818 Chestnut St., New Orleans 70130
(504) 522-5575

Flanders & Flanders (AFM)
600 Loyola (201), New Orleans 70113
(504) 586-1441

Lipscomb Mediation (AFM)
8011 1/2 Maple St., New Orleans 70118
(504) 861-0505

Maine

Houlton
Chase Mediation (AFM)
PO Box 323, Houlton 04730
(207) 764-0311

Portland
Court Mediation Service
PO Box 328 D.T.S., Portland 04112
(207) 879-4700

Long Mediation (AFM)
75 Pearl St., Portland 04101
(207) 761-1817

Maryland

Annapolis
Community Arbitration
1623 Forest, Annapolis 21401
(301) 263-0707

Neighborhood Mediation Program
Office State Attorney, 101 S. St., Annapolis
    21401

National Center for Mediation & Education
2083 W. St. (3C), Annapolis 21401
(301) 224-3322

Mediation Services of Annapolis (AFM)
2083 West St. (3C), Annapolis 21401
(301) 261-8445/268-4072

Baltimore
Divorce Mediation Services
408 E. Quadrangle, Village of Cross Keys,
    Baltimore 21210
(301) 435-9280

Bel Air
Hartford County Circuit Court (AFM)
Courthouse (2-54), Bel Air 21014
(301) 838-6000

Chevy Chase
National Academy of Conciliators (C)
5530 Wisconsin Ave. (1130), Chevy Chase
    20815
800-638-8242

Boren Mediation (AFM)
3515 Chevy Chase Lake Dr., Chevy Chase
    20815
(301) 654-1577

Pickard Mediation (AFM)
5400 Trent St., Chevy Chase 20815
(301) 986-0010

College Park
Custody Mediation Services
Benjamin Bldg. (3304), University of Mary-
    land, College Park 20742
(301) 454-2036

Gaithersburg
Quinlan Mediation (AFM)
102 S. Frederick Ave., Gaithersburg 20877
(301) 840-2022

Hagerstown
Consumer-Business Binding Arbitration
138 E. Antietam St. (210), Hagerstown
    21740-5684
(301) 791-4780

Kensington
Family Center for Mediation & Counseling
    (AFM)
3514 Plyers Mill Rd. (100), Kensington
    20895
(301) 946-3400

Rockville
County Consumer Affairs
100 Maryland Ave. (330), Rockville 20852
(202) 251-7373

Family & Child Associates (AFM)
414 Hungerford Drive (240), Rockville
    20850
(301) 340-2060

National Criminal Justice Reference Service
Box 6000, Rockville 20850
(202) 251-5500

Towson
Divorce Mediation Services
204 E. Joppa Rd. (PH 10), Towson 21204
(301) 435-9280

Massachusetts

Amherst
U. of Massachusetts Mediation Project
425 Amity St., Amherst 01002
(413) 545-2462

Athol
Community Mediation Program
100 Main St., Athol 01331
(508) 249-9926/4422

Barnstable
Cpae Cod Mediation Program
PO Box 930, Barnstable 02630
(508) 362-3410

Boston
American Arbitration Assn. (C)
230 Congress St., Boston 02110-2409
(617) 451-6600

United States Arbitration & Mediation of
New England (C)
105 Union Wharf, Boston 02109-1286
(617) 742-0064

Alternative Dispute Resolution Project
Dept. Att. Gen., 1 Ashburton Place, Boston
02108
(617) 727-7122

ADR, INC.
200 State St., Boston 02109
(617) 439-9720

Face-to-Face Mediation Program
City Hall (613), Boston 02201
(617) 725-3320

Mediation Clinic
Downtown Law Center, University of Massachusetts, Boston 02125
(617) 956-1088

Common Ground/Center for Policy Negotiation, Inc.
20 Park Plaza, Boston 02116-4303
(617) 482-8660

New England Environmental Mediation
Center
200 Lincoln St., Boston 02111-2404
(617) 451-3670

Center Negotiation & Public Policy
Statler Office Bldg. (520), Boston 02116
(617) 482-8660

ERM New England, Inc.
205 Portland St., Boston 02114-1708
(617) 742-8228

Family Mediation Associates (AFM)
264 Beacon St., Boston 02116
(617) 876-8036

Mediation Program
Crime & Justice Foundation, 20 West St.,
Boston 02111
(617) 426-9800

Massachusetts Mediation Service
State House (373), Boston 02133
(617) 727-2224

Brighton
Faneuil Mediation Program
276 N. Beacon St. (26), Brighton 02135
(617) 254-4088

Brockton
Brockton Mediation Program
45 School St., City Hall, Brockton 02401
(508) 580-7184

Brookline
Mediation Group (C)
74 Salisbury Rd., Brookline 02146
(617) 277-9232

Brookline Mediation Collaborative
43 Garrison Rd., Brookline 02146
(617) 734-5871

Cambridge
Harvard Program on Negotiation
500 Pound Hall, Harvard Law School,
Cambridge 02138
(617) 495-4615

Harvard Mediation Program
Pound Hall, Harvard Law School, Cambridge 02138
(617) 495-1854

Dispute Settlement Center
1 West St., Cambridge 02139
(617) 876-5376

ENDISPUTE of Boston (C)
12 Arrow St., Cambridge 02138-5105
(617) 868-0200

Interaction Associates, Inc.
124 Mount Auburn St., Cambridge 02138
(617) 354-2000

Center for Law Education (E)
Gutman Library, 6 Appian Way, Cambridge
  02138
(617) 495-4666

Children's Hearings Project (E)
99 Bishop Allen Dr., Cambridge 02139
(617) 661-4700

Children's Judicial Resource Council
34 Royal St., Cambridge 02138
(617) 267-3590

Ombudsman M.I.T.
Room 10-213, Mass. Inst. Technology,
  Cambridge 02139
(617) 253-5921

Educators for Social Responsibility (E)
23 Garden St., Cambridge 02138
(617) 492-1764

Welsh Assn. for Negotiation Training (E)
1105 Massachusetts Ave. (12E), Cambridge
  02138
(617) 576-2137

Dorchester
Housing Authority Mediation
100 Ames St., Dorchester 02120
(617) 282-7081

Urban Mediation Project
1486 Dorchester Ave., Dorchester 02122
(617) 288-7163/6816

Dudley
Mediation Services
District Court, West Main St., Dudley
  01570
(508) 943-7123 (Ext. 40)

Edgartown
Edgartown Mediation Program
Box 1284, Edgartown 02539
(508) 627-3751

Fitchburg
Fitchburg Mediation Project
District Court, 100 Elm St., Fitchburg
  01420
(508) 345-2111

Framingham
Court Mediation Services, Inc.
600 Concord St., Framingham 01701
(508) 872-9495

Gloucester
New England Environmental Mediation
125 Main St., Gloucester 02111
(508) 283-1153

Greenfield
Franklin County Mediation Project
13 Prospect St., Greenfield 01301
(413) 772-0035/774-7931

Haverhill
Mediation Dispute Resolution Project
25 Locust St., Haverhill 01830
(508) 373-1971

Kingston
South Shore Mediation Program
169 Summer St., Kingston 02364
(508) 585-3885

Lowell
Alternative Dispute Resolution Program
167 Dutton St., Lowell 01852
(508) 459-0551 (Ext. 138)

Lynn
Lynn Youth Resource Bureau
19 Sutton St., Lynn 01901
(617) 598-4874

Needham
Agreement, Inc. (C)
18 Border Rd., Needham 02192
(617) 444-2346

New Bedford
Probate & Family Court Mediation
505 Pleasant St., New Bedford 02740
(617) 996-5669

Community Mediation Project
167 William St., New Bedford 02740
(508) 999-9935

Newton Centre
Mediation Associates
1280 Centre St. (240), Newton Centre
  02159
(617) 244-0084

Northampton
Parent-Adolescent Mediation Program
17 New South St., Northampton 01060
(413) 584-1087

Orleans
Family Mediation Program
81 Old Colony Way, Orleans 02633
(508) 255-2981

Plymouth
Family Mediation Program
374 Court St., Plymouth 02360
(617) 746-9025

Quincy
District Court Mediation Services
District Court, 1 Dennis F. Ryan Pkwy.,
   Quincy 02169
(617) 471-1650

Salem
District Court Mediation Headquarters
Holyoke Square, Salem 01970
(508) 745-9010

Salem Mediation Program
1st District Court, 65 Washington St.,
   Salem 01970
(508) 745-4165

Somerville
Somerville Mediation Program
1 Summer St., Somerville 02143
(617) 776-5931

Springfield
Dispute Rsolution Services, Inc.
9 Stockbridge St., Springfield 01103
(413) 787-6480

Family Mediation Service
155 Maple St. (3rd Floor), Springfield 01105
(413) 733-6624

Neighborhood Youth Mediation
2345 Main St., Springfield 01107
(413) 737-2632

Wenham
Mediation Resources (AFM)
161 Main St., Wenham 01984
(617) 468-2579

Worcester
Mediation Services
81 Plantation St., Worcester 01608
(508) 755-7660

Community Mediation Center
340 Main St. (555), Worcester 01608
(508) 754-5322

Michigan

Ann Arbor
Dispute Resolution Center
PO Box 8645, 4133 Washtenaw Rd., Ann
   Arbor 48107
(313) 971-6054

Environmental Conflict Project
2036 Dana Bldg., University of Michigan,
   Ann Arbor 48109
(313) 764-1511

Ann Arbor Mediation Center (AFM)
405 N. Main St., Ann Arbor 48104
(313) 663-1155

Dispute Resolution (E)
4028 B Lit., Science & Art Bldg., U. of
   Michigan, Ann Arbor 48109
(313) 764-7487

Dearborn
Ford Consumer Appeals Board
PO Box 1805, Dearborn 48126
(313) 337-6950

Detroit
Family Counseling & Mediation, Friend of
   Court
65 Cadillac Square (556), Detroit 48226
(313) 224-5266

Society Professionals in Dispute Resolution
4140 Second Ave., Detroit 48201
(313) 832-0682

Federal Bldg. (431), 231 W. Lafayette St.,
   Detroit 48226
(313) 226-2114

Michigan Arbitration Services, Inc. (C)
25505 W. 12 Mile Rd. (2713), Southfield
   48034
(313) 350-3060

Interaction Associates, Inc.
46671 Greenridge Dr., Northville 48167
(313) 349-5780

Volunteer Mediation Program
150 Michigan Ave. (4th Floor), Detroit
48226
(313) 224-4950

Chrysler Customer Arbitration
PO Box 1718, Detroit 28288
(313) 956-5970

Gaylord
Uhlmann Mediation (AFM)
1557 Wilkinson Rd., Gaylord 49735
(517) 732-1178

Grand Rapids
Family Service Assn.
1122 Leonard NE, Grand Rapids 49503
(616) 774-0633

Smith, Haughey, Rice & Roegge (L)
200 Calder Plaza Bldg. (200), Grand Rapids
49503
(616) 774-8000

Lansing
Christian Conciliation Service
1441 1/2 East Michigan, Lansing 48912
(517) 485-2270

Consumer Protection Division
690 Law Bldg., 525 W. Ottawa St., Lansing
48913
(517) 373-1140

Midland
Joseph Mediation (AFM)
5810 Evergreen, Midland 48640
(517) 835-1116

Mt. Clemens
Citizens Dispute Settlement
40700 Romeo Plank Rd., Mt. Clemens
48044
(313) 386-8010

Mt. Pleasant
Mid-Michigan Family & Divorce Mediation
302 1/2 E. Chippewa, Mt. Pleasant 48858
(517) 773-9600

Pontiac
Friend of the Court
1200 N. Telegraph Rd., Pontiac 48053
(313) 858-5560

Redford
Christian Conciliation Service
27350 W. Chicago St., Redford 48239
(313) 937-3939

St. Joseph
Fisher, Troff & Fisher (L)
PO Box 67, St. Joseph 449085
(616) 983-0160

The Samaritan Center
2001 Niles Ave., St. Joseph 49085
(616) 443-4422

Southfield
American Arbitration Association (C)
Ten Oak Hollow (170), 48034-7405
(313) 352-5500

Minnesota

Alexandria
D.E.O. Family Center
2210 Lincoln Ave. East, Alexandria 56308
(612) 763-3700

Brooklyn Center
North Hennepin Mediation Project
5136 N. Lilac Drive, Brooklyn Center 55429
(612) 536-1121

Duluth
Custody/Visitation
424 W. Superior St. (600), Duluth 55802
(218) 726-4826

Northland Mediation Service
802 Torrey Bldg., Duluth 55802
(218) 723-4003

Edina
Family Mediation Service (AFM)
4570 W. 77th St. (223), Edina 55435
(612) 893-0501

Fridley
Primary Mediation Services (AFM)
7260 University Ave. NE (320), Fridley
55432
(612) 571-7132

Minneapolis
American Arbitration Assn. (C)
514 Nicollet Mall, Minneapolis 55402-2975
(612) 332-6545

Christian Conciliation Service
5701 Normandale Rd. (326), Minneapolis
   55424
(612) 922-2048

Americord, Inc. (C)
Renaissance Square (375), 512 Nicollet
   Mall, Minneapolis 55402
(612) 344-1999

Park Nicollet Medical Center
500 W. 39th St., Minneapolis 55416
(612) 937-3060

Citizens Dispute Settlement
A-1700 Hennepin Government Center
Minneapolis 55487
(612) 348-7496

Society Professionals in Dispute Resolution
University of Minnesota Law School, 229
   19th St., Minneapolis 55454
(612) 373-4841

Neighborhood Dispute Serivce
2507 Fremont Ave. North, Minneapolis
   55411
(612) 529-6440

Divorce Mediation Services
2205 Minneapolis Ave., Minneapolis 55406
(612) 339-6242

Michael Shea & Associates
1730 Clifton Place (100), Minneapolis 55403
(612) 871-2165

Resources (E)
Sociology Dept. (1114), 267 19th Ave.
   South, Minneapolis 55455
(612) 376-2740

Osseo
North Hennepin Mediation Service
33 Fourth St. NW, Osseo 55369
(612) 425-4116

Rochester
Family Consultation Center
903 W. Center St. (220), Rochester 55902
(507) 287-2010

Dunlap, Keith, Finseth, Berndt & Sandberg
   (L)
505 Marquette Bank Bldg., Rochester 55903
(507) 288-9111

St. Paul
Society Professionals in Dispute Resolution
Minn. Bureau Mediation Services, 205 Aurora, St. Paul 55103
(612) 296-2525

Customer-Business Disputes
1745 University Ave., St. Paul 55104
(612) 646-4637

Consumer Services Unit
117 University Ave., St. Paul 55155
(612) 296-3353

Customer Service, Public Utilities Commission
American Center Bldg. (708), 160 E. Kellogg, St. Paul 55101
(612) 296-7126

Dispute Resolution Center
911 Lafond Ave., St. Paul 55104
(612) 489-4051

Domestic Relations Division
Commerce Bldg. (700), 1745 Court House,
   St. Paul 55101
(612) 298-4379

Fee Arbitration Committee
Ramsey County Bar, W952 1st Nat. Bank
   Bldg., St. Paul 55101
(612) 222-0846

4-H Family Mediation
340 Coffey Hall, University of Minnesota,
   St. Paul 55108
(612) 625-9700

Macalester College Mediation
1600 Grand Ave., St. Paul 55104
(612) 696-6297

Workers Compensation Mediation
Dept. Labor & Industry, 444 Lafayette Rd.,
   St. Paul 55101
(612) 296-4534

Mediation Center
Midway Bldg., 1821 University Ave., St.
   Paul 55104
(612) 644-1453

Mediation Alternative (C)
23 Empire Dr. St. Paul 55103
(612) 223-8662

Davis Mediation (AFM)
1828 Wordsworth Ave., St. Paul 55116
(612) 699-4763

Stillwater
Associates & Emery Barrette (AFM)
815 McKusick Rd., Circle N., Stillwater
  55082
(612) 430-2710

Missouri

Hannibal
Legal Aid
PO Box 1276, Hannibal 63401

Kansas City
American Arbitration Assn. (C)
1101 Walnut St., Kansas City 64106-2110
(816) 221-6401

Midwest Arbitration & Mediation Services
  (C)
PO Box 26064, Kansas City 64196
(913) 791-4050

Lathrop Koontz & Norquist (L)
2345 Grand Ave., Kansas City 64108
(816) 842-0820

Housing Information
3810 Paseo, Kansas City 64109-2721
(816) 842-2440

St. Louis
Neighborhood Dispute Center
3700 Lindell Blvd. (310), St. Louis 63108
(314) 535-2061

Missouri Arbitration Servcie, Inc. (C)
915 Olive St. (1001 C), St. Louis 63101
(314) 231-4642

Americn Arbitration Assn. (C)
One Mercantile Center (2512), St. Louis
  63101-1643
(314) 621-7175

Mediation Services of St. Louis (AFM)
8000 Bonhomme St. (201), St. Louis 63105
(314) 721-4333

Law & Education Unit, Public Schools (E)
5183 Raymond St., St. Louis 63113
(314) 361-5500

Family Mediation Assn.
141 N. Meramee St. (307), St. Louis 63105
(314) 862-2305

Institute for Peace & Justice
4144 Lindell St. (400), St. Louis 63108
(314) 533-4445

Springfield
Ozark Christian Counseling Service
1500 E. Sunshine St. (B), Springfield 65804
(417) 881-3285

Montana

Missoula
Northern Rockies Arbitration & Mediation
  Services (C)
126 E. Broadway (25), Missoula 59802
(406) 728-4681

Nebraska

Lincoln
Willard Crime Prevention Justice
1245 S. Folsom St., Lincoln 68522
(402) 475-0805

Omaha
United States Arbitration & Mediation of
  Nebraska (C)
8712 W. Dodge Rd. (300), Omaha 68114
(402) 392-1250

County Conciliation Court
Hall of Justice (1st Floor), Omaha 68183
(402) 444-7168/69

Nevada

Las Vegas
Consumer Affairs
2501 E. Sahara (304), Las Vegas 89104
(702) 386-5293

Child Custody Div., District Court (AFM)
200 S. 3rd St. (407), Las Vegas 89155
(702) 455-4185

Sparks
Juris-Amicus, Inc. (AFM)
835 N. Rock Blvd., Sparks 89431
(702) 825-8382

New Hampshire

Concord
New Hampshire Mediation Service
33 Stickney St., Concord 03301
(603) 224-8043

Exeter
Resolve Mediation Service (AFM)
22 Epping Rd., Exeter 03833
(603) 772-4112

New Jersey

Atlantic City
Community Justice Institute
1201 Bacharach Blvd., Atlantic City 08401
(609) 345-7267

Belle Mead
Unitarian University Counsel/Education Service
27 Tall Cedar Court, RD 6, Belle Mead 08502
(201) 359-2097

East Orange
Family Counseling Unit
Municipal Court, 221 Freeway Dr. East, East Orange 07018
(201) 266-5073

Hackensack
Neighborhood Dispute Center
355 Main St., Hackensack 07601
(201) 646-2121

Small Claims Settlement
Hackensack Courthouse (430), Hackensack 07601
(201) 646-2000

Jersey City
Neighborhood & Family Dispute Settlement
Murdoch Hall (9th Floor), 114 Clifton Place, Jersey City 07306
(201) 451-0165

Millville
Neighborhood Dispute Panel
18 S. High St., Millville 08332
(609) 825-7000 (Ext. 317)

Morristown
County Family Mediation
Hall of Records Bldg., Morristown 07960
(201) 829-8408

New Brunswick
Citizens Dispute Settlement
PO Box 789, New Brunswick 08903
(201) 745-3886

Newark
Center for Negotiation & Conflict Resolution
15 Washington St., Newark 07102
(201) 648-5048

Dispute Resolution Project
Essex County Bar, Gateway (16th Floor), Newark 07102
(201) 622-6207

Office of Consumer Protection
1100 Raymond Blvd. (405), Newark 07102
(201) 648-3622

Municipal Court, Neighborhood Service Div.
31 Green St., Newark 07102

Pomona
Community Justice Institute
Stockton State College, Pomona 08240
(609) 345-7267

Princeton Junction
Divorce Mediation, Felmeister & Isaacs
Princeton-Windsor Office Park, Princeton Junction 08550
(609) 448-4550

Red Bank
Muise Mediation (AFM)
10 Spring St., Red Bank 07701
(201) 530-2951

Somerset
American Arbitration Assn. (C)
265 Davidson Ave., Somerset 08873-4002
(201) 560-9560

South Orange
Police-Citizen Mediation Study (E)
Seton Hall University, South Orange 07079
(201) 786-9170/(212) 849-9166

Toms River
Family Intake Services
New Justice Complex (209), Toms River
08753
(201) 929-2062

Trenton
County Mediation Unit
Family Court, 650 S. Broad St., Trenton
08611
(609) 989-6080/6081

Center for Public Dispute Resolution
Public Advocate, CN 850, Trenton 08625
(609) 292-1773

Society Professionals in Dispute Resolution
860 Lower Ferry Rd., Trenton 08628
(201) 560-9560

Union City
Help Center (AFM)
1906 Kennedy Blvd., Union City 07087
(201) 868-0922

New Mexico

Albuquerque
Christian Conciliation Service
616 Central SE (211), Albuquerque 87102
(505) 243-6887

Wheeler, McElwee, Sprague & Long (L)
3401 Carlisle NE, Albuquerque 87110
(505) 881-8998

New Mexico Center for Dispute Resolution
510 Second St. NW (209), Albuquerque
87102
(505) 843-9410

Conflict Resolution in the Schools (E)
PO Box 25883, Albuquerque 87125
(505) 842-6136

Second District Family Court Clinic (AFM)
PO Box 488, Albuquerque 87103
(505) 841-7409

Egan Mediation (AFM)
1228 Central SW, Albuquerque 87102
(505) 242-0660

Bernalillo County Court Clinic (AFM)
1340 Wellesley NE, Albuquerque 87106
(505) 268-0867

Los Alamos
Los Alamos Family Council
1505 15th St., Los Alamos 87544
(505) 662-3264

Moore & Golden
PO Box 1226, 1650 Trinity Dr., Los Alamos
87544
(505) 662-5112

Santa Fe
Western Network
1215 Paseo de Peralta, Santa Fe 87501-2748
(505) 982-9805

Taos
Environmental Mediation
PO Box 2231, Taos 87581
(505) 758-0043

New York

Albany
Albany Mediation Program
PO Box 9140, Albany 12209
(518) 436-4958

Consumer Protection
NY Dept. of Law, Albany 12224
(518) 474-5481

N.Y. Community Dispute Resolution Centers Program
Agency Bldg. 4 (10th Floor), Empire State
Plaza, Albany 12223
(518) 473-4160

Albion
Dispute Settlement Center of Orleans
County
Orleans County Admin. Bldg., Route 31,
Albion 14411
(716) 589-5673

Baldwin
Barsky Mediation (AFM)
8977 Lorenz Ave., Baldwin 11510
(516) 223-2025

Batavia
Dispute Settlement Center, Genesee County
Main Street, Batavia 14020
(716) 343-8180 (Ext. 250)

Binghamton
ACCORD
Cutler House, 834 Front St., Binghamton
13905
(607) 724-5153

Brooklyn
Brooklyn Mediation Center
210 Joralemon St. (618), Brooklyn 11201
(718) 834-6671

Dispute Resolution Center
1106 James Hall, Brooklyn College, Brooklyn 11210
(718) 780-4148

Buffalo
Dispute Settlement Center (Regional Office)
346 Delaware Ave., Buffalo 14202
(716) 856-7180

Canastota
Resolve—Center For Dispute Settlement, Inc.
120 E. Center St., Canastota 13032
(315) 697-3809

Caneadea
Dispute Resolution Center
PO Box 577, Caneadea 14717
(716) 373-5133

Canton
Center for Conflict Resolution, Inc.
PO Box 70, Canton 13617
(315) 386-4677

Carmel
Putnam County Mediation Program
PO Box 776, Carmel 10512
(914) 225-9555

Catskill
Common Ground
PO Box 329, 1 Bridge St., Catskill 12414
(518) 943-9205

Centereach
Conflict Resolution & Mediation Service (E)
8 43rd St., Centereach 11720
(516) 467-3610

Coram
Community Mediation Center
356 Middle Country Rd., Coram 11727
(516) 736-2626

Corning
Neighborhood Justice Project of Southern
Tier
147 E. 2nd St., Corning 14830
(607) 936-8807

Cortland
Cortland County Resolve
111 Port Watson St., Cortland 13045
(607) 753-6952

Croton-on-Hudson
Kimmelman Mediation (AFM)
29 Scenic Circle, Croton-on-Hudson 10520
(914) 271-9280

Delhi
Delaware County Dispute Resolution Center
72 Main St., Delhi 13753
(607) 746-6392

Elizabethtown
Center for Conflict Resolution, Inc.
North County Community College, Elizabethtown 12932
(518) 873-9910

Elmira
Neighborhood Justice Project
451 E. Market St., Elmira 14901
(607) 734-3338

Fayetteville
Family Mediation Center (AFM)
7000 E. Genesee St. (Bldg. A), Fayetteville
13066
(315) 446-5513

Fonda
Center for Dispute Resolution
39 E. Main St., Fonda 12068
(518) 853-4611

Fulton
Oswego County Resolve
365 W. 1st St., Fulton 13069
(315) 598-3980

Garden City
American Arbitration Assn. (C)
585 Stewart Ave., Garden City 11530-4789
(516) 222-1660

Nassau County Community Dispute Center
585 Stewart Ave. (302), Garden City 11530
(516) 222-1660

Marlow Mediation (AFM)
300 Garden City Plaza (410), Garden City
   11530
(516) 294-5848

Geneseo
Center for Dispute Settlement, Inc.
4241 Lakeville Road, Geneseo 14454
(716) 243-4410

Geneva
Center for Dispute Settlement
One Franklin Square, Geneva 14456
(315) 789-0364

Granville
Washington County Mediation Services
5 North St., Granville 12832
(518) 642-1237

Herkimer
Community Dispute Resolution Program
Catholic Family & Community Services
216 Henry St., Herkimer 13350
(315) 866-4268

Hudson
Common Ground
Box 1, Hudson 12534
(518) 828-4611

Huntington
Haynes Mediation Associates (AFM)
161 E. Main St., Huntington 11743
(516) 385-2490

Construction Mediation, Inc.
PO Box 181, Huntington 11743
(516) 271-7697

Ithaca
Dispute Resolution Center
124 The Commons, Ithaca 14850
(607) 273-9347

Jamestown
Dispute Settlement Center
Municipal Bldg., 300 E. 3rd St., Jamestown
   14701
(716) 664-4223

Jamaica
Mediation for Youth
89-25 Parsons Blvd., Jamaica 11432
(718) 523-6868

Kew Gardens
Queens Mediation Center
119-45 Union Turnpike, Kew Gardens
   11375
(718) 793-1900

Lake George
Adirondack Mediation Services
Warren County Municipal Center, Lake
   George 12845
(518) 761-6401

Lockport
Dispute Settlement Center, Niagara County
1 Locks Plaza, Lockport 14094
(716) 439-6684

Long Island City
SMART Mediation Program (E)
William Cullen Bryant H.S., 48-10 31st St.,
   Long Island City 11103
(718) 721-5404 (Ext. 24)

Lowville
Lewis Mediation Service
5402 Dayan St., Lowville 13637
(315) 376-7991

Lyons
Center for Dispute Settlement
26 Church St., Lyons 14489
(315) 946-9300

Malone
Center for Conflict Resolution
64 Elm St., PO Box 270, Malone 12953
(518) 483-5470

Manhasset Hills
Crootof Mediation (AFM)
54 Crest Rd., Manhasset Hills 11040
(516) 624-7421

Middletown
Orange County Mediation Project, Inc.
57 North St., PO Box 520, Middletown
   10940
(914) 342-6807

Mineola
Mediation Alternative Project
100 E. Old Country Rd., Mineola 11051
(516) 741-5580

Monsey
Center for Family & Divorce Mediation
   (AFM)
146 Willow Tree Rd., Monsey 10952
(914) 638-4666

Monticello
Ulster-Sullivan Mediation, Inc.
PO Box 947, Monticello 12701
(914) 794-3377

Mount Vernon
Family Institute of Westchester
147 Archer Ave., Mount Vernon 10550
(914) 699-4300

New City
Volunter Counseling Service
151 S. Main St., New City 10956
(914) 634-5729

New Paltz
Ulster-Sullivan Mediation, Inc.
PO Box 726, New Paltz 12561
(914) 691-6944

New York City
American Arbitration Assn. (C)
140 W. 51st St., New York 10020-1203
(212) 484-4000

IMCR Dispute Resolution Center
425 W. 144th St., New York City 10031
(212) 690-5700

Washington Heights–Inwood Coalition
652 W. 187th St., New York City 10033
(212) 781-6722

Victim Services Agency
2 Lafayette St., New York City 10007
(212) 577-7700

Davidson, Dawson & Clark (L)
320 Madison Ave., New York City 10017
(212) 557-7700

Donovan, Leisure, Newton & Irvine (L)
30 Rockefeller Plaza, New York City 10112
(212) 632-3000

Shearman & Sterling (L)
599 Lexington Ave. at 53rd St., New York
   City 10022
(212) 848-4000

Skadden, Arps, Slate, Meagher & Flom (L)
919 Third Ave., New York City 10022-9931
(212) 735-3000

Webster & Sheffield (L)
237 Park Ave., New York City 10017
(212) 808-6000

Society Professionals in Dispute Resolution
   (George Nicolau)
125 E. 10th St., New York City 10003
(212) 777-5032

Center for Public Resources (C)
680 Fifth Ave., New York City 10019
(212) 541-9830

Institute for Mediation & Conflict Resolution
99 Hudson St., (11th Floor), New York City
   10013
(212) 966-3660

Brach Mediation (AFM)
146 Central Park West, New York City
   10023
(212) 580-0471

Institute of Judicial Administration
1 Washington Square Village, New York
   City 10012
(212) 949-4929

Scientists Institute for Public Information
355 Lexington Ave., New York City 10017
(212) 661-9110

School Conflict Resolution Project (E)
49 E. 68th St., New York City 10021
(212) 570-9400

Dept. Consumer Affairs
80 Lafayette St., New York City 10013
(212) 577-0111

Center Family Treatment & Divorce Mediation (AFM)
1 W. 91st St., New York City 10024
(212) 595-3444

Dispute Resolution Project
John Jay College of Criminal Justice
445 W. 59th St., New York City 10019
(212) 489-3287

Center for Law and Human Values (E)
2901 Broadway (120), New York City 10025
(212) 316-1267

Center for Study Bargaining in Higher Education (E)
Baruch College, CUNY, 17 Lexington Ave.,
   New York City 10010
(212) 725-3390

Negotiation Institute, Inc.
230 Park Ave. (460), New York City 10017
(212) 986-5557

PINS Mediation Project
105 E. 22nd St. (514), New York City
10010
(212) 949-4929

Niagara Falls
O'Connor Mediation (AFM)
710 Cedar Ave., Niagara Falls 14301
(716) 282-2008

Northport
Project PATCH (E)
110 Elwood Rd., Northport 11768
(516) 261-9000 (Ext. 284)

Norwich
Dispute Resolution Center, Chenango
County
Norwich Center Office Plaza, 27 W. Main
St., Norwich 13815
(607) 336-5442

Nyack
Children's Creative Response to Conflict (E)
Box 272, Nyack 10960
(914) 358-4601

Olean
Dispute Settlement Center
255 N. Union St., Olean 14760
(716) 373-5133

Oneonta
AGREE—Center for Dispute Settlement
9 S. Main St., Oneonta 13820
(607) 432-5484

Oswego
Resolve—Center for Dispute Settlement,
Inc.
1198 W. First St., Oswego 13126
(315) 342-3092

ACCORD
55 North Ave., Oswego 13827
(607) 687-4864

Pittsford
Divorce Mediation Associates (AFM)
47 Round Trail Dr., Pittsford 14534
(716) 385-2648

Plattsburg
Center for Conflict Resolution, Inc.
Clinton County Center, Ward Hall (212A),
SUNY at Plattsburg
Plattsburg 12901
(518) 564-2327

Port Washington
Mediation Alternative
382 Main St., Port Washington 11050
(516) 883-3006

Poughkeepsie
Community Dispute Resolution Center
327 Mill St., Poughkeepsie 12601
(914) 471-7213

PROUD, Poughkeepsie School District (E)
11 College Ave., PO Box 3010, Poughkeepsie 12603
(914) 471-5030

Rochester
Center for Dispute Settlement, Inc.
87 N. Clinton Ave. (510), Rochester 14604
(716) 546-5110

Society Professionals in Dispute Resolution
(Mona Miller)
NYSSILR, Cornell University
305 Andrews St., Rochester 14604
(716) 428-9906

Divorce Mediation Center (AFM)
2024 W. Henrietta Rd. (5G), Rochester
14623
(716) 272-1990

Saratoga
Dispute Settlement Program
10 Franklin St., Saratoga 12866
(518) 587-9826/583-0756

Scarsdale
Gateway Counseling
56 Hutchinson Blvd., Scarsdale 10583
(914) 725-1244

Schenectady
Community Dispute Settlement
161 Jay St., Schenectady 12305
(518) 346-1281

Antokol & Coffin
514 State St., Schenectady 12305
(518) 370-2500

South Setauket
Society Professionals in Dispute Resolution
(Charles Zoffer)
NYS Dept. Transportation, 56 Bellwood
South Setauket 11720
(516) 360-6100

Speculator
Dispute Resolution Coordination
Village Hall, Elm Lake Rd., PO Box 356,
Speculator 12164
(518) 548-8213

Staten Island
Community Dispute Resolution
111 Canal St., Staten Island 10304
(212) 720-9410

Divorce Mediation Service
190 Hart Blvd., Staten Island 10301
(718) 273-7216

Syracuse
American Arbitration Assn. (C)
109 S. Warren St., 720 State Tower Bldg.,
Syracuse 13202-1838
(315) 472-5483

Dispute Resolution Center
Onondaga County Civic Center (12th
Floor), Syracuse 13202
(315) 425-3053

Resolve—Center for Dispute Settlement,
Inc.
210 E. Fayette St. (7th Floor), Syracuse
13202
(315) 471-4676

Mediation Network of Syracuse
501 Stolp Ave., Syracuse 13207
(315) 475-2158

Dispute Resolution Project
Sociology Dept., 500 University Place,
Syracuse 13244
(315) 423-2572

Tarrytown
Arbitration Forums, Inc. (C)
200 White Plains Rd., PO Box 66, Tarry-
town 10591-0066
(914) 332-4770/800-426-8889

Troy
Community Dispute Settlement
35 State St., Troy 12180
(518) 274-5920

Utica
Community Dispute Resolution
214 Rutger St., Utica 13501
(315) 797-6473

Watertown
Dispute Resolution Center
PO Box 899, Watertown 13601
(315) 782-4900

Watkins Glen
Neighborhood Justice Project
PO Box 366, 111 9th St., Watkins Glen
14891
(607) 535-4757

Weedsport
Cayuga County Dispute Resolution Center,
Inc.
9021 N. Seneca St., Weedsport 13166
(315) 834-6881

White Plains
American Arbitration Assn. (C)
34 S. Broadway, White Plains 10601-4485
(914) 946-1119

Friedman Mediation (AFM)
10 Mitchell Place, White Plains 10601
(914) 997-8352

Yonkers
Westchester Mediation Center of CLUSTER
201 Palisade Ave., Box 201, Yonkers 10703
(914) 963-6500

North Carolina
Asheville
Mediation Center
County Courthouse (408), Box 7171, Asheville 28801-3576
(704) 251-6089

Divorce Mediation Associates
PO Box 15689, Asheville 28813
(704) 274-5588

Neville Mediation (AFM)
PO Box 15689, Asheville 28813
(704) 254-1058

Burlington
Family Counseling & Mediation (AFM)
108 W. Kime St., Burlington 27215
(919) 227-8412

Carrboro
Dispute Settlement Center
302 Weaver St., Carrboro 27510
(919) 929-8800

Chapel Hill
Dispute Settlement Center
01 Steele Bldg. 050A, U. of North Carolina
Chapel Hill 27514
(919) 966-4041

Charlotte
American Arbitration Assn. (C)
7301 Carmel Executive Park, Charlotte
28226-8297
(704) 541-1367

Community Relations Council
623 E. Trade St. (410), Charlotte 28202
(704) 336-2424

United Family Services (AFM)
301 S. Brevard St., Charlotte 28202
(704) 332-9034

Durham
Dispute Settlement Center
800 Watts St., Durham 27702
(919) 683-1978

Private Adjudication Center, Inc. (C)
Duke University, Durham 22706-7706
(919) 493-7770

Adult Counseling Services
3500 West Gate Dr. (403), Durham 27707
(919) 493-2674

Fayetteville
Dispute Resolution Center
310 Green St., Fayetteville 28301
(919) 486-9465

Goldsboro
Dispute Settlement Center
PO Drawer A, Goldsboro 27523
(919) 735-6121

Graham
Alamance County Dispute Settlement Center
PO Box 982, Graham 27252
(919) 228-7394

Greensboro
Mediation Services
1105 E. Wendover Ave., Greensboro 27405
(919) 273-5667

Green Mediation (AFM)
1210 B Westridge Rd., Greensboro 27410
(919) 292-3663

Hendersonville
Henderson County Dispute Settlement Center
Federal Bldg., 140 4th Ave. West, Hendersonville 28739
(704) 697-7055

Lynn
Polk County Dispute Settlement Center
PO Box 112, Lynn 28750
(704) 859-9819

Pittsboro
Dispute Settlement Center
PO Box 1151, Pittsboro 27312
(919) 542-4075

Raleigh
Fontaine Mediation (AFM)
114 Byron Place, Raleigh 27609
(919) 782-4354

Mediation Services of Wake County
PO Box 1462, Raleigh 27602
(919) 821-1296

Statesville
Piedmont Mediation Center
PO Box 169, Statesville 28677
(704) 873-7624

Wilmington
Neighborhood Justice Program
414 Chestnut St. (301), Wilmington 28401
(919) 341-7159

Winston-Salem
Neighborhood Justice Center
PO Box 436, Winston-Salem 27102
(919) 724-2870

Family Service Mediation Center
610 Coliseum Dr., Winston-Salem 27106
(919) 722-8173

Stafford Mediation (AFM)
4139 Rosalie St. (100), Winston-Salem 27104
(919) 765-0587

North Dakota

Bismarck
Fee Arbitration Panel
PO Box 2136, Bismarck 58502
(701) 255-1404

Christian Conciliation Service
1501 N. 12th St., PO Box 2599, Bismarck 58502
(701) 255-6601

Legal Counsel for Indigents
514 E. Tahyer Ave., Bismarck 58501
(701) 224-5636

Fargo
Dept. Child/Family Science
North Dakota State University (H.E. 283), Fargo 58105
(701) 237-8280

Ohio

Beachwood
Weiss & Eisenhardt
4 Commerce Park Square (600), 23200 Chagrin Blvd., Beachwood 44122
(216) 292-8171

Canton
Mennonite Conciliation Service of Ohio
1939 Third St. SE, Canton 44707
(216) 453-1044

Cincinnati
American Arbitration Assn. (C)
441 Vine St. (3308), Cincinnati 45202-2809
(513) 241-8434

Private Complaint Program
County Justice Center (111), 1000 Sycamore St., Cincinnati 45202
(513) 763-5130

Cincinnati Institute of Justice
222 E. Central Pkwy. (408-A), Cincinnati 45202-1215
(513) 421-2022

Christian Conciliation Service
P.O. Box 19167, Cincinnati 45219
(513) 861-HOPE

Cleveland
American Arbitration Assn. (C)
1127 Euclid Ave., Cleveland 44115-1632
(216) 241-4741

Prosecutor Mediation Program
1200 Ontario St. (8th Floor), Cleveland 44113
(216) 664-4800

Community Youth Mediation (E)
3000 Bridge Ave., Cleveland 44113
(216) 771-7297

Law & Public Service Magnet H.S. (E)
1651 E. 71st St., Cleveland 44112
(216) 431-6858

Jewish Family Service Assn.
28790 Chagrin Blvd., Cleveland 44122
(216) 292-3999

Settlement Program
12510 Mayfield Rd., Cleveland 44106

Blue & Associates
20310 Chagrin Blvd. (6), Cleveland 44122
(216) 761-6373

Cleveland Heights
Divorce Equity, Inc.
3130 Mayfield Rd. (W-200), Cleveland Heights 44118
(216) 321-8587

The Foresight Group
Five Severance Circle, Cleveland Heights 44118
(216) 291-2107/2109

Columbus
Night Prosecutor's Program
Municipal Court (7th Floor), 375 S. High St., Columbus 43215
(614) 222-7483

Small Claims
375 S. High St., Columbus 43215
(614) 222-7381

Ohio Dispute Resolution, Inc. (C)
6797 N. High St. (332), Columbus 43085
(614) 885-1992

Family Counseling & Crittenton Services
185 S. 5th St., Columbus 43215
(614) 221-7608

Family Counseling & Crittenton Services
1229 Sunbury Rd., Columbus 43219
(614) 252-5229

Family Counseling & Crittenton Services
4770 Indianola Ave. (104), Columbus 43214
(614) 885-8259

Columbus Grove
Psychosocial Associates
200 N. High St., Columbus Grove 45830
(419) 659-5998

Dayton
Night Prosecutor's Program
Safety Bldg. (338), 335 W. 3rd St., Dayton
    45402
(513) 443-4400

Elyria
Reconciliation Ministries, Inc.
121 Keep Court, Elyria 44035
(216) 324-3550/236-8833

Findlay
Hancock Co. Mental Health Clinic
2515 N. Main St., Findlay 45840
(419) 422-3711

Betts, Miller & Russo (L)
101 W. Sandusky St., Findlay 45840
(419) 422-5565

North Canton
Professional Mediation Services
PO Box 2277, North Canton 44720
(216) 863-0712

Norton
Mennonite Conciliation Services
3595 Everett Dr., Norton 44203
(216) 825-3322

Reynoldsburg
Family Counseling & Crittenton Services
6420 E. Main St., Reynoldsburg 43068
(614) 863-6631

Sylvania
Christian Conciliation Service
5271 Alexis Rd., Sylvania 43560
(419) 885-7026

Toledo
Citizens Dispute Settlement
555 N. Erie St., Toledo 43624
(419) 245-1951

Warren
Presource of Warren
680 Perkins Dr. NW, Warren 44483
(216) 394-3792

Oklahoma

Oklahoma City
Oklahoma Mediation/Arbitration Service (C)
5929 N. May Ave. (204), Oklahoma City
    73112-4276
(405) 848-6627

Complaints, Engineering Div.
Oklahoma Corp. Commission, Jim Thorpe
    Bldg., Oklahoma City 73105
(405) 521-2331

Dispute Mediation Service
1613 N. Broadway, Oklahoma City 73103
(405) 236-0413

Mediation Component
Consumer Div., 112 State Capitol, Okla-
    homa City 73105
(405) 521-3921

Victim-Offender Program
Dept. Corrections, 3400 Martin Luther
    King, Oklahoma City 73136
(405) 427-6511 (Ext. 476)

Christian Conciliation Service
8800 Northridge Terrace, Oklahoma City
    73132
(405) 720-9207

Owasso
Oklahoma Mediation/Arbitration Service (C)
202 S. Cedar St., PO Box 116, Owasso
    74055-0116
(918) 272-5338

Stillwater
Dispute Services
230 N. Murray Hall, Oklahoma State Uni-
    versity, Stillwater 74078
(405) 624-5671

Tulsa
Early Settlement
600 Civic Center, Tulsa 74103
(918) 592-7786

Christian Conciliation Service
228 W. 17th Place, Tulsa 74119
(918) 584-4187

Oregon

Corvallis
Consulting Associates
Po Box 2029, Corvallis 97339
(503) 757-8623

Harding Mediation Service
226 SW 8th St., Corvallis 97333
(503) 757-7594

Eugene
Community Mediation Board
PO Box 11222, Eugene 97440
(503) 683-5574

Mediation Service
2271 Birch Lane, Eugene 97403
(503) 683-0780

Open Adoption & Family Services (AFM)
239 East 14th Ave., Eugene 97401
(503) 343-4825

The Mediation Center (AFM)
1158 High St. (202), Eugene 97401
(503) 345-1456

Mennonite Conciliation Service Affiliate
1475 Ferry St., Eugene 97401
(503) 683-0780

Academy of Family Mediators (AFM)
PO Box 10501, Eugene 97440
(503) 345-1205

Hillsboro
Taylor Mediation (AFM)
511 NE Birchwood Dr., Hillsboro 97124
(503) 293-3440

Lake Oswego
Western Arbitration Associates
4350 SW Galewood St., PO Box 2029, Lake
    Oswego 97034
(503) 635-9915

Portland
Neighborhood Mediation Center
4815 NE 7th St. (20), Portland 97211
(503) 243-7320

Family Mediation Center (AFM)
1020 SW Taylor St. (845), Portland 97205
(503) 248-9740

Mediation Services, Inc.
529 SE Grand Ave., Portland 97214
(503) 235-2493

Association of Family & Conciliation Courts
3181 SW Sam Jackson Park Rd., Portland
    97201
(503) 279-5651

Christian Conciliation Service
PO Box 9070, Portland 97207
(503) 667-1776

Arbitration Services of Portland
620 SW 5th Ave. (1010), Portland 97204
(503) 226-3109

Lewis & Clark Law School (AFM)
10015 SW Terwillinger Blvd., Portland
    97219
(503) 244-1181

Oster Mediation (AFM)
2630 SW Nevada Court, Portland 97219
(503) 655-8342

Society Professionals in Dispute Resolution
    (Carlton Snow)
College of Law, Willamette University,
    Salem 97301
(503) 370-6433

Salem
Neighbor to Neighbor
PO Box 3653, Salem 97301

Marion County Family Court Conciliation
    Service
303 Center St., Salem 97301
(503) 588-5088

Seaside
North Coast Counseling Services
815 S. Holladay St., Seaside 97138
(503) 738-6227

Pennsylvania

Akron
Mennonite Conciliation Service
21 S. 12th St., Akron 17501
(717) 859-1151

Butler
Christian Conciliation Service
PO Box 1805, Butler 16003
(412) 285-5102

Darby
Community Dispute Settlement
844-B Main St., Darby 19023
(215) 532-2375

Fallsington
Bucks County Mediation Service
9300 New Falls Rd., Fallsington 19054
(215) 295-8154

Harrisburg
ADR Committee, Penn. Bar Assn.
PO Box 186, Harrisburg 17108
(717) 236-6715

Hepford, Swartz, Menaker & Morgan (L)
111 N. Front St., Harrisburg 17108
(717) 234-4121

Lancaster
Mediation Center
900 E. King St., PO Box 1078, Lancaster
17603
(717) 397-1137

Lemoyne
Behavioral Medicine & Psychological Services
650 N. 12th St., Lemoyne 17043
(717) 761-8303

Levittown
New Horizon Counseling & Mediation
64 Turf Rd., Levittown 19054
(215) 946-5161

Media
Family & Community Service
100 W. Front St., Media 19063
(215) 566-7540

Mount Joy
BIC Bd. of Brotherhood Concerns
PO Box 246, Mount Joy 17552
(717) 653-8251

Philadelphia
American Arbitration Assn. (C)
230 S. Broad St., Philadelphia 19102-4121
(215) 732-5260

JUDICATE (C)
1608 Walnut St., (1200), Philadelphia
19103
(215) 546-6200/1-800-631-9900

Arbitration & Mediation Services
Municipal Court, City Hall Annex (1224),
Philadelphia 19107
(215) 686-2974

Bauman, Millison & Cohen (AFM)
2043 Naudain St., Philadelphia 19146
(215) 985-9336

American Intermediation Service—Philadelphia (C)
10 Penn Center (1000), Philadelphia 19103
(215) 557-6501/800-826-5605

Society Professionals in Dispute Resolution
Fed. Mediation Servcie, 600 Arch St.
(3456), Philadelphia 19106
(215) 597-4796

United States Arbitration—Mediation Northeast, Inc. (C)
924 Cherry St. (521), Philadelphia 19107
(215) 238-0191

Blumstein/Perlmutter Associates (AFM)
634 W. Cliveden St., Philadelphia 19119
(215) 843-2425

Rosenberg Mediation (AFM)
1 East Penn Square (307), Philadelphia
19107
(215) 686-3745

Dispute Resolution Program
601 City Hall Annex, Philadelphia 19107
(215) 686-2872

Cohen, Shapiro, Polisher, Shiekman &
Cohen (L)
12 S. 12th St. (22nd Floor), Philadelphia
19107
(215) 922-1300

Mediation, Good Shepherd House
5356 Chew Ave., Philadelphia 19138
(215) 843-5413

Wisch Mediation (AFM)
1700 Sansom St. (701), Philadelphia 19103
(215) 988-9104

Conflict Analysis, U. of Pennsylvania (E)
3418 Locust Walk (130), Philadelphia 19104
(215) 898-8412

Nonviolence & Children Program (E)
1515 Cherry St., Philadelphia 19102
(215) 241-7239

Pittsburgh
American Arbitration Assn. (C)
Four Gateway Center (221), Pittsburgh
  15222-1207
(412) 261-3617

Society Professionals in Dispute Resolution
  Board of Arbitration (Elizabeth Neumeier)
  530 Oliver Bldg., Pittsburgh 15222
(412) 471-1558

5978 Alder St. (Mark Lefcowitz), Pittsburgh 15232
(412) 661-3333

Christian Conciliation Service
114 Smithfield St., Pittsburgh 15222
(412) 391-3800

Court of Common Pleas (AFM)
605 City-County Bldg. (Judge Kaplan), Pittsburgh 15219
(412) 355-7127

Divorce & Separation Mediation Center
  (AFM)
7514 Kensington St., Pittsburgh 15221
(412) 371-1000

Souderton
Eastern Penn. Mediation Service
105 W. Chestnut St., Souderton 18964
(215) 721-1813

West Chester
Environmental Resources Management, Inc.
999 West Chester Pike, West Chester 19382
(215) 696-9110

York
Family Service of York
800 E. King St., York 17403
(717) 563-1368

Rhode Island

Pawtucket
Bettigole Mediation (AFM)
29 Wilcox Ave., Pawtucket 02860
(401) 331-1244

Providence
Tillinghast, Collins & Graham (L)
1 Old Stone Square, Providence 02903-7104
(401) 456-1200

South Carolina

Columbia
Ombudsman, Office of Governor
1205 Pendleton, Columbia 29201
(803) 734-0457

Associates in Marriage & Family Therapy
2229 Bull St., Columbia 29201
(803) 252-5300

Lexington
Juvenile Arbitration
105 S. Lake Drive, Lexington 29072
(803) 359-8355

Spartanburg
Christian Conciliation Service
180 Library St., Spartanburg 29301
(803) 582-3740

South Dakota

Pierre
Consumer Affairs
Off. Attorney General, Anderson Bldg.,
  Pierre 57501
(605) 773-4400

Tennessee

Brentwood
H. L. Mills & Associates (AFM)
PO Box 1772, Brentwood 37027
(615) 371-9583

Germantown
Germantown Psychological Associates
7516 Enterprise Ave. (1), Germantown
  38138
(901) 755-5802

Kingsport
First Broad St. United Methodist Church
PO Box 1346, Kingsport 37662
(615) 246-4471

Knoxville
Baptist Center Dispute Program
1230 W. Scott St., Knoxville 37921
(615) 525-9068

Christian Conciliation Service
7323 Bennington Dr. NW, Knoxville 37909
(615) 694-8906

Memphis
Citizens Dispute Office
201 Poplar Ave. (LL20), Memphis 38103
(901) 576-2520

Family & Health Institute
965 Reddoch Cove, Memphis 38119
(901) 682-6993

Memphis Citizen Dispute
28 Adams St. (120), Memphis 38103

Nashville
American Arbitration Assn. (C)
162 Fourth Ave. N. (103), Nashville 37219-2412
(615) 256-5857

Consumer Affairs
1808 West End Bldg. (105), Nashville 37219
(615) 741-4737/800-342-8385

Christian Conciliation Service
2114 Parkway Towers, Nashville 37219
(615) 244-6632

Texas

Amarillo
The Samaritan Counseling Center (AFM)
2929 Duniven Circle, Amarillo 79109
(806) 353-1668

Austin
Dispute Resolution Center
512 E. Riverside (206), Austin 78104
(512) 443-5981

Slaikeu Mediation (AFM)
1717 W. 6th St. (2156), Austin 78703
(512) 474-5132

Beaumont
Mediation Center of Jefferson County
John Gray Institute, 8545 Florida Ave.,
Beaumont 77705
(409) 835-8747

Corpus Christi
Nueces County Dispute Resolution Center
County Courthouse, 901 Leopard (110),
Corpus Christi 78401
(512) 888-0650

Dallas
American Arbitration Assn. (C)
Two Galleria Tower (1440), Dallas 75240-6620
(214) 702-8222

Dispute Mediation Service
3310 Live Oak (202-LB 9), Dallas 75204-6133
(214) 821-4380

Settlement Consultants International, Inc.
(AFM)
12115 Self Plaza (209A), Dallas 75218-1418
(214) 321-8624

United States Arbitration & Mediation of
Dallas/Ft. Worth (C)
12700 Hillcrest Rd. (211), Dallas 75230
(214) 490-6394

The Mediation Group of Dallas (AFM)
14001 Goldmark (101), Dallas 75240
(214) 680-2911

Family Mediation Service
6200 LBJ Frwy. (250), Dallas 75240
(214) 239-2301

Christian Conciliation Service
1209 N. Haskell Ave. (A), Dallas 75204
(214) 824-0521

Leviton & Greenstone (AFM)
PO Box 670292, Dallas 75367-6292
(214) 361-0209

Hahn Mediation (AFM)
Old Courthouse (3rd Floor), 100 S. Houston
St., Dallas 75202
(214) 749-8679

Juvenile Court Mediation
4711 Harry Hines Blvd., Dallas 75235
(214) 920-7700

Hack Mediation (AFM)
PO Box 595314, Dallas 75359
(214) 528-7651

Kirkpatrick Mediation (AFM)
3503 Fairmont, Dallas 75219
(214) 528-2830

Fort Worth
Dispute Resolution Services
1025 S. Jennings St. (102), Fort Worth
76104
(817) 877-4554

Neurology Associates of Ft. Worth
1400 S. Main St. (211), Fort Worth 76104
(817) 334-0011

Garland
Yingling Mediation (AFM)
1002 Woburn, Unit 1, Box 1, Garland
75043
(214) 278-6557

Houston
American Arbitration Assn. (C)
1 Allen Center (1000), Houston 77002-4891
(713) 739-1302

Dispute Resolution Centers
Criminal Court Bldg. (315), 301 San Jacinto
St., Houston 77002
(713) 221-8274

United States Arbitration & Mediation, Inc.
(C)
PO Box 6968, Houston 77265
(713) 622-8033

Family Mediation Service (AFM)
909 Kipling St., Houston 77006
(713) 521-9551

Christian Conciliation Service
One Park Place (200), Houston 77084
(713) 578-8787

Divorce & Family Mediation Services
(AFM)
6065 Hillcroft St. (300), Houston 77081
(713) 777-8808

Special Committee Multi-Door
1307 San Jacinto St. (10th Floor), Houston
77002

Adam's Mediation & Financial Resource
Center
1200 Blalock St. (204), Houston 77055
(713) 465-2347

Graul Mediation (AFM)
24 Greenway Plaza (1509), Houston 77046
(713) 629-4146

Hurst
PSA Counseling Center, Inc.
1237 Southridge Court (100), Hurst 76053
(817) 268-2673

Lewisville
Center for Dispute Resolution
102 West M St., Lewisville 75067
(214) 221-9333

San Antonio
Mediation Center
212 Stumberg St. (214), San Antonio 78204
(512) 220-2128

Utah

Salt Lake City
Consumer Protection
160 E. 300 South St., Salt Lake City 84145-
0801
(801) 530-6601

Rental Dispute Mediation
637 E. 400 South St., Salt Lake City 84102
(801) 328-8891

United States Arbitration & Mediation of
Salt Lake City, Inc. (C)
3075 E. 4590 South, Salt Lake City 84117
(801) 272-6923

Mediation/Arbitration Center
1382 E. 1300, Salt Lake City

Western Arbitration Association
2480 S. Main St. (203), Salt Lake City
84115
(801) 583-3004

Vermont

Brattleboro
Brattleboro Family Institute
50 Elliott St., Brattleboro 05301
(802) 257-1660

Brattleboro Retreat
75 Linden St., Brattleboro 05301
(802) 257-7785

Montpelier
Dispute Resolution Clinic
659 Elm St., Montpelier 05602
(802) 229-0516

Mediation Courses (E)
Woodbury College, Montpelier 05602
(802) 229-0516

Rutland
Family Mediation & Arbitration
40 S. Main St., Rutland 05701
(802) 775-2471

Shelburne
Resolve
Route 7, PO Box 637, Shelburne 05482
(802) 985-9712

South Royalton
Environmental Law Center
Vermont Law School, PO Box 96, South
    Royalton 05068
(802) 763-8303

White River Junction
Mental Health Services of Southeastern Vt.
Gilman Office Complex, Bldg. 4, White
    River Junction 05001
(802) 295-3031

Virginia

Alexandria
Mediation for the 80s
2418 Menokin Dr. (202), Alexandria 22302
(703) 671-3959

Clean Sites, Inc.
1199 N. Fairfax St., Alexandria 22314-1437
(703) 683-8522

Conflict Resolution Newsletter
3404 Wessynton Way, Alexandria 22304
(703) 780-4403

Counseling & Mediation
424 S. Washington St., Alexandria 22314
(703) 548-0101

Arlington
Juvenile & Domestic Relations Mediation
PO Box 925, 1400 N. Courthouse Rd., Ar-
    lington 22216
(703) 558-2231

Divorce & Marital Stress Clinic (AFM)
1925 N. Lynn St. (810), Arlington 22209
(703) 528-3900

Council Better Business Bureaus
1515 Wilson Blvd., Arlington 22209
(703) 276-0100

Family Mediation (AFM)
1515 N. Courthouse Rd. (605), Arlington
    22201
(703) 522-7631

Burke
Burke Family Counseling Center
5206-B Rolling Rd., Burke 22015
(703) 978-8330

Charlottesville
Institute for Environmental Negotiation
Campbell Hall, University of Virginia,
    Charlottesville 22903
(804) 924-1970

Lowe & Jacobs, Ltd. (L)
300 Court Square, Charlottesville 22901
(804) 296-8188

Danville
Associates in Mental Health Services
145 Holbrook Ave., Danville 24541
(804) 791-2059

Fairfax
Center for Conflict Resolution/Conflict
    Clinic, Inc.
George Mason University, 4400 University
    Dr., Fairfax 22030
(703) 323-2086/764-6225

ICF, Inc. (C)
9300 Lee Highway, Fairfax 22031-1207
(703) 934-3000

Falls Church
Family Relations Institute
3705 S. George Mason Drive, Falls Church
  22041
(703) 998-5550

Public Mediation Services
1130 S. Washington St. (T-2), Falls Church
  22046
(703) 543-1526

Harrisonburg
Community Mediation Center
298 Green St., Harrisonburg 22801
(703) 434-0059

Mennonite Conciliation Services
251 Park Place, Harrisonburg 22801
(703) 433-9879

Manassas
Juvenile & Domestic Relations, Court Service Unit (AFM)
9311 Lee Ave., Manassas 22110
(703) 335-6232

McLean
Washington Mediation Center (AFM)
1508 Emerson Ave., McLean 22101
(703) 442-9090

Quantico
Family Service Center
Little Hall, Marine Corps Development
  Com., Quantico 22134
(703) 640-2659

Richmond
Community Incentive Program
PO Box 26963, Richmond 23261
(804) 257-6419

ADR Center
701 E. Franklin St. (712), Richmond 23219

Psychological & Counseling Resources, Inc.
  (AFM)
6901 Patterson Ave., Richmond 23226
(804) 288-7227

Vienna
Center for Mediation, Counseling
8148-A Electric Ave., Vienna 22180
(703) 573-1110

Williamsburg
National Center for State Courts
300 Newport Ave., Williamsburg 23187-
  8798
(804) 253-2000

Washington

Bellingham
Family Mediation Services
1155 N. State St. (524), Bellingham 98225
(206) 671-6416

Edmonds
Tribal Community Boards
121 Fifth Ave. N. (305), Edmonds 98020
(206) 774-5808

Everett
Rental Housing Mediation
2801 Lombard St., Everett 98201
(206) 339-1335

Kirkland
Northwest Mediation Service, Inc.
135 Lake St. South (100), Kirkland 98033
(206) 455-3989

Seattle
American Arbitration Assn. (C)
811 First Ave. (200), Seattle 98104-1455
(206) 622-6435

Washington Arbitration & Mediation Services (C)
525 Westland Bldg., 100 S. King St., Seattle
  98104
(206) 467-0793

Ombudsman, Citizen Complaints
C-213 King County Courthouse, Seattle
  98104
(206) 344-3452

Northwest Renewable Center
1133 Dexter Horton Bldg., 710 2nd Ave.,
  Seattle 98104
(206) 623-7361

Christian Conciliation Service
424 N. Both St., Seattle 98133
(206) 367-2245

West Virginia

Charleston
Family Service of Kanawha Valley
1036 Quarrier St. (317), Charleston 25301
(304) 340-3676

Wisconsin

Eau Claire
Try Resolution Yourself, Inc.
721 Oxford Ave. (258), Eau Claire 54703
(715) 839-6995

Green Bay
Am. Found. Rel. & Psychology
130 E. Walnut St. (706), Green Bay 54301
(414) 437-8256

Madison
Assn. Family Conciliation Courts (AFM)
314 E. Mifflin St., Madison 53703
(608) 251-0604

Consumer Protection
123 W. Washington St. (170), PO Box
 7856, Madison 53707
(608) 266-1852/800-362-8189

Center for Public Representation
520 University Ave., Madison 53703
(608) 251-4008

Civil Litigation Research (E)
University of Wisconsin Law School, 209
 Law Bldg., Madison 53706
(608) 263-2545

Marshfield
Marshfield Clinic
1000 N. Oak Ave., Marshfield 54449
(715) 387-5182

Milwaukee
North Shore Psychotherapy Assn.
633 E. Henry Clay, Milwaukee 53217
(414) 961-1314

Divorce Mediation Center
11805 W. Hampton Ave., Milwaukee 53225
(414) 466-9988

U.S. Arbitration & Mediation of Wisconsin,
 Inc. (C)
2631 N. Downer Ave., PO Box 11913, Milwaukee 53211
(414) 962-3502

Oshkosh
County Family Court
415 Jackson St., PO Box 2808, Oshkosh
 54903
(414) 235-2500

Racine
Dispute Settlement Center
730 Wisconsin Ave. (4th Floor), Racine
 53403
(414) 636-3277

River Falls
The Mediation Center (AFM)
710 N. Main St., Box 405, River Falls
 54022
(715) 425-9558

Waukesha
County Mediation Program
414 W. Moreland Blvd. (107), Waukesha
 53188
(414) 544-5431

Wausau
Henderson Mediation (AFM)
1335 Torney Ave., Wausau 54401
(715) 848-1381 (Ext. 246)

Wyoming

Casper
U.S. Arbitration & Mediation of Wyoming,
 Inc. (C)
100 Center St. (6th Floor), PO Box 636,
 Casper 82602
(307) 234-1116

Guam

Agana
Christian Conciliation Service
PO Box CE, Agana 96910
(671) 646-1527

Puerto Rico

San Juan

American Arbitration Assn. (C)
Esquire Bldg. (800), San Juan 00918-3628
(809) 764-8515

Dispute Resolution Center
San Juan Judicial Center, Box CJ, Hato
Rey, San Juan 00918
(809) 763-4813

The Academy of Family Mediators stipulated that the following statement be carried in connection with the listing of members in this directory:

Membership in the Academy is open to individuals who practice as family mediators and who meet the Academy's standards for formal education, specialized training and work experience. There are two categories: Member and Associate Member. Both require either a law degree or a master's degree in one of the behavioral sciences, as well as 40 hours of specialized family mediation training. In the absence of a post-graduate degree, the Academy has defined equivalency criteria. Full Member status additionally requires the completion of 15 mediations and 10 hours consultation with an experienced mediator.

Although the Academy does set standards for membership, we do not certify competency nor do we monitor the professional mediation practices of individual members.